FASHION
The Twentieth Century

W9-ATZ-293

Front cover:
Yohji Yamamoto
Photograph by Nick Knight
Autumn/Winter 1987–1988

Page 4:
Renée
Photograph taken in Biarritz
by Jacques-Henri Lartigue
1930

Translated from the French *Mode du Siècle*
by Jane Brenton

First published in the United States of America in 1999
by Universe Publishing
A division of Rizzoli International Publications, Inc.
300 Park Avenue South
New York, NY 10010
www.rizzoliusa.com

Revised edition 2006

2006 2007 2008 2009 / 10 9 8 7 6 5 4 3 2

ISBN 0-7893-1397-9
Library of Congress Control Number 2005928098

Printed and bound in China

FRANÇOIS BAUDOT

FASHION
The Twentieth Century

Universe

Contents

8 **Foreword**

11 **Introduction**

29 **Chapter 1** 1900–1960

30 **The Belle Époque** 1900–1914

30 Historical Review
36 Jacques Doucet
40 Paul Poiret
46 Mariano Fortuny
50 **And Also:** Redfern, Creed, Paquin,
Chéruit, Callot Soeurs, Margaine-Lacroix,
Drecoll, Lewis, Legroux and others
54 People
56 Menswear

60 **The First World War** 1914–1918

62 **Between the Wars** 1919–1939

62 Historical Review
66 Jeanne Lanvin
70 Jean Patou
72 Sportswear
74 Gabrielle Chanel
80 Jewelry
82 Madeleine Vionnet
86 Lucien Lelong
88 Elsa Schiaparelli
92 **And Also:** Mainbocher, Molyneux, Ricci,
Revillon, Valentina, Irfé, the *parfumeurs*,
Reboux, Perugia, Ferragamo and others
100 People
102 Menswear
104 The Influence of American Film

106 **The Second World War** 1939–1945

106 Historical Review
114 The Reign of the Milliners
116 Grès
118 Charles James
122 American Ready-to-Wear
126 Claire McCardell
128 Menswear
130 Liberation
132 Jacques Fath

136 **The Theatre of Fashion**

140 **The Fifties**

140 Historical Review
144 Christian Dior
150 Pierre Balmain and Norman Norell
152 Roger Vivier
154 Balenciaga
160 Givenchy
162 The Return of Chanel
164 **And Also:** Guy Laroche, Jacques Griffe,
Jean Dessès, Carven, Line Vautrin,
Lola Prusac, Jacques Esterel and others
168 People
170 From Couture to Mass Manufacturing
174 Lempereur and the Pioneer Stylists
178 Pierre Cardin
182 Menswear

185 **Chapter 2** | 1960–2000

186 **The Sixties**

186 Historical Review
192 Yves Saint Laurent
196 André Courrèges
198 Paco Rabanne
200 Emilio Pucci and Rudi Gernreich
202 And Also: Louis Féraud, Ted Lapidus,
    Torrente, Jean-Louis Scherrer, Lesage,
    Emanuel Ungaro, Oleg Cassini, Anne Klein,
    Pauline Trigère, Giorgio di Sant'Angelo,
    Valentino, Simonetta, Capucci and others
208 Swinging London
210 The Empire of Style: Maïmé Arnodin
    and Denise Fayolle, Emmanuelle Khanh,
    Christiane Bailly, Cacharel, Dorothée Bis,
    Michèle Rosier, Prisunic and others
218 People
220 Menswear

224 **Street Fashion
    and Anti-Fashion** | 1968–1972

232 Anti-Fashion Becomes Big Business

234 **The Seventies**

234 Historical Review
238 France: Marc Bohan, Sonia Rykiel,
    Karl Lagerfeld, Kenzo, Issey Miyake
    and others
248 London: Mr Freedom, Ossie Clark,
    Zandra Rhodes and Anthony Price
250 Italy: Capucci, Mila Schön, Krizia, Cerruti,
    Gianfranco Ferre, Giorgio Armani, Walter
    Albini, Laura Biagiotti, Missoni and others

258 United States: Bill Blass, John Anthony,
    Oscar de la Renta, Halston, Geoffrey Beene,
    Adolfo, Stephen Burrows, James Galanos
    and others
266 Basics
268 Agnès B.
270 People
272 Menswear

276 **The Eighties**

276 Historical Review
282 Azzedine Alaïa
286 Thierry Mugler
288 Stephen Jones
    and Claude Montana
290 Jean-Paul Gaultier
292 Giorgio Armani
294 Ralph Lauren
296 Manolo Blahnik and Adidas
298 Zoran and Lagerfeld at Chanel
302 Sybilla and Romeo Gigli
304 Christian Lacroix
306 Marithé & François Girbaud and
    Jean-Charles de Castelbajac
308 And Also: Myrène de Prémonville,
    Michel Klein, Chantal Thomass,
    Guy Paulin, Anne-Marie Beretta,
    Marc Audibet, Jean-Rémy Daumas,
    Jean Colonna, Kansai Yamamoto,
    Junko Koshino, Junko Shimada,
    Walter Steiger, Carolina Herrera,
    Carolyne Roehm, Perry Ellis,
    Isaac Mizrahi and others
313 The Japanese Phenomenon
314 People

316 **The Nineties**

316 Historical Review
322 Yohji Yamamoto
324 Gianni Versace
326 Comme des Garçons
328 Martine Sitbon
330 Vivienne Westwood
332 Gucci
334 Prada
336 **The Life of a De-Luxe Label:** Hermès, Céline,
     Vuitton, Trussardi, Loewe and others
340 Jil Sander and Martin Margiela
342 Paul Smith, Philip Treacy and Patrick Cox
344 Helmut Lang and Dolce & Gabbana
346 Marc Jacobs and Michael Kors
348 Dries Van Noten and
     Ann Demeulemeester
350 John Galliano and Alexander McQueen
352 Dior and Givenchy
354 Gianfranco Ferre and Alberta Ferretti
356 Thierry Mugler and Jean-Paul Gaultier
358 Adeline André and Chanel
360 Walter Van Beirendonck and Rifat Ozbek
362 Donna Karan and Gap
364 Calvin Klein
366 **And Also:** Thimister, Ocimar Versolato,
     Christophe Rouxel, Dominique Sirop,
     Narciso Rodriguez, Cristina Ortiz,
     Stella McCartney, Alber Elbaz, Isabel Marant,
     Todd Oldham, Dirk Bikkembergs, Nike
     and others
372 **The Future**
374 **People**

377 Conclusion

385 Bibliography
390 Picture Credits
394 Acknowledgments
396 Index

Foreword

What is fashion, but a series of trends? Often slow to take hold, they blaze for a while before gradually dying out. Like striking a match, sometimes you will burn your fingers, but sometimes the flames take hold and are fanned by the winds of change, only to be extinguished later on by a pall of indifference, the sheer weight of habit and the boredom that sets in over time. By then the wind will already have changed direction. Other fashions will have sprung up that are even more brilliant and dazzling than their predecessors. Some people will be scandalized, but there will also be admirers and imitators. The word spreads like wildfire. Then, one day, such and such a garment, or line, or style is consigned to dust, but not always for ever. Some fashions languish in obscurity, while others return – resurrected, embellished and transposed into new forms by lapses of memory – to delight future generations. The freedoms enjoyed by the couturiers of the past are the means of infinitely extending those of today's creators.

Drawing by Ruben Toledo for Louis Vuitton
From *The New York Scrap Book.*

In the seventeenth century, fashion related, above all, to a way of life and, only by extension, to a way of dressing. In fact, the French still use the expression *mode de vie* to mean 'way of life'. Fashion governed the sort of behaviour that was acceptable, what you could wear and what you were allowed to say; it also required arbiters of taste. Princes, dandies, aesthetes, Louis XIV, Beau Brummell and Baudelaire have all dictated fashion simply by using it to suit themselves. It was in France, under the Second Empire and with the approval of the powers that be, that an Englishman called Charles Frederick Worth first laid down the rules of Parisian haute couture.

Fabrics, colours, motifs and forms changed from one season to the next. Instead of people developing their own interpretation of fashion by following the broad guidelines laid down by the arbiters, fashion became a matter for the experts. Originally no more than tradesmen, these people gradually climbed to the very top of the social scale. Once they were the servants of a society that clung jealously to its privileges, but today they dictate to the masses and increasingly frequently are supported by financial groups that include some very powerful people indeed. Fashion has always been a game, but now the stakes have been raised dramatically. It all goes to show that the two sides of life are inseparable: you cannot divorce the ephemeral, the frivolous and the inessential from the serious world of lasting consequences.

This evolution is echoed linguistically. We rarely talk about fashions, preferring instead the term 'product'. Where once 'fashion', in the old sense of the word, implied a mature and settled judgment, today it is more likely to conjure an image of constant ferment, of instant favourites and of ever-new concepts. From this organized chaos, designed to mutate at regular intervals, and from this profitable alliance between chance and necessity, between art and industry, between the need to express yourself and the need to clothe yourself, it is impossible to extract a coherent narrative – the history of costume is not the same as that of fashion. The moment a garment ceases to be worn, it no longer exists. This book, therefore, does not claim to offer an exhaustive account and even less to deliver any sort of verdict. It is more a gentle stroll through a century of fashion, with plenty of opportunity to express personal opinions and enjoy chance encounters.

Introduction

Fashion has grown from strength to strength, in the last hundred years,
winning hearts and favourable opinion on all sides. Beyond its primary
functions of determining how people should look and providing pleasure,
it has also served as a catalyst for the economy, uniting the two opposite
poles of contemporary culture: the desire for creativity and the need
for production.

The duel between man and machine that has been fought for nearly
two hundred years has found in fashion its ideal field of combat. The
couturier is on the one hand a creative person, on the other an industrialist.
In some ways, he functions like an artist and, yet, the moment that what
he produces falls out of favour, he ceases to exist. True artists, on the
other hand, never submit to market forces. The designer is in a vulnerable
position and one that can only become more precarious. The industrialist,
meanwhile, has different priorities. He stands for stability, continuity
and the need to rationalize his specialist product. He thinks in multiples,
whereas the creative artist thinks in the singular.

Paris was the birthplace of fashion, in the sense that we understand the
term today. Right from the outset, in the early years of the twentieth century,
it divided this creative industry into two distinct professional classes, which
were rigorously kept apart. On the one side was the world of couture, which
was very much a closed shop and catered for made-to-measure. On the
other, off-the-peg clothes were manufactured for the masses.

The first chapter of this chronological account posed few problems.
Right up until the Sixties, the development of fashion was linear. It operated

under the aegis of haute couture, which, as
a reflection of the society it served, addressed
only a social elite. The handmade garment was
created for the salons, not the streets, and was
an unattainable luxury for ordinary mortals.
Haute couture was unique and it alone determined
what was à la mode. Once the *dernier cri*, or latest
fashion, had been adopted in polite circles,
it would filter down in waves to reach the lower
classes of Western society. It spread by a number
of different mechanisms: skilled workshops,
anonymous little dressmakers and housewives
toiling over their sewing machines. They
reproduced with charm and skill, though
sometimes more by luck than judgment, the various patterns, models
and silhouettes that were published, sometimes after a considerable delay,
in the fashion magazines, or simply picked up ideas that were floating about
the Parisian streets.

For the peasants and workers who belonged to the subterranean
world that the bourgeoisie still referred to as 'the people', fashion had never
been anything other than hearsay. At the start of the twentieth century, most
people still wore clothes appropriate to their work and these hardly varied
in the course of a lifetime. You could indeed judge people by appearances.
Until after the Second World War, you could almost always tell who you were
dealing with simply by their clothes. It was not until the Sixties that the full
effects of the upheavals set in motion by the pan-European conflict filtered
through, inaugurating the second and considerably more complex part of
this history of contemporary clothing. In the latter half of this century, as a
result of an expanding economy and social changes, the traditional divide
that existed in the West between high society and workers became simply
untenable. In particular, a new young generation wanted to reap the benefits
of a booming consumer society. Privilege was less blatantly advertised and

differences were glossed over. America, the victorious big brother, imposed its model of democracy. As the ancient European hierarchies were overturned, the external marks of distinction faded with them. By the time the first rockets were launched into space, Europe was more than ready for a quality ready-to-wear garment on American lines, something to occupy the middle ground between off-the-peg and couture. The need was all the more pressing because increases in overheads and raw material costs were beginning to relegate handmade fashion to the sidelines. At the same time, rapidly developing new technologies made it easier and easier to manufacture an ever-improving high-quality product.

In around 1963, a group of young fashion draughtsmen and designers established contact with the big manufacturers. Before long they took over from the factories' accredited designers, who themselves were more than

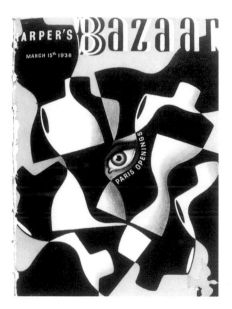

willing to shed their technicians' white coats and embrace the freshness and creativity of what in France was then called *style* and in the Anglo-Saxon countries, design. Faced with the threat of a factory-made fashion-based product, Parisian haute couture mounted its defences, but to little effect. It could not stop fashion leaking out on to the streets. In these years when the old world was taking its final bow, the changes in fashion were one of the most visible manifestations of the general shake-up in society. Before long, whole categories of women hitherto restricted to inferior substitutes for haute couture would enjoy a greatly enlarged freedom of choice.

As ready-to-wear developed, it brought about another major change. Dealing in far larger quantities, production cycles were longer than those of couture workshops, which meant that stylists planning their lines for the twice-yearly collections had to try to guess more than a year in advance what their customers would want.

Roy Lichtenstein
Untitled Shirt
The Fabric Workshop
and Philadephia
Museum,
Philadelphia.
1979

How would they react when the collections finally reached the shops?
A new power was afoot, that of the street, constituting a further threat
to the dictatorship of the masters of couture.

In just thirty years, the gentle revolution of ready-to-wear was to
transform the immutable code which had governed peoples' appearances
since the year dot. As rules were relaxed, clothing ceased to be a matter of
costumes for the different social classes. Novelty, the spirit of the times,
fantasy and chance all now played their part. Haute couture continued to
dazzle, in the new state of affairs, but was now no more than a prelude to
ready-to-wear. During the Seventies, most of the couture designers launched
subsidiary ranges which they sold in their own boutiques. A new kind of shop

Hardy Amies
The English royal
dressmaker.
Photograph by
Frank Horvat.
1961

**Drawing by
René Gruau**
The famous
illustrator produced
this drawing for the
cover of *International
Textiles.*
1955

flourished, alongside the boutiques, which marketed an original but accessible own-label product (Dorothée Bis, Gudule and Mic Mac on the Left Bank, in Paris, and Mary Quant, Let It Rock and Biba in London). At the same time, popular consumption rocketed and distribution and product choice were vastly improved. There was just one last step to be taken before fashion took on the form we know today. This coincided with the emergence, in France, of the *jeunes créateurs* (young designers), who completed the revolution set in motion by their predecessors, the so-called stylists. In future, a product would be created under the name, aegis and exclusive control of a single individual, the *créateur* or fashion designer, and it would be manufactured by an industrialist whose role was purely that of a contractor. Clothes were no longer made by a company but created by an individual talent, a designer who was on your wavelength and with whom you, and every other customer, enjoyed a special relationship. Fashions were like love affairs, with the press recording every passing fad and fancy. From the Seventies onwards, partly due to the vogue for retro and under the influence of people such as Diana Vreeland (former editor of American *Vogue* and consultant to the Costume Institute of the Metropolitan Museum in New York from 1973 to 1986), collections of old fashions were assembled and exhibited – organized thematically, monographically or chronologically.

At the same time, the old-established haute couture houses, like Yves Saint Laurent, began to create systematic archives of the models their workshops had produced. With the aid of museums and these new centres of documentation, twenty years before the end of the century, the arts of fashion and textiles started to develop a cultural hinterland.

These new labels we have been discussing, with the support of individual designers, continued to multiply and diversify during the

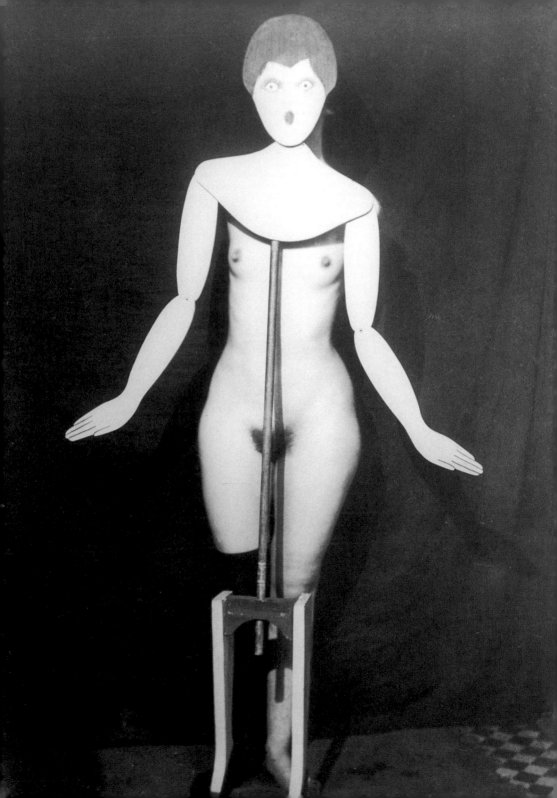

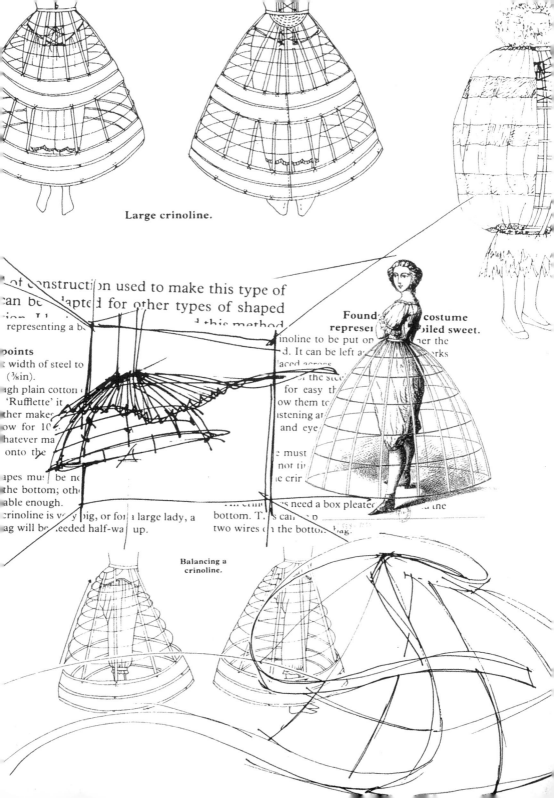

Large crinoline.

Found... costume
represen...iled sweet.

...of construction used to make this type of
...can be...adapted for other types of shaped
...representing a b...
...this method...

...points
...width of steel to...
...(⅜in).
...gh plain cotton...
...'Rufflette' it...
...ther makes...
...ow for 10...
...hatever ma...
...onto the...

...apes mu... be n...
...the bottom; oth...
...able enough.
...crinoline is v...y big, or for a large lady, a
...ag will be...eeded half-wa... up.

...noline to be put on...er the
...d. It can be left a...rks
...laced across...
...the ste...
...for easy th...
...ow them to...
...stening ar...
...and eye...

...e must...
...not ti...
...e crir...

...s need a box pleate...the
bottom. T... can...
two wires on the bottom...g.

Balancing a
crinoline.

Preceding pages:
Man Ray
Coat Stand
Published in *New York Dada.*
1920

The Crinoline
Montage taken from the catalogue of the Florence Biennale *Il Tempo e la Moda.*
1996

Left:
Isabel Toledo
The Cuban designer and her husband, illustrator Ruben Toledo, are among the brightest talents on the contemporary New York scene.
1999

Eighties and Nineties. It is important to distinguish them, however, from two other categories. On the one hand, there were the high-quality or de-luxe labels belonging to old-established companies that originally were not necessarily related to the clothing industry (among them, Hermès, Vuitton, Gucci and Prada). Their production of timeless classics, which were less dependent on vagaries of taste, have tended to consolidate and expand over the years. The fashion sides of their operations, however, were something quite separate and, therefore, limited in scope. Diversification, in these instances, was bound to be slow.

The other category is that of the 'concept' or 'designer' label, large numbers of which were established in the Eighties, especially in the United States. Their products, frequently of high quality, are underpinned by a formidable image-promoting operation. What they sell is a global concept, a lifestyle, based on solid market research and supported by a relentless PR campaign. These concept labels are, in fact, the heirs of the big European off-the-peg manufacturers from the beginning of the century. Their widely distributed lines copy the most accessible products to have emerged in preceding seasons. Long ago, French industrialists let slip this attractive market, which was invented more or less under their noses. Much more dynamic, over the last forty years, have been the many Italian companies, often family firms, which present their new ranges at the twice-yearly Milanese ready-to-wear shows that are the counterparts of the Paris collections.

After this first wave of emancipation, it was New York's turn to free itself, during the Nineties, from the French yoke. Now, at the dawn of the third millennium, the audience for the mass-manufactured product is international, served by an efficient worldwide network of boutiques. Their interiors are carefully designed to reflect the concept of the label, allowing us all to share in the dream. However, in the medium term, that concept risks becoming so formulaic that it could lead to a decline in consumer interest. No doubt it is in response to this danger that a new sort of enterprise has been quietly laying its foundations in recent seasons.

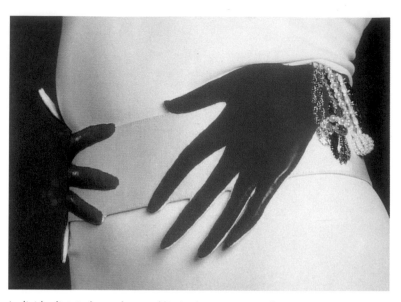

Individualist, independent and limited in resources, these new
operations signal a return both to the values of made-to-measure
and to a more personalized form of design. If this young generation of
designers and craftsmen can satisfy the requirements of a new clientele,
they may lead the way for the reinterpretation and triumphant restoration
of haute couture.

Disadvantaged by foreign competitors and, since the late Eighties,
by the effects of economic recession, Paris has neglected its trump card.
Without particularly going into the reason why this should be so, it
is a simple fact that, for the past century, no creative talents, whatever
their origins, have ever achieved international fame without submitting
themselves to the verdict of Paris. Not that French haute couture is the
expression of national genius, far from it. Where would it be without the
Englishman Worth, the Basque Balenciaga, Lagerfeld who comes from
Germany, Kenzo from Japan and Margiela from Antwerp? And yet, there
are countless numbers of international fashion designers who have never
joined the ranks of fashion's true stars for want of making the trip to Paris.
It is a city where, as we shall see in the course of this book, over the past
150 years, a succession of talents have handed the baton from one

Pierre et Gilles,
Snow White
Whether in
photography or
painting, fashion or
illustration, Pierre et
Gilles epitomized the
last years of the
twentieth century.
1990

Karl Lagerfeld
Self-Portrait
The artistic director
of Chanel and
photographer at
work in the splendid
library of his house
in Paris.

generation to the next. Until the Sixties, the way the system worked was that prestigious labels lent younger designers credibility, while they, in their turn, gave their elders a new lease of life. By neglecting this link between the two generations, haute couture began to decline. As the twentieth century drew to a close, new creative designers have taken over old houses that were losing their way. Some – and not the least of them – now combine ready-to-wear with made-to-measure, demonstrating once and for all that the two disciplines are perfectly capable of living in harmony within one organization and of addressing different occasions in the same woman's life. Today, it is increasingly obvious that the future of fashion rests with designers who are receptive to industry and with industrialists showing creative flair.

CHAPTER 1

1900-1960

Gabrielle Chanel
Coco before she cut
her hair short. For a
fancy-dress ball, she
has chosen to dress
up as a best man at
a village wedding.
The fitted jacket,
black bow and round-
brimmed hat reveal
an early penchant
for appropriating
clothes from the
male wardrobe.
1912

The Belle Époque | 1900–1914

Historical Review

Fashion, like all the applied arts in the nineteenth and early twentieth century, was essentially the preserve of Paris, although not so much the geographical capital of France as the autonomous world that existed at the cosmopolitan heart of the city. Powerful, prosperous, populous and of international reputation, it was the undisputed centre of the luxury industries. Pioneers and creators benefited from the support of skilled workers who passed down from one generation to the next a body of accumulated knowledge and experience, along with all their jealously guarded secrets and an innate feeling for beauty and fine workmanship. Embracing fashion, textiles and accessories of every description, notably jewelry – where Chaumet and Fabergé were the leading names – the industry employed a substantial workforce. A hive of creativity, its antennae were also attuned, in everything it produced, to the intangible rules of polite society, which determined the conventions of behaviour – and therefore governed external appearances – in a closed world that was as confident in its own invulnerability as in the soundness of the French franc.

For Paris, the Parisians and all who lived with and worked for them, the period between the Franco-Prussian War of 1870 and the cataclysm of 1914–1918 was one of the most prosperous in history. The France of 1900 still clung to certainties, confident of its status and wealth. It had not yet come to terms with the notion that art and innovation, or creativity which in any way enhances reputation or lifestyle, tend to progress as a result of

Princess Alexandra
It was for Alexandra, queen consort of England from 1901 to 1910, that Redfern originally invented the tailored suit.
1880

clashes and breaks with the past. The sort of ruptures, in fact, that were to spark off the twentieth-century avant-gardes.

Modernity, having lurked unrecognized in the wings of the former world, would emerge in the few years preceding the First World War to deploy its advance troops, notably Apollinaire, Picasso, Stravinsky, Diaghilev, Cocteau, Santos-Dumont and many other foreigners living and working in Paris around 1910. From them, Paul Poiret would take his cue and tag along with his cortège of dresses. But this band of innovators was soon to be halted in its tracks by the declaration of war, which would set back the true beginnings of modern art and the modern sensibility by at least a decade. Back in 1900, however, the world that Marcel Proust had so expertly described and decoded in *Remembrance of Things Past* did not yet know that polite society was doomed. The ancient aristocracy, Empire nobility, new money and the aspiring middle classes had all taken pains to detach themselves from the lower classes, but, whether they liked it or not, they were part of a republic, of which, historically speaking, the Belle Époque was just one aspect.

If life at the imperial court had survived the carnage of the Battle of Sedan, the leading couturiers would probably not have enjoyed the same post-1870 freedom in which to express their originality and impose their views. In particular, the figure of the inspirational designer would not have been able to set himself up as more or less the sole authority on matters of style. France had no policies to reduce expenditure and, unlike the other nations of the old Europe, was content to let such talents flourish. Although it was chauvinist and corporatist, wary of anything foreign or even – horror of horrors – provincial, the Paris of the Belle Époque, of the Place Vendôme and its adjacent streets, nevertheless acted as a formidable catalyst for a variety of energizing influences and trends. For centuries, a stream of visitors had converged on the City of Light. Nourished and cross-fertilized by its influx of cosmopolitan talent, the capital would sift through what was on offer and then calmly pre-empt and appropriate for itself ideas, trends, sources and outside viewpoints with which to buttress its own hegemony.

Since the beginnings of haute couture, this highly developed skill of assimilation had demonstrated, in an exemplary way, the Parisian ability not only to conceptualize and refine, but also to find concrete expression for such abstractions as the mood of the times, good taste, contemporary style and the exotic. At the close of the nineteenth century, horizons were generally broadened, as a result of the exponential growth of all types of communications and of the improvements in transport that facilitated travel

Jean Béraud
(1849–1936)
Une soirée
Oil on canvas
Musée d'Orsay,
Paris.
1878

Avenue des Acacias, Paris
Photograph by
Jacques-Henri
Lartigue.
1911

at home and abroad. Is that not what industry has always promised: a future of consumer delights for ever-larger sections of the population?

In 1878, 1889 and 1900, world fairs held in Paris and a number of other foreign capitals opened a window on to the wider world. For industry, they provided an international showcase for their wares. The first to benefit were the luxury trades, followed, in their wake, by a thousand and one peripheral businesses that appealed to the masses. It was the same mass audience whose everyday needs were served by Parisian department stores, such as Le Bon Marché, Le Printemps and Autre Bonheur des Dames, which – after a considerable interval, admittedly, but employing the same process of assimilation – offered them a breed of luxury that imitated that of the elite. As the wheel turned full circle and as a precursor of street fashion, the discreet and often rather well-made clothes sold on the counters of the department stores began to familiarize the elegantly dressed woman with the concept of a garment that – although perhaps not yet to be described as 'practical' – was certainly much less elaborate. The reason, of course, was that these exotically plumed beauties were beginning to step in and out of cars and indulge – timidly at first – in the delights of the open air. Also, with increasing frequency, their conversation included a new and somewhat fearsome word, redolent of the English style. That word was 'sport'.

Yet, the fact remains that, as the nineteenth century drew to a close, the outfits worn by the men and women of polite society remained strikingly similar to those of the past. The basic cut of a man's suit had been defined at the end of the eighteenth century and, even up to the present day, it is only the details that have changed. We shall have more to say on that subject later. The woman had taken on the more visible role within the couple, to reflect the rank of a partner who was restricted to dark colours and

anonymous attire. However, while ringing the changes in colours, materials and trimmings, a woman's silhouette had remained essentially unchanged since the Renaissance. With the exception of the Directoire and Empire periods, with their brief interludes of an antique style, female garments had adopted the same hourglass shape for four centuries. The body was divided into two distinct but unequal parts, demarcated by the nipped-in waist of a corset. No fashionable woman ever could, or would, lace up or unlace this restraint without the help of a third party. Poiret would be the first to design garments that could be put on unassisted.

Between 1870 and 1900, from the heyday of pioneer Charles Worth to the discreet rule of the last great nineteenth-century designer, Jacques Doucet, the appearance of fashionable women changed very little. The use of different trimmings were all that distinguished one season from the next. These over-elaborate outfits have been described as belonging to the *style tapissier* (upholstery style), owing to their strong resemblance to the chairs, canopies and curtains being designed by decorators operating in the best parts of town. With the dawn of the new century and the advent of the 'modern style', the silhouette, echoing, as always, the trend in the decorative arts, moved away from the padded look of 1880 to something much more fluid and lithe.

Besides being artists, great twentieth-century designers cannot neglect the need to shock, to produce something new to keep up sales, if they are to maintain their appeal. At the time of Jacques Doucet, however, that constant desperation for radical change, which is now essential for the survival of fashion within the existing system, was literally unthinkable. Yet in 1908, with the advent of Paul Poiret, a turning point was reached. Four years of a literally suicidal war then shook the world to its foundations and completed this break with the past. Fashion was ready to take off.

Jacques Doucet

What is left today of Jacques Doucet, so famous in his day, beyond his name, which is attached to the two libraries he established and left to the French nation? He was born in 1853 into a prosperous family whose business, Doucet Lingerie, had flourished in the Rue de la Paix since 1816. An elegant and distinguished member of the wealthy middle classes, Doucet must constantly have aspired, without success, to belong to the society whose refined women he dressed. Following the example of his predecessor Worth, he transformed, in the closing years of the nineteenth century, the family business in de-luxe hosiery, lingerie and lace, fine linens and made-to-measure shirts, which he had inherited, into a couture house. Monsieur Jacques, as his illustrious customers called him, perhaps with a hint of condescension, never lost a taste for flimsy, translucent materials and fluid lines. He excelled in superimposing pastel colours and his ornate gossamery dresses suggest not only the eighteenth-century visions of Watteau, but also Impressionist shimmers of reflected light. This elegance of the boudoir, more distinguished than *déshabillé*, supplied a privileged clientele with the numerous outfits needed to fulfil a society calendar that was as strictly regulated as a musical score. Whether she was attending the season in Paris or staying on her country estate, the fashionable woman would change her clothes as many as five times a day. Her confections were essentially designed to perpetuate a social ideal. Obeying imperatives that left little to the imagination of the couturier, they therefore

La Chaîne fleurie
(The Floral Chain)
Dinner gown by
Jacques Doucet.
Gazette du bon ton.
March 1913

Jacques Doucet
(1853–1929)
In his dressing gown.
c. 1925

excluded any element of surprise. Doucet reserved his most original designs for actresses – both on and off the stage. With Sarah Bernhardt, Cécile Sorel and Réjane, he would experiment with effects that would later be adopted by his other clients, once they had been deemed acceptable. As a vehicle for introducing new ideas, the role of the theatre was comparable to that of couture collections today.

The tea gowns created by the Maison Doucet for women of the *demi-monde* were perfectly suited to these hothouse flowers – the tarts and hookers of their day, sometimes known as 'horizontals'. The frills, sinuous curving lines and lace ruffles the colours of faded flowers were typical elements of a Belle Époque style, to which Doucet, the last costumier of a declining society, adhered, with perhaps more conscientiousness than inspiration. But he deserves to be remembered for other reasons. Beneath the veneer of a prosperous gentleman, the couturier concealed a keen sensitivity and a grand passion for collecting. He built up an outstanding assortment of eighteenth-century furniture, objets d'art, paintings and sculptures, that were fashionable at the time, and then, on one memorable occasion in 1912, sold the entire collection at auction. He then moved on to pursue an interest in Post-Impressionism and the nascent Cubism. At the end of his life, having abandoned all ambition of worldly success, he became

Réjane as a young woman
(1856–1920)
The Parisian actress who was Jacques Doucet's muse starred in many successful plays and ran her own Théâtre Réjane from 1906 to 1918.

the close friend of Francis Picabia and Marcel Duchamp. André Breton, Louis Aragon and Pierre Reverdy were employed as librarians and helped him assemble an impressive collection of manuscripts by contemporary authors. From 1925, Jacques Doucet's collections were housed in a small modern house in Neuilly. As well as major works by De Chirico, Brancusi, Braque, Miró and Masson, they included furniture by Pierre Legrain, Eileen Gray and Marcel Coard, Douanier Rousseau's *The Snake Charmer* (bequeathed to the state) and *Les Demoiselles d'Avignon*, which he bought direct from Picasso's studio. The enigmatic Monsieur Jacques also took on the young

Paul Poiret (whose most notable creation, in the course of a rather turbulent passage through the fashion house, was the famous white costume immortalized by Sarah Bernhardt in *L'Aiglon*).

Between these two men, who to all appearances had nothing in common, there existed a powerful mutual respect that bridged their two worlds. The old master had demonstrated his ability not only to identify but also to appreciate and support some of the most revolutionary aesthetic movements that were then in the making. What he was not capable of doing, and no doubt would not have wanted to do, was to translate that insight into practical terms in the world of fashion. He was content to be remembered as a designer of taste and discrimination. Many have tried that role since, but rarely with Doucet's degree of success.

Paul Poiret

L'Embarras du choix
(Spoilt for Choice)
Tailored suit by
Paul Poiret.
Gazette du bon ton.
March 1914

Paul Poiret
(1879–1947)
September 1924

Born in 1879, the son of a tradesman at Les Halles, Paul Poiret was taken on by Doucet as a draughtsman. He completed his apprenticeship with Worth and opened his own house in 1904, which, in the course of its numerous reincarnations and expansions, proceeded to turn the conventions of the fashion world upside down. Not only did he exert a decisive influence on the development of clothing, but he also made contributions to other aesthetic fields. He was an unusual man who shot to fame in very much the sensational manner we expect in fashion today. He continually strove to ennoble the applied arts as a whole, through his lively and abundant creations. None of those inspired by his example have succeeded in matching his achievement of designing, in the early years of the century, a global range of clothes united by the same label and co-ordinated by the same sensitivity. Anticipating the diversification that is the aim of virtually all big houses today, Poiret put his visionary ideas into practice in a series of collections that marked a complete break with everything that had gone before.

In 1908, Prometheus was unchained and the designer introduced his Directoire line.

Skirts fell straight from the waist to within two inches (five or six centimetres) of the ground, while the waist rose to just below the bust, encouraging women to abandon their corsets in favour of high-fitting boned belts. Once the initial shock had been absorbed, it took only two years for the new softer look to be universally accepted. In 1909, with the first visit to Paris of the Ballets Russes, the elite discovered the charms of Orientalism. Poiret's clients were at once transformed into harem girls in flowing pantaloons, turbans and vivid colours. In the same year, as the luxury trade expanded towards the west of Paris, Poiret moved into an eighteenth-century building on the Rue du Faubourg Saint Honoré, which he redecorated with the help of Louis Süe in the newly fashionable Art Deco style. The talk of the town, the Caliph of Fashion's designs were enthusiastically received in most of the major capitals, as he experimented with every form of exoticism, from the geisha's kimono to the garb of the Ukrainian peasant. Evidence of his influence can still be found today, season after season, in the work of various young contemporary designers.

Batik
Evening coat
with long train and
fur-trimmed collar
and cuffs.
April 1911

Salome
Evening dress
by Paul Poiret.
Gazette du bon ton.
March 1914

Anticipating Chanel by ten years and Lanvin by fifteen, Paul Poiret, in 1911, launched the first perfume to be marketed by a couturier, personally co-ordinating the fragrance, bottle design, packaging, publicity material and distribution. It was called Rosine, after his eldest daughter. He was, of course, encroaching on the jealously guarded territory of the French *parfumeur*, but, as we know, his initiative enjoyed long-term success. He then turned his hand to fabric design. With the support of an atelier and the help of the young Raoul Dufy, he set about revolutionizing the comfortable world of textile printing with his ideas for furniture and clothing fabrics. An ardent supporter of

modern art, of which he was a discriminating collector, Poiret summoned innovatory artists, writers, graphic designers and model makers to join his enterprise. Better still, in 1911, he founded a Paris-based atelier for the teaching of decorative arts, which he called the École Martine after his second daughter. Its purpose was to instruct young women of modest means in the design of carpets, light fittings, fabrics and accessories for the home. To distribute these original products, which today are much sought after by collectors, a Martine shop opened; displays were also set up in the big department stores. At the same time, the group took on a number of design jobs, treating all the elements, including furnishings and accessories, as a unified whole. The results were photographed and reproduced in the newspapers to publicize this innovative approach to interior design. Still receptive to new ideas, even in his old age, the indefatigable Doucet was among the few enthusiasts to place an order.

As a pioneer in the fields of communication and publicity, Poiret was a brilliant organizer of shows and functions. However, the inspirations and follies that ensured his fame later led to his demise.

The experience of serving in the First World War profoundly affected this effusive humanist. Worse, when peace was restored, it became clear that women had grown accustomed to the active lives that they had led while the men had been away and no longer fitted his dreamy visions of reclining madonnas. Poiret watched his support ebb away. And yet, as though liberated from the need to please, he went on to produce some of his finest designs. Always an innovator, he launched the suspender belt, flesh-coloured stockings and culottes and introduced the modern brassiere. He was also the first to present both the

Le Collier nouveau
(The New Necklace)
Evening dress
by Paul Poiret.
Drawing by
Georges Lepape.
Gazette du bon ton.
January 1914

Faune
Denise Poiret wears
a gold lamé bodice
with a V-back and
corded halter-neck.
The skirt is fringed
with monkey fur and
gold braid and the
shoes are also gold.
1919–1920

sheath and the sack dress. After signing
his first contracts for the manufacture of a
range of licensed goods, he dreamed up a
weekly publication in which women would
be encouraged to design their own original
patterns under the Poiret label. Nothing much
came of it. Times had changed. A whimsical
approach to the serious business of management
and a disastrous lack of vision forced Paul the
Magnificent to close his doors in 1926. The sale
of paintings by Matisse, Derain, Van Dongen,
Picasso and Vlaminck, among others, was
not enough to avert the catastrophe that
then engulfed this unique and multi-talented
individual. Ruined, but not defeated, Paul
Poiret took to the stage with his friend Colette
in *La Vagabonde*. Between 1930 and 1934, he
published various volumes, including a book
of recipes and his memoirs which have been
translated as *My First Fifty Years*. Destitute, forgotten and alone, he then
devoted his life to his great passion, painting.

Within an ace of having to beg for his living, he barely survived
the Occupation. In 1947, a retrospective of his work was organized
by the faithful Jean Cocteau. But there was to be no final triumph for
Paul Poiret. He died a few days before the opening, leaving us food
for thought and a direction for fashion to pursue.

Mariano Fortuny

Mariano Fortuny y Madrazo was an unusual figure, with few parallels in any age, whose links with the world of fashion comprise only a small part of his œuvre. Yet his influence on dress design is still felt today. Together with the enlightened patron Jacques Doucet and the inspired innovator Paul Poiret, Fortuny, in the role of artist, constitutes the third element of the triptych of early twentieth-century fashion.

Natasha Rambova
Photograph by James Abbe of the actress wearing the famous Delphos dress.
c. 1924

Mariano Fortuny
(1871–1949)

Born in Granada in 1871, he belonged to a family of cosmopolitan artists of Spanish origin and was himself a great traveller, making his home in Venice in 1905. With his partner Henriette Negrin, whom he had met in Paris and whom he subsequently married, he shared forty-seven years of creative activity during which they explored painting, sculpture, photography, textiles and theatre and furniture design, while also collecting works of art. He invented stage-lighting systems, which anticipated those now used in photographic studios today, and also took out patents on his dress designs, for which he devised a special pleating process and new dyeing techniques.

Delphos was the name he gave to his long clinging sheath dresses that undulated with colour. Each was made of a single piece of the finest silk, its distinctive colour obtained by repeated immersions in dyes whose shades were reminiscent of moonlight or of the watery reflections of the Venetian lagoon. Mexican cochineal, Breton straw and indigo from the Far East were among

the ingredients that the Fortunys carefully imported themselves for
this alchemical process. It seems in a way ridiculous to use the term
fashion to describe these works of art, which are rooted in notions of
symbolism, memory and an idealized vision of the future, united by
a sense of virtuoso plasticity.

Proust's Oriane de Guermantes receives the narrator wearing a kimono
wrap by Fortuny and the author also clothes his Albertine in the same
manner. Isadora Duncan, Eleonora Duse, the Marquise Casati, Cléo de
Mérode, Liane de Pougy and Émilienne d'Alençon all wore his tunics that
breathed the very spirit of Venice. Our nostalgia for such luxuriousness
is tempered only by the fact that the principle of the Delphos dress has
resurfaced in simpler form in contemporary fashion. Adapted to suit the
techniques and fabrics of the late twentieth century by Issey Miyake in his
famous Pleats Please collection, this style of garment now enjoys worldwide
success. Many women who have never heard of the Venetian master
are eager to include in their wardrobe a timeless dress that is not only
lightweight but endlessly versatile.

And Also

In the Belle Époque, English tailors were regarded as the best in the world and attracted a large clientele, including a number of women. London was therefore Paris's only real competitor. The ancient rivalry that had existed between France and England did not prevent English tailors from opening shops in Paris – which was perhaps one of the first practical consequences of the Entente Cordiale. At the same time, subsidiaries of the great French fashion houses opened their doors in London. Worth was followed across the Channel to Paris by Redfern, Lucile, Creed and Molyneux, while Paquin, Poiret and then Chanel made the journey in the opposite direction.

The most successful of the English newcomers was Charles Poynter Redfern, whose label managed to ally the unquestionable distinction of the great London tailors with the notion of 'Parisian chic'; he was the first to offer women a tailored suit based directly on its male counterpart. It was the Princess of Wales, seeking to simplify her wardrobe for official engagements, who helped to spread the popularity of this eminently practical garment, which was immediately taken up by a whole generation of fashionable women. Its sober elegance has served it in good stead ever since.

Founded in 1891, Paquin, the first fashion house to be run by a woman, was highly influential. It was responsible for a number of innovations, among them, the use of publicity stunts; the setting-up of foreign partnerships; its own resolutely modern designs; and the employment of outside designers, such as illustrators Léon Bakst and Paul Iribe and architects Louis Süe and Robert Mallet-Stevens. The label continued until 1956.

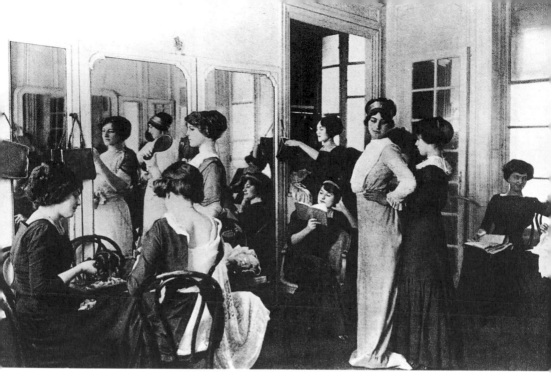

The House of Paquin
Final preparations in
the ateliers before the
collection is shown.
From *L'Illustration*.

Other notable houses of the Belle Époque were Chéruit (1906–1935),
Callot Soeurs (1895–1954), where Madeleine Vionnet worked as a leading
seamstress, and Margaine-Lacroix (1868–1930), which introduced the *robe-sylphide* (sylphlike dress) with its sinuous Art Nouveau curves. Between
1906 and 1909, the house of Agnès sold 'dresses, coats, fine lingerie,
petticoats, dressing gowns and négligées'. Christoff von Drecoll, designer
to the imperial court of Austria since 1902, opened a branch in Paris. In the
context of these names and many others now forgotten, it is worth pointing
out that, at the beginning of the century, the distinction between couture
and ready-to-wear was not sharply defined. The two different modes of
production, represented at the heart of the same professional group, were
still far from being competitors. Indeed, they often co-existed in houses
where the seamstresses moved freely, in response to demand and without
fuss or sense of hierarchy, between made-to-measure and ready-made.
Although invented in 1831, Barthélemy Thimonnier's revolutionary sewing
machine had not yet transformed working practices. In 1910, a historic date

for the profession, the first warning peal of thunder disturbed this settled state of affairs, as couture moved to protect itself by seceding and establishing itself as a separate profession. Yet it was not until the hardships of the German Occupation that a code was finally agreed, in 1945, which defined the status of the *grand couturier*. Nevertheless, by 1910, there were two distinct worlds, each with clearly specified functions: one reserved for the privileged few, the other serving the needs of the average woman. Couture or off-the-peg, each profession played to its strengths. The former boasted luxury, skill and a creativity that could find instant expression. The latter, more dynamic and more competitive, supplied social classes, not necessarily inferior, but certainly more populous. We shall have more to say later about the division of fashion into two distinct worlds.

It could be said that the designers of the Belle Époque were mad as hatters. In the late nineteenth century, the indispensable headgear for women was a tiny little confection that perched on top of, rather than fitted, a well-groomed head. In the early years of the twentieth century, this understated sophistication took on alarming proportions that were further accentuated by an increasingly willowy silhouette. From about 1910 onwards, hats had broad, straight brims and were trimmed with ribbons, flowers

Hat
c. 1910

and even exotic ostrich feathers, which required long pointed hatpins – precious items of jewelry in themselves – to attach them to the carefully coiffed hairstyle. Caroline Reboux, E. Lewis and Legroux were the most sought-after names. Poiret offered, as an alternative, his turbans, simple felt hats and clouds of tulle. And a still largely unknown young woman emerged from obscurity to open a hat shop. A few photographs of celebrities sporting her creations appeared in the papers and her name began to be noticed. Mademoiselle Chanel had made her mark.

Since the end of the eighteenth century, fashion magazines had played a significant role in forming

Lingerie
c. 1900

and guiding public taste. When, in 1890, they began to include photographs, their influence became even more pronounced. In cities throughout Europe, even in Moscow, people fought over the latest issues from Paris. The actresses, society beauties and women about town who were featured in them were in effect the fashion models of their day. Talented illustrators – among them, Paul Iribe and Georges Lepape – drew exquisite fashion plates for these magazines which covered the most recent developments in fashion and beauty and all the events in a modern woman's busy lifestyle. Among the best was the *Gazette du bon ton* founded in 1912 by Lucien Vogel, which (with the exception of the war years) was regularly published until 1925.

Until the end of the nineteenth century, women wore body linen, or undergarments, beneath their dresses. Frilled and flounced, these items were a source of easy profit for the cheaper traders. Both fetishistic objects and indispensable elements of a trousseau, their quality indicated the status of the wearer. For a long time women had remained bare-bottomed beneath their dresses. However, knickers and breeches, which had first appeared in the sixteenth century, began to be widely adopted during the nineteenth. They represented a victory for modesty and hygiene and were also a declaration of independence. For the first time, men were not the only ones to wear the trousers.

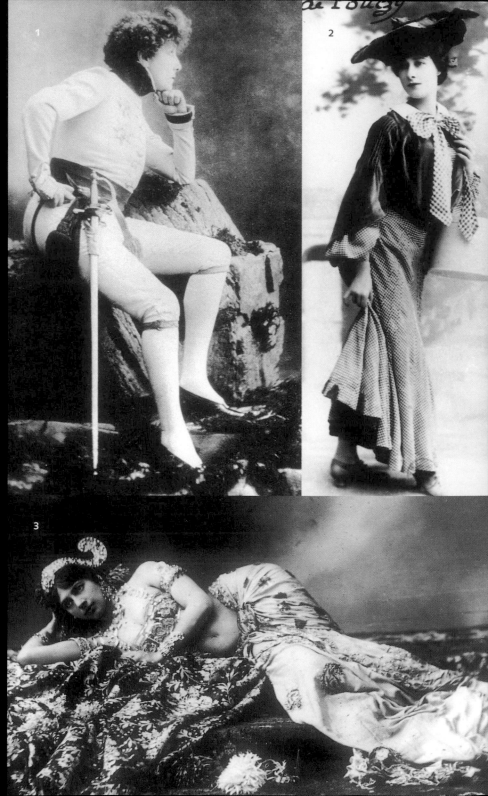

1 **Sarah Bernhardt**. For her performance in Edmond Rostand's *L'Aiglon* in 1900, the actress wore a costume designed by Paul Poiret.

2 **Liane de Pougy**. One of the most famous courtesans of the Belle Époque.

3 **Mata Hari**. Dancer and adventurer from the Netherlands. She was accused of spying for Germany and shot by the French in 1917.

4 **Léon Bakst**, *The Princess*, 1910. Sketch of a costume for Igor Stravinsky's ballet *The Firebird*.

5 **Mrs Evalyn Walsh McLean** wearing the Star of the East diamond in her hair and the Hope diamond on her necklace.

6 **Cléo de Mérode**. Dancer and mistress to the kings of the Belle Époque.

Menswear

**Comte Étienne
de Beaumont**
Photograph by
Adolf de Meyer.
1919

**Comte Robert
de Montesquiou**
Painting by
Giovanni Boldini.
1897

Men's fashion has not undergone a structural transformation anything like as rapid as women's. From a twentieth-century perspective, we should probably think more in terms of a history of the development of male attire. Little has changed in respect of the dress code put in place at the end of the eighteenth century, comprising jacket and trousers, waistcoat and tie. The gentleman's suit was perfected in London's Savile Row, at about the same time as the collapse of the Ancien Régime in France. With the demise of the French monarchy, the figure of the elaborately powdered and plumed courtier who attended the Sun King, Louis XIV, at his palace in Versailles also disappeared.

Anglo-Saxon society, dividing its time between town and country estate and with its hunting, love of travel and relaxed attitude to life, had something to teach the average Continental about an alternative way of living. As a consequence of home-grown liberalism, the eighteenth-century English gentleman had the opportunity – still denied to the French nobility – to make money. As a result, he often owned and administered large estates, and spent much of his time outdoors.

His clothes reflected it, just as they reflected the development of the English wool trade. Throughout Europe, an Anglomania took hold and determined the vocabulary and rationale of men's clothing for

two centuries. Its much vaunted simplicity – the last refuge of a complex people – was, in fact, no more than the affectation of a democratic exterior, which helped the player to keep his advantage and stay ahead in the game.

A man's clothes were a mark of his distinction and proof that he cared about his appearance and the effect it produced. Yet such a concern had on no account to betray itself. Since the time of Beau Brummell, archetype of the dandy, it has been taboo for the well-dressed man to discuss his clothes.

Plain, sober and dark-coloured – but with infinite variations – were the prerequisites of the fashionable male wardrobe for more than two centuries.

Darius Milhaud and Jean Cocteau

The frock coat (French *redingote*, from the English 'riding-coat') was the accepted day wear, replaced in the evening by tails. From 1820, breeches began to give way to trousers. At first, they were tight-fitting and ankle-length, then with straps under the feet, then button-up flies. Trousers were modernity's major contribution to men's outfitting. Finally came the dress suit and the smoking jacket, which were envisaged as more informal options for evening wear.

From being an anonymous craftsman, the tailor became a central figure in society. The fact that people ran up debts with him was indicative of his standing. In Romantic literature, we find countless examples of young men for whom clothes and paying their tailor's bill were the main preoccupations in life.

The paletot was originally inspired by a sailor's jacket and appeared as a mass-produced garment in around 1835. It fell like a sack from the shoulders down to the hips, with no waist. Also called a pea-jacket, this garment was easy to reproduce, fitted more or less any shape or size and did not require individual cutting. It was the forerunner of a whole new industry in off-the-peg clothes that was quietly beginning to emerge. Originally aimed at the

Edmond Rostand and his sons Jean and Maurice at their villa near Biarritz.

working classes, ready-to-wear garments soon attracted all sections of the bourgeoisie. The new god of the modern age was speed and everything now had to be done as fast as possible, including buying clothes.

The nineteenth and twentieth centuries continued to reaffirm the essential masculine principle of discretion. Restraint, fitting behaviour, giving women precedence and knowing when to keep quiet remained the best ways for gentlemen to distinguish themselves. Brummell said that true elegance passes unnoticed. Or rather *claimed* that it should do so.

The First World War | 1914–1918

Fashion and war don't mix, yet it is true that the latter has an indirect influence on the outward appearances of the survivors. All conflicts bring with them a legacy of social change and research undertaken for military purposes tends to accelerate technical progress, producing spin-offs in other areas.

At the start of the First World War, no one could have predicted the upheavals that were about to take place. The absence of large numbers of men encouraged women to take over the role that society had traditionally reserved for those who were now away at war. Conceived as a stopgap, this measure was to have irreversible consequences. As mothers, wives and daughters were forced to work, often in factories, they demanded clothes that were better suited to their new activities. Social events had to be postponed in favour of more pressing engagements, such as caring for the wounded. Women donned nurses' overalls or wore trousers in the arms factories, unaware that a whole new way of life was being born. The need to mourn the increasing numbers of dead, visits to the wounded and the general gravity of the hour meant that darker colours became the norm during the First World War. They ushered in a monochrome look that was, at that time, unfamiliar to young women in comfortable circumstances. Inevitably, by 1915, skirts rose above the ankle, and then to mid-calf. For men escaping on leave from the horrors of the front, the fact that so much freedom has been discovered in their absence was the cause of considerable concern.

1 **Woman wearing the new shorter-length dress, with dropped waist**
This style became fashionable at the end of the First World War.
1919

2 **Women working the land in Suffolk**
1916

3 **Marylebone Station, London**
Two women porters at work during the First World War.
1915

Between the Wars | 1919–1939

Historical Review

At the heart of the myth that even today perpetuates Paris's position as the capital of couture and luxury goods are the great fashion houses that were the glory of France in the Twenties and Thirties.

As in many other spheres, the major revolutions in fashion had already begun before the First World War. But peace had to be restored before the effects of such profound changes could be felt. The upheavals constituted a dividing line that separated the old world, a Europe of great families governed by tradition, from the new, with its altered social composition and emergent customs and objectives that had little in common with the nineteenth century. Carriages gave way to cars, bouffant coiffures to short hairstyles, dresses with long trains to above-the-knee pinafores. Princes and princesses lost their crowns. Women abandoned their corsets. There was no more leisurely remembrance of Proust's *Things Past*. Instead, a whole new society, one which liked to sunbathe and swim in the sea, was intent on broadening its horizons. Even bodies changed shape. While women borrowed their clothes from the male wardrobe and chose to dress like boys, haute couture recruited new clients from the ranks of film actresses, American heiresses and the wives and daughters of rich industrialists. Old money rubbed shoulders with the nouveaux riches, as new rules came into play. And for those who wanted to take part, life was there for the taking. Jean Cocteau, Josephine Baker, Picasso, Ernest Hemingway, Maurice Ravel, Colette and all those who flocked to hang out at the Bœuf sur le Toit were

Models on the terrace of the casino at Monte Carlo *1928*

equally enthusiastic about jazz, African art, transatlantic cruises, the new developments in cinema, modern communications and the thrill of speed. They lived life to the full and that meant adopting a new sort of fashion, one which started from first principles. The *garçonne* or bachelor girl became the symbol of women's desire to retain their new-found emancipation. No more chaperones, fewer hats and, sadly, fewer men, since so many had been killed in the war.

The couturiers were hesitant at first about the new androgynous look, but embraced it wholeheartedly from 1925. This was the year of the great Paris Exposition Internationale des Arts Décoratifs which gave its name to Art Deco, synonymous with a bustless, waistless silhouette. The bachelor girl still wanted to look seductive, but was now armed with different weapons. Aggressive dressing-down was mitigated by feather boas, embroidery and showy accessories. The woman of elegance, in the meantime, rubbed shoulders with the avant-gardes, and was allowed to demonstrate an intelligence that had hitherto been the preserve of her less glamorous sisters. Like new movements in the arts, each period in fashion begins as a scandal. Trends start suddenly and come to abrupt ends, defined not so much by what they espouse as by what they repudiate.

The euphoria of the Twenties, with its appetite for change and progress, was halted in its tracks by the crash of 1929. Its effects were felt first on the New York stock exchange, hurling millionaires downwards from the giddy heights of their skyscrapers. It then hit Europe, causing unemployment, inflation and the rise of totalitarian movements that were the inevitable consequence of troubled times. Women in modest circumstances, who could not afford couture clothes, resorted to their sewing machines.

Alexander Rodchenko
Textile design.
c. 1920

With characteristic ingenuity and dexterity, Parisian women managed to run up outfits whose innate stylishness made the French capital a byword for elegance during the inter-war period.

The flattened contours of the early Twenties gave way to a new emphasis on the body in the following decade. Fashion became more compromising, aiming to preserve feminism's victories while rediscovering a subtle and reassuring elegance. Crises are not the time for experimenting. The waist was restored to its proper position, hair was grown back to a more feminine length and often softly waved. Thin, toned and sporty bodies were back in fashion, with a renewed appreciation of the bust. Naturalness, harmony and simplicity were the catchwords. The furniture designs of Jean-Michel Frank, André Arbus, Louis Süe and André Mare reflected this interest in the neoclassical. The period has often been regarded as the apogee of good taste in the lifestyle arts and is still considered a touchstone today, especially in the fashion world where it remains a constant source of reference for designers.

With the 1936 introduction in France of paid holidays, the Popular Front packed enthusiastic crowds off to the seaside. The vogue for outdoor

Garçonne or
bachelor girl

fashions encouraged couturiers to produce what today we would call sportswear. Nobody yet used the term 'ready-to-wear', but the boutiques already described such clothes as being 'for sport'. With their trousers, bathing costumes, pareos and sweaters, the great houses began to cater for the long holidays enjoyed by their wealthy clients. In the whole history of fashion design, this period between the wars is the only one to be dominated by women designers.

Foremost among them were Madeleine Vionnet and Gabrielle Chanel, two outstanding but very different women. The former was a hardworking technician, whose interest lay in the production of garments. The latter, already known to all of Paris as Coco, was a liberated woman, a media-conscious subversive, whose ambition was to devise a dress code for the new woman. Where Vionnet was the architect, Chanel took the role of stylist. The two axes of future fashion were clearly delineated: on the one hand, it was to be sculpture in movement, on the other, a living language. Twenty years later, factory mass-production methods would universalize their made-to-measure templates. In the meantime, the female trio was completed by Elsa Schiaparelli, who brought to couture an inimitable wit and a range of accessories that anticipated the most adventurous developments in contemporary ready-to-wear.

Jeanne Lanvin

Jupiter
This evening coat offers a foretaste of the stylized designs of Art Deco.
Winter 1919

Jeanne Lanvin and her daughter dressed to go to a ball
This photograph inspired Paul Iribe's design for the Lanvin logo.
1907

The history of Jeanne Lanvin, the little milliner girl, reads like a fairy story. An unassuming but quietly determined young Parisienne, born in 1867, she found employment trimming hats and set up on her own in 1885.

When her daughter was born twelve years later, she made her such beautiful clothes that they attracted the attention of a number of wealthy people, who asked for copies. Her fortune was made. It was then only a small bridge to cross from making dresses for little girls to designing outfits for their mothers. Lanvin's name appeared in the fashion yearbook from 1901 onwards. Edmond Rostand was the first of many eminent writers to ask her to make him the traditional green coat worn by members of the Académie Française, a curious twist of fate for a woman who was notorious for her lack of volubility. In 1920, the talented decorator Armand-Albert Rateau designed the interiors of the Maison Lanvin, at 15 and 22 Rue du Faubourg Saint Honoré. The clientele included many lifelong devotees, as well as some of the most famous names in Europe. For women of classical beauty, Madame Lanvin's was the perfect style. Without fuss, it espoused the taste of the day, with its skilful use of intricate trimmings, virtuoso embroideries and the beaded decorations in clear, light, floral colours that became a Lanvin trademark.

In 1925, the Maison Lanvin comprised twenty-three ateliers employing over eight hundred women.

On top of that, there were the employees of the various other departments, such as made-to-measure, sportswear, furs, lingerie and, later, men's fashion, as well as an interior design shop overseen at one point by Rateau. Their global approach to lifestyle products foreshadowed the strategies that all the big contemporary fashion houses would later adopt in their efforts to diversify.

From 1923 onwards, Jeanne Lanvin's empire also included a dye factory, where the wonderfully subtle colours that gave the Lanvin palette its reputation were created. Then, in 1925, while Jeanne Lanvin was vice-president of the Pavillon de l'Élégance and playing an active part in the historic Exposition Internationale des Arts Décoratifs, she launched, under her own label, My Sin, the first scent to be an overnight success in the United States. Arpège followed in 1927. The spherical black bottle bore a gold motif representing, in Paul Iribe's stylized design, a woman holding her young daughter by the hand.

Besides her love of craftsmanship that she developed to the heights of perfection, Jeanne Lanvin's passion and talisman, right up until the day she died, aged seventy-nine in 1946, was her only child, Marie-Blanche. Her daughter was a fine pianist and it was her practising her scales that inspired the name of the perfume Arpège, or arpeggio, that is synonymous with the Maison Lanvin, whose first customer she had been and the direction of which she took over in the Fifties.

Arpège by Lanvin
Spherical bottle designed by Armand-Albert Rateau, bearing Paul Iribe's logo.
1927

Lee Miller
The American actress wears a Lanvin evening dress in this photograph taken by Hoyningen-Huene for *Vogue* magazine.
1932

Jean Patou

Born in 1880 and a serving soldier until 1918, Jean Patou, who died prematurely in 1936, enjoyed a dazzling career and occupies a unique position in Twenties couture. The war was barely over when this tanner's son, who had been an apprentice furrier before turning to dressmaking, opened a salon that bore his name in the Rue Saint Florentin, in Paris. His style was never mainstream, but full of originality and characterized by a studied simplicity which was to win him fame, especially in the American markets. With their clean lines, their geometric and even Cubist motifs and their combination of practicality and luxury, many of his garments were designed to satisfy the new craze for the outdoor life. They bear an uncanny resemblance to modern sportswear.

With its deliberately restrained palette of blue and white, combined – and we should remember that this was something new – with every shade of beige, this look was in perfect symbiosis with the early jazz bands and the Art Deco style. Its most famous proponent was the tennis champion Suzanne Lenglen. After Jean Patou's death in 1936, his house continued to give young designers the chance to make their mark right up until the Eighties. All that remains today is the perfumery business, launched with the customary efficiency of a man who was truly progressive.

Afternoon suit
Suit with navy and yellow stripes, with matching scarf, cloche hat and clutch bag.
1927

Sweater
Jean Patou's monogram figures prominently.
1930

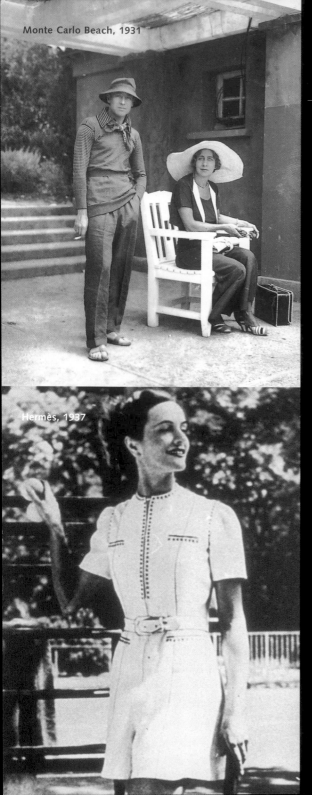

Monte Carlo Beach, 1931

Hermès, 1937

Sportswear

Sportswear has little to do with sport
in the competitive sense of the word;
its connotations are more of leisure,
the open air and relaxation. Implying
nonetheless a fair degree of physical
activity, it is not surprising that
sportswear was introduced into the
male wardrobe during the Twenties
by the social classes that were
sufficiently privileged to expend
their energy in the pursuit of
pleasure. It enabled the well-dressed
man, without in any way demeaning
himself, to escape temporarily from
the strict code that still governed
what he should wear. Jersey, soft
knits, flannel, short-sleeved polo
shirts, windbreakers, caps, reefer
jackets and sailors' overshirts began
to infiltrate wardrobes, influencing
the way that people looked. Women
also benefited from this new
freedom and, with Chanel and Patou
leading the way, couturiers gradually
began to adapt to the resulting state
of affairs that for once was not of
their making. The thin, tanned
and healthy woman of the Thirties
was sport's finest achievement.

USA, 1938

Monte Carlo, 1931

Suzanne Lenglen, 1921

Gabrielle Chanel

Gabrielle Chanel
(1883–1971)
The great couturière
is photographed here
in the grounds of
her villa, La Pausa,
in the Thirties.

Because the House of Chanel continues to exist today, we have a tendency
to attribute all the fashion innovations of the Twenties to its founder.
In fact, she was not the first to cut her hair short, but she did make the
style fashionable. Poiret had already devised an outfit which women could
put on without the help of a maid, but it was Mademoiselle Chanel who
actually sold it to the public. Because raw materials were still in short
supply after the war, she pioneered the use of jersey knit, hitherto reserved
for men's underwear. She also ennobled the status of both knitwear and
costume jewelry.

The inventor of 'poor chic' (which has grown from strength to
strength ever since), Coco Chanel was a bit of a loose cannon and a loner,
who invented a whole new look while, all about her, others were merely
churning out models, season after season. Without being aware of it, she,
as a designer, echoed the stance of the great writers on modernity. With her
background in the *demi-monde* of the Belle Époque, this daughter of poverty-
stricken peasants had realized that work was her only means of salvation.
Attaining a level of excellence in everything she attempted, she took men on
and equalled them, by being quite simply better than they were. This entirely
unprecedented attitude introduced a new dimension into the history of
fashion: morality.

Thereafter, the well-dressed woman would be the lesser-dressed woman,
demanding her right to enjoy herself before seducing a man with a fat wallet.
Furthermore, as an instigator of this type of behaviour, Chanel was also
claiming to be an arbiter of style – her own. Occupying, as she did,

**The woman everyone
knew as Coco**
30 May 1929

**Coco Chanel
accompanied
by Serge Lifar**
Attending a dinner
in Monte Carlo.
1933

a marginal position within Parisian couture, Mademoiselle Chanel, with her
lovers, her magnetic personality and her silver tongue, was the first designer
to behave as though she was on a par with her customers. Similarly, her
designs were born in response to her own personal needs and corresponded
to an image that she wanted to create for herself. If she designed evening
dresses, it was because she herself was going out. When she used tweed,
in a masculine cut, with knitwear, it was because she was going riding with
the Duke of Westminster. Or she may have been sunbathing on the Riviera
with Serge Lifar, or curling up on his sofa. Her view of the world was
uncompromising. The press photographed her captivating *belle-laide*

Fulco di Verdura cuff bracelet
Sicilian by birth, the Duke of Verdura was famous in the Thirties for designing some of Chanel's finest jewelry. This lacquered ivory bracelet encrusted with faceted coloured crystals is a fine example.
1930

Chanel on holiday
For a stroll with Serge Lifar, Coco Chanel wears linen trousers and espadrilles.

features – which were striking but not in the conventional sense of beauty – and quoted her every witticism and outrageous comment. People laughed, but they took notice, since Paris was the last city where ridicule could still kill. And many fell victim to Mademoiselle Chanel, as she set about consigning every previous fashion to history.

In 1921 Chanel opened the fashion house that still bears her name at 31 Rue Cambon. In the same year, she launched her first perfume. Presented in a plain, unembellished bottle marked only with its registered number, Chanel No. 5 unashamedly employed synthetic products which modern perfumery did not yet admit to using. Its eighty or so ingredients are blended together in a fragrance as abstract as Chanel fashion itself. The magic formula quickly outstripped all the rest to become an outright best-seller. It was to prove a veritable gold mine and would play a disproportionately large role, given the size of the product, in perpetuating the style, glamour and influence of a designer who now looms as large in our recollections of the century as Picasso, Warhol and Cocteau. One final peculiarity is that at a time when fashions were short-lived, Chanel's success spanned two distinct periods. The first ended with the German invasion; the second began in 1954 when the great designer reopened her salons and confounded expectations by staging a comeback.

Van Cleef & Arpels

Boivin

Jewelry

In the period between the wars,
jewelry, too, reflected the economic
and social changes that contributed
to modifying female appearance.
'A woman's neckline is not a safe,'
ruled Mademoiselle Chanel,
who was the first to use costume
jewelry, of Byzantine inspiration, to
accessorize her little black dresses.
At the same time, largely under the
influence of Louis Cartier and his
successor Jeanne Toussaint, quality
jewelry began to make increasing use
of platinum (which, although hard-
wearing and malleable, had been
disregarded for some time) in
infinitely discreet settings of jewels
that now became the focus of the
piece. While its combinations of
precious and semi-precious stones,
platinum and various colours of
gold sometimes achieved effects
of wonderful simplicity, never before
had Parisian jewelry used gemstones
of such high quality. Under the
influence of Art Deco, designers
devised forms of Cubist inspiration,
incorporating into their decorative
schemes a whole gamut of non-
precious objects, such as enamel,
Bakelite, glass beads and moulded,
nickel-plated and lustred metals.
On the other side of the Atlantic,
under the fresh eyes of the craftsmen
who supplied the Hollywood film
industry, costume jewelry developed
a complete new range of forms,
of dazzling originality, during
the Thirties.

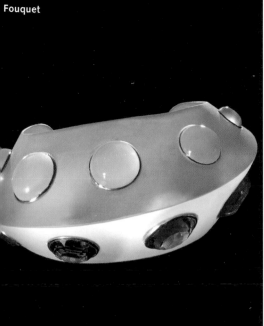

Boucheron

Cartier

Van Cleef & Arpels

Madeleine Vionnet

**Ivory-coloured
evening dress in
Moroccan crêpe**
Musée des
Tissus, Lyon.
Winter 1935–1936

Madeleine Vionnet
(1876–1975)
Vionnet usually
worked with dolls to
create her designs.

'Insofar as one can talk of a Vionnet school, it comes mostly from my having been an enemy of fashion. There is something superficial and volatile about the seasonal and elusive whims of fashion which offends my sense of beauty', confided Madeleine Vionnet in 1937. And indeed the creations produced by this great architect of the dress, who found her inspiration in Greek statues, do seem utterly timeless. That no doubt is what makes her today the most universally respected of the fashion designers of the past. Queen of the bias cut, which she began to experiment with before the First World War, she created evening dresses that fitted the body without excessive elaboration or dissimulation, employing a flowing line that would not seem out of place on a Greek frieze.

Yet this apparent simplicity concealed a lengthy preparation process. Vionnet produced her designs by cutting, draping and pinning fabric on to dolls, before making up full-scale models in chiffon, silk or Moroccan crêpe. Her perfect draping of these delicate materials created a wonderfully poised and sensual effect. Her designs were also hugely influential in respect of the freedom of movement they allowed. The unequalled success of Vionnet's cuts assured her reputation right up to her retirement in 1939, making hers the most elegant clientele of the period between the wars.

Madeleine Vionnet, 1931

Lucien Lelong

In the late nineteenth century, Arthur and Eléonore Lelong opened a couture business to supply foreign courts. Their son Lucien left the army in 1910, joined the house and began to contribute his own ideas; by 1926 the business had 1,200 employees. Lucien's wife Natalie Paley, daughter of Grand Duke Paul of Russia, was a noted beauty. She used to wear her husband's designs and, for a time, they formed one of the most prestigious and best-matched couples in Paris in the Thirties.

Like Jacques Doucet and many other heads of great fashion houses in the pre-Liberation period, Lelong was not really a creative innovator. His forte was as a co-ordinator, combining the roles of businessman and artistic director in a commercial enterprise that, at various times, employed such talents as Pierre Balmain, Christian Dior and Hubert de Givenchy on the design side. He also served on a number of official bodies, both abroad and within the profession at home.

Aware of developments in America, in 1935, this shrewd and far-sighted entrepreneur set up a department of ready-made dresses in parallel with his busy couture operation. The garments were produced in limited numbers and could be fitted with minimal alterations. Marketed under the label Lucien Lelong Éditions, they were one of the first products of the emergent ready-to-wear industry.

**Woman in
a sedan chair**
Photograph by
Man Ray.
1937

Lucien Lelong
(1889–1952)

Elsa Schiaparelli

Along with Vionnet, Lanvin and Chanel, the other female designer
of distinction in this period was Schiaparelli.

Elsa did not show her first proper collection until 1929, when she was
promptly hailed by the press as 'one of the rare innovators' of her day.
Just ten years later, the German invasion forced her into exile in the United
States. In a pulsatingly exciting and inventive career, Schiap, as she was
called, did not so much revolutionize fashion as shatter its very foundations.
Although, unusually, she did not depend on the traditional expertise of
French craftsmen working in the luxury trades, this young Italian woman
could only have achieved what she did in Paris, where she knew many
of the most influential artists and was adept at pulling the strings.

She was born in 1890 into a highly cultured and patrician Roman family.
Married at twenty-four, she went first to the United States, where she met,
among others, Marcel Duchamp, Francis Picabia,
Man Ray and Alfred Stieglitz. Having moved to Paris
in 1922, she designed and sold, not without difficulty,
her first knitwear designs. Poiret supported her. Boosted
by a degree of early success and blessed with huge self-
belief and a spirit of adventure, coupled with a streak of
ruthlessness, she opened her own boutique in the Rue
de la Paix. The first pullover she displayed in her windows
caused a sensation: it was knitted in black with a *trompe-
l'œil* white bow. She turned out dazzling collections hard
and fast thereafter, mesmerizing the public and attracting

**Three Schiaparelli
silhouettes, sketched
by Christian Bérard**
Cape in pink silk
embroidered with
a golden sun, for
the astrological
collection.
1938

**Padlock motif
in gold thread,**
embroidered by
the Maison Lesage.
1939

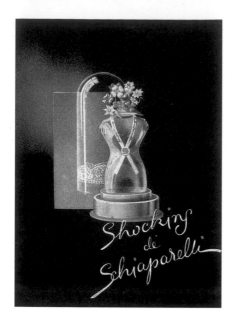

Shocking
Advertisement for
Elsa Schiaparelli's
first perfume; the
shape of the bottle
is inspired by Mae
West's bust.
1938

**Shocking pink
bow-sash**
A classic look
adapted for
haute couture by
Elsa Schiaparelli,
photographed
by Horst.
1938

a devoted clientele, much to the chagrin of
Mademoiselle Chanel. There are endless contrasts
and parallels that could be drawn between these
two women who chose to live independently
of men, so different in spite of all they had
in common.

Elsa Schiaparelli was a close friend of Jean
Cocteau, Christian Bérard and also Salvador Dalí,
who designed embroidery motifs for her and
provided inspiration for models like the desk suit
with drawers for pockets, the shoe-shaped hat,
the silk dress painted with flies and the one
bearing a picture of a large lobster. At about
this time, in 1935, Jean-Michel Frank decorated
her salon, now moved to 21 Place Vendôme, in his revolutionary style.
Giacometti and the Duchess of Windsor, Greta Garbo and Arletty,
all of Paris flocked to this temple of eccentric elegance as collection
succeeded collection: in 1936, the parachute dress; 1937, the telescopic hat;
1938, launch of the scent Shocking, its bottle an unequivocal representation
of Mae West's bust; 1939, the Cash and Carry collection.

After a period in the United States supporting the war effort, the designer
returned to Paris in 1945, where her salon had survived the Occupation.
Pierre Cardin and Hubert de Givenchy were among those who graced her
workshops. In 1946, Dalí designed the bottle for her Roi Soleil fragrance.
Schiaparelli subsequently launched a line of luggage designed for modern
methods of transport and distributed a range of ready-to-wear in the United
States. But her heart was no longer in it and, besides, the rules of the game
had changed. Financial difficulties forced her to stop trading in 1954;
she was still wealthy, but disillusioned. Before her death at the age of
eighty-three in 1973, she published a delightful book of memoirs called
Shocking Life, after the vibrant pink that was her signature colour.

And Also

Evening dress in black silk crêpe by Mainbocher
Severe elegance is the latest New York look.
1945

In the Paris of the Thirties, quite apart from all these distinguished and successful fashion houses, one name stood out, that of Mainbocher. A native of Chicago (1890–1974), he was the first American designer to live and work in Paris, having emigrated to Europe in 1911. A graphic designer working in advertising and then a sergeant major during the First World War, by 1925 he had landed the job of *Vogue*'s American correspondent in Paris. Four years later, more or less on a whim, he opened his own couture house. His designs were plain in style but had supreme elegance, often employing the bias cut pioneered by Vionnet. They attracted the attention of his compatriot Wallis Simpson, who, in 1936, asked him to create an outfit which became a worldwide sensation and which, for the first time in the history of couture, was ripped off and reproduced in thousands of copies. This was the wedding dress that brought about the abdication of Edward VIII and made Mainbocher's name.

Edward Molyneux (1891–1974) was of Irish extraction and originally wanted to become a painter. Instead, his drawings attracted attention and won him a job as a fashion draughtsman, first in the United States and then in Paris. In 1919 he set up on his own. Success was almost instant, with his commission to design the trousseau and elegant wedding dress worn

Evening dress by Norman Hartnell
A classic British look in the romantic style of the dressmaker to the English royal family. Victoria and Albert Museum, London.
1933–1934

by Princess Marina of Greece for her marriage to the Duke of Kent. Innovative and well-bred, with pure lines and discreet Anglo-Saxon colours, Molyneux's style is best represented by his matching ensembles, tailored suits and coats and evening pyjamas.

Still with us today is the house of Nina Ricci which, from modest beginnings, has won a deserved reputation for middle-of-the-range couture. Founded by the Italian designer in 1932, after an apprenticeship that began when she was thirteen, its quality of workmanship was outstanding in the period before the Second World War. During the Occupation, Nina Ricci's son, Robert, embarked on a policy of diversification, which was amply vindicated by the launch in 1948 of one of the most acclaimed post-war fragrances, L'Air du Temps. It alone guaranteed the future of a house that had long been synonymous with romantic dresses favoured by the daughters of the wealthy bourgeoisie.

The fur coat, introduced by Revillon, became the most luxurious item of an elegant woman's winter wardrobe. Beaver, astrakhan and sealskin were at that time still more popular than mink. Fox stoles were worn draped around the neck, like a scarf or cravat, and monkey skin was used for bolero jackets.

Hermès had existed as a saddlery in the Rue du Faubourg Saint Honoré since 1837. Then, in 1933, it started selling the handmade printed silk square scarves with which its name has become synonymous. It also popularized the zip and many other practical inventions. The new passion for sport spawned not only bathing costumes, but a whole range of other outfits. Shorts for cycling, beachwear, ski clothes and printed pareos all prefigured a ready-to-wear industry that would operate in parallel with couture.

Describing the outlets as 'boutiques' betrayed a degree of coyness about marketing the standard finish of the first mass-produced objects under couture labels. Slowly but inevitably, however, designer off-the-peg ranges became the norm.

Jenny, Martial et Armand, Augustabernard, Premet.... There are too many to list them all, but each couture house in the Thirties had its own place in the market, with its own style, clientele and philosophy to distinguish it from all the rest. In this respect, at least, we can compare the proliferation of couture houses in the period between the wars with today's manufacturers of off-the-peg designer clothes. In neither of these cases will you find an operation or a label that is the exact counterpart of any other. Big or small, each house has its own niche and offers a very specific range of designs to clients appreciative of its style. It is this patchwork of industries, each with its own formulae and manufacturing secrets, that has always been the distinguishing feature of Paris fashion, from the Thirties to the present day.

Liu by Guerlain
1929

Paris is also the city where the White Russians took refuge. Ruined by the October Revolution, some of these aristocratic ladies became *vendeuses*, models or designers in the couture houses. Princess Irene, with Prince Felix Yusupov, scraped together the necessary capital to start her own label. This was the Maison Irfé, founded in 1924. Valentina was another who arrived in Paris after the Revolution, headed for New York and four years later opened her own house. Princess Irene Galitzine emigrated to Rome in 1918, although she did not launch her own label until 1959.

Other luxury goods were soon introduced to complement the elegance of couture, notably designer perfumes. Influenced by the success

The Coty boutique in the Place Vendôme
The discreetly luxurious interior is designed to complement the products on display.

of Chanel No. 5, most of the larger houses opened their own perfumery departments. In 1900, the composition of the precious liquid, its bottling and its distribution were still the exclusive preserve of *parfumeurs*, who jealously guarded their unique role. The perfumers Viollet, Lubin, Gellé, Pinaud, Delettrez and Molinard had all first opened their doors during the Restoration or under the July Monarchy, whereas Rigaud, Agnel and Roger et Gallet were names that appeared during the Second Empire. Guerlain, established in 1828, held pride of place in the aristocracy of fragrance, with such winners as Jicky (1889), Après l'Ondée (1906) and L'Heure Bleue (1912). It was Paul Poiret, influenced by Gaston Leroux's *The Perfume of the Lady in Black*, who invented the designer perfume. People laughed at his presumption, but he single-handedly destroyed the monopoly.

**Hat by Caroline
Reboux**
The Baronne
d'Almeïda also wears
a boa by Patou.
1932

In the late nineteenth century, although scents were created largely from
synthetic substances – transforming the traditional chemistry of fragrance –
they still hid behind poetic floral names appropriate to the comparatively
few natural ingredients they contained, such as jasmine, rose, lavender,
patchouli, cloves and bergamot. The surreptitious admixture of synthetic
products was rarely confessed to, even though it considerably enriched
the range of fragrances and made them last longer on the skin. It was
Chanel No. 5 that first abandoned this polite fiction and, in 1921,
declared itself unequivocally the first perfume not to be one hundred
per cent natural. This veritable alchemist's elixir enjoyed legendary
success. Radically different, it transformed a whole ancient tradition

of perfumery and revealed a scope for future development that continues to be exploited today.

Even though the female look became progressively more informal during the Twenties and Thirties, hats nevertheless remained de rigueur for day wear. As the essential finishing touch to any elegant ensemble, there was one for every hour of the day, every outfit and every woman. For the morning, there were felt hats in masculine styles. For the races, broad brims in lightweight materials were popular. In the evening, on the other hand, little veils and feathers, and sometimes jewels, were worn. Caroline Reboux continued to be the dominant influence in this important sphere of Paris fashion.

The market in handmade shoes was led by the French designer André Perugia. The son of a cobbler who had emigrated to Nice, he was apprenticed to the trade at sixteen. The manager's wife at the Hôtel Negresco noticed his work and allowed him to display some of his early models in a window of the foyer. Paul Poiret chanced to see them and was so impressed that he invited the young man to Paris. In 1920, Perugia opened his first boutique in the Rue du Faubourg Saint Honoré. As well as producing shoes in classic styles, the House of Perugia produced models of unrivalled fantasy and extravagance.

Shoe by André Perugia
The Salome model has a woven upper and Art Deco motifs on the heel.
c. 1927

In 1935, Salvatore Ferragamo set up a shoe-making workshop which was to blossom into of one of the biggest fashion empires in Italy. It still occupies its original premises in the Palazzo Spini Ferroni in Florence. Shortages of materials in the Italy of the Thirties led him to experiment with materials such as hemp, straw, paper and some of the early synthetics. He also, famously, invented the platform sole and, later, the so-called invisible shoe, with uppers made of clear nylon thread. Most of these models may be seen today at the Ferragamo Museum in Florence.

In contrast to the seductive underwear favoured in the Belle Époque, all that was needed for the liberated woman dancing

Sandal by Salvatore Ferragamo
With adjustable straps in red suede and a platform sole in incised and painted wood.
1935–1936

Brassière
Model designed by Madame Denise Ferreiro, 21 Rue Washington, Paris.
1935

the charleston, in a dress with neither bust nor waist, was a lightly elasticated girdle and jersey-knit pants and sometimes a band to flatten the bust, instead of a bra. The resulting effect emphasized the androgynous look. As underwear began to be machine produced, the notion of the sacramental trousseau was abandoned. Fine lingerie was not only standardized but also democratized by mass production. In the Thirties, the waist reverted to its natural position. The female body was remodelled to a more neoclassical shape with the aid of the brassiere, the girdle and the lightweight corset. The resultant slim and sharply defined line would be skimmed by a silk slip, worn beneath a dark sheath dress or a draped antique-style gown. At the same time, the constricting garter was replaced by the suspender belt, which echoed the natural curve of the body. While the free-love philosophy of the Twenties had encouraged many liberated women to adopt pyjamas, 1930 saw the return of the nightdress and the frothy negligées that were so popular in Hollywood films.

1 **Nancy Cunard**, 1926. The wealthy heiress was a patron of the Surrealists and a passionate collector of African art. Photograph by Man Ray.

2 **Josephine Baker** in the *Can Can*, Mairie du Larrotto, 1923. Her first appearance in Paris was in *La Revue nègre* at the Théâtre des Champs-Elysées, in 1925.

3 **Lee Miller**. The American beauty was discovered by Condé Nast. She appeared in Jean Cocteau's *The Blood of a Poet*, before becoming Man Ray's mistress and collaborator. Photograph by Man Ray.

4 **Lady Mountbatten**, 1925. A relative of the English royal family, her distinguished elegance helped to popularize Norman Hartnell's designs on the Continent.

Menswear

Tennis outfit
Casual male elegance
at Monte Carlo.
1935

After the First World War, not only was there a huge expansion in menswear for the colonies, where troops had been raised to fight in the war, but there was a growing mood of informality, among Americans in particular, which was reflected in styles that emphasized youthfulness and relaxation.

Until the turn of the century, there was an appropriate outfit prescribed for every event in the well-dressed gentleman's day. But young men in the Twenties, no longer afraid to show their youthfulness, began to wear the same soft wool suit all day long. In some quarters this was frowned upon, although it was considered not nearly as shocking as the wearing of soft collars. At the same time, beards and moustaches, signs of virility, disappeared with Gillette's popularization of the electric razor.

With the more widespread practice of sport (the Lacoste shirt first appeared in 1933), men became accustomed to a more active life and the male body grew leaner and more toned. The London cut, with its slim lines, padded shoulders and loose-fitting sleeves, perfected by the English tailor Scholte, offered that blend of casual and classic favoured by Edward Prince of Wales, a man who, in the end, opted for comfort rather than the formality of the court and English tailoring rather than royal duty. The great Hollywood actors took their cue from him and did their bit in popularizing a style whose elegance remains unsurpassed.

Louise Brooks

Katharine Hepburn

The Influence of American Film

During the Thirties, the Hollywood dream factory provided entertainment and escape for its viewers. Its stars were the new gods and a costume worn by Travis Banton, Edith Head or Gilbert Adrian would be seen by millions. Quantitatively speaking, that costume would have a larger audience than the photograph of a dress designed by a great couturier illustrated in a magazine read by no more than a few thousand people.

Without even attempting to keep track of all the latest Paris fashions, its costume designers concentrated on their own version of classicism, which was intended to be timeless, flattering and photogenic. Using ostensibly luxurious materials (sequins, fur and chiffon, rarely patterned fabrics), the clothes were simply cut. Often, however, they included some memorable detail, such as a low-cut back to a dress – which was only revealed when the actress turned her back to the cameras – or some particularly striking accessory. A further development was the prototype of the busty Hollywood pin-up, who first appeared in 1943 when Howard Hughes designed a bra with pointed cups for Jane Russell.

Carole Lombard

Greta Garbo

Marlene Dietrich

The Second World War | 1939–1945

Historical Review

Abri, a camouflage one-piece by Elsa Schiaparelli
With its large patch pockets, this overalls-style garment was designed for dashing down to the bomb shelter when the alert was sounded.
1939

Guyla Batthyany
The Sisters of Gamos
Budapest.
1943–1944

The posturings of the phoney war did not prevent the haute couture industry from functioning during the season of 1939–1940. With most clients doing their bit for the war effort, however, some degree of restraint was called for. General Gamelin's wife, for example, would ostentatiously knit a khaki wool balaclava while she attended fashion shows. Dress designs tended to have names like Alert, Leave and No Shelter. Blues were called Maginot Line and reds Foreign Legion. Yet, at the same time, skirts were already being designed with side-slits, to make it easier to ride a bicycle.

After the invasion of Poland, the American Mainbocher moved his couture operation to Manhattan, in 1941. The ageing Madeleine Vionnet had closed down her business in 1939. Mademoiselle Chanel sensibly headed south in her chauffeur's car and was not to reopen her salon until the war was over. Only the boutique in the Rue Cambon remained in business. The German soldiers used to stock up on Chanel No. 5 there, until Paris was liberated; then the Yankees took their place, queueing patiently for hours.

In the great intellectual and moral re-education programme undertaken by the French state, under the direction of Marshal Pétain, couture was not spared, given over as it was, or so he claimed, to outsiders and prey therefore to moral decadence. In contrast to the elegant, emancipated Parisienne, Vichy promoted the model of the wife and mother,

the healthy, sporty young woman, a figure who was much more in line with the new political criteria.

In the meantime, Germany was requisitioning more than half of what France produced. People faced genuine hardship as they struggled to keep going. Haute couture was no more immune than the rest of the country to the conquerors' greed. Where Vichy had wanted to rationalize, Germany wanted to take over and was planning quite seriously to transfer French couture to Berlin and Vienna, placing it under German control. The archives of the Chambre Syndicale de la Couture were seized, most significantly the client list. The couturiers themselves were invited, in pressing terms, to move their workshops to the two foreign capitals, neither of which had any tradition of fashion. The real point of all of this was to break up a monopoly that threatened the supremacy of the Reich.

Lucien Lelong had been president of the Chambre Syndicale since 1937 and he mounted a vigorous counter-offensive. With the backing of the collaborationist government, which recognized that thousands of jobs were at stake, he went to Berlin. There, he discovered, not entirely to his surprise, that the Germans were setting up a heavily subsidized couture industry of their own. Insisting on the right of each country to create its own

Presentation of wooden-soled shoes

fashions, the French delegate told the German officials that they would have to fight their own battles, independently of the Paris industry that they seemed to regard as such a threat. 'It does not lie within the power of any nation to take away from Paris the creative genius of fashion, which, in the city where it belongs, is not only a spontaneous outburst of talent but the result of a tradition maintained by a body of specialist male and female workers employed in a number of different crafts.'

The above extract from the 'Lelong Report on French Fashion from July 1940 to August 1944' represents a declaration of belief that is just as

AVENUE DES CHAMPS ÉLYSÉES

ZUR NORMANDIE FRONT

Rüstungs u. Beschaffungsstab Frankreich
Paris Avenue des Champs Élysées 131

Zentra·Kraft
Paris Rond-Point des Champs Élysées 14.

NSKK Gruppe Todt
Abschnittsführung West
31, Avenue des Champs Élysées 79

K.I.P. 513

Cycling stockingless through the streets of Paris

relevant today. It was couched in terms that were sufficiently compelling to persuade the Germans, even after the autumn of 1940, to allow Parisian couture to retain its autonomy. In those difficult times, one of its considerable achievements was to employ the largest possible labour force to handle a minimum of raw materials. Limiting the models in shows to seventy-five; shortening evening wear; making day wear skimpier; and using substitute materials wherever possible, Parisian couture was determined to survive. It was backed up by a professional sector which demonstrated, as never before, its ability to adapt, a flexibility it retained even after peace was declared.

In the meantime, for most people, it was a question of recycling old garments and juggling clothing coupons. Viscose manufactured out of wood pulp, rayon, bonded fibres and man-made fabrics were the only materials available to protect them against the particularly harsh winters of those Occupation years.

As the Parisienne grew thinner, her clothes, like the wooden soles of her shoes, grew thicker. Regulations governing the clothing industry were introduced. From 1940 onwards, no more than thirteen feet (four metres) of cloth could be used for a coat and just over three feet (one metre) was all that was allowed for a blouse, with special dispensations for pregnant women. No leather belt could be more than 1 ½ inches (four centimetres) wide and one particularly narrow model was nicknamed Another Notch. Humour and frivolity became a way of defying the occupying powers.

While most of the French population became increasingly resourceful, relying heavily on their imagination, haute couture tried to keep its flag flying. In this, it was oddly successful. Some have argued that it survived because its customers were the wives of rich Nazis. In fact, records reveal that, apart from wealthy Parisiennes, it was wives of foreign ambassadors, clients from the black market and a whole eclectic mix of people who continued to frequent the salons, among whom German women were a minority. Social life during the Occupation was frenetic, since it was too cold to stay at home. There were even new houses opening up. Jacques Fath, Nina Ricci, Marcel Rochas, Maggy Rouff, Robert Piguet, Jeanne Lafaurie and Madeleine Vramant were among the names that brought life and colour to this dark period, as couture, by its refusal to shut up shop, safeguarded its essential tradition of knowledge and experience. If, as the occupying forces wanted, the workshops had closed down from 1939 to 1945, the continuity maintained by handing down information by word of mouth would have been destroyed. In just one generation, an oral tradition can die out completely.

In Great Britain, during this period, the Board of Trade asked the Fashion Group of Great Britain to set up a committee to design attractive clothing within the terms of the textile restrictions that had been in force since 1941. The group was headed by Edward Molyneux, who had returned to England in 1939, and included among its members Hardy Amies and Norman Hartnell – both of whom were to become royal dressmakers during the Fifties – as well as Digby Morton and Victor Stiebel. Thirty-two of these Utility garments were selected for mass production, among them, the legendary and elegant women's uniform which the Americans called the Victory Suit.

Woollen suit by Jacques Fath for everyday wear
This style of double-breasted jacket, with vertical pockets partially concealed by folds in the basque, was a favourite of Fath's until 1945. Bibliothèque Nationale, Paris.
1942

Maggy Rouff

Martial et Armand

Bruyère

Molyneux

Henriette Beaujeu

Worth

Henriette Beaujeu

Robert Piguet

Molyneux

Mad Carpentier

Il fait

Balenciaga

Carven

Jacques Fath

Marcelle Dormoy

Carven

Schiaparelli

Jean Patou

Carven

Mad Carpentier

frais

The Reign of the Milliners

Flaunting their own extravagance, hats seemed to defy the prevailing austerity. Made of scraps of material that would otherwise have been thrown away and sometimes incorporating bits of paper, butter muslin and wood shavings, they were the perfect way to brighten up drab outfits in need of a lift.

Pauline Adam was a former model and *vendeuse* who, in 1929, opened her own millinery shop, under the name of Paulette. From her early successes of 1939, right up to the Sixties, she exercised an enormous influence on hat design. During the Occupation, she produced variations on the turban, developed ingenious uses of veiling and also worked on many films and plays. Together with Claude Saint-Cyr, this elegant and capable woman ranks among the last of the great milliners.

Under the name Claude Saint-Cyr, Simone Naudet opened a hat shop whose creations soon adorned the heads of the capital's best-dressed women. Although more modest by nature, she sometimes experimented with the excessive proportions that were in vogue during the Occupation. In the Fifties, she was appointed milliner to Queen Elizabeth II of England.

As with many accessories that are now deemed superfluous, it was during the Sixties that hats suffered an irreversible decline. Women relegated them to special occasions only, preferring to have their hair permed and dyed, or even to wear wigs – a trend that led to the virtual disappearance of the milliner, in the second half of the twentieth century, and to the rise of the celebrity hairdresser.

Grès

For many generations, the name of Madame Grès was synonymous with beautifully draped and moulded fabrics. She opened her house in Paris in 1941, but was almost immediately forced to close down after devoting her first show to patriotic models in blue, white and red. The Germans allowed her to reopen a year later and she lost no opportunity to demonstrate her mastery of the twin skills of intricate drapery and impeccable cut. Inspired by the antique peplum, she created evening wear that was utterly individual and timeless. Unrivalled at pleating jersey silk in monochrome sculptural designs, she also produced beautifully crafted suits, coats and burnouses for day wear. The success of her perfume Cabochard, launched in 1960, enabled this small beturbanned designer to postpone until 1980 her decision to branch into ready-to-wear. But it was too late and the 1984 takeover of her house, by businessman Bernard Tapie, came as a rude shock for a proud woman who had devoted her whole life to an ideal that was no longer viable. But the memory of her designs lives on and many of her creations are today regarded as works of art in their own right. The closure of the Maison Grès marked the end of an era. The doyenne of her profession and ex-president of the Chambre Syndicale de la Couture, Madame Grès passed away, in poverty and obscurity, in 1993.

The quest for timeless elegance
Photograph by Willy Maywald.
1939

Madame Grès
(1903–1993)

Charles James

The Sirène
This dress is an exercise in draping soft fabric over a rigid structure, giving the illusion of a natural flowing line.
1938

Charles James
(1906–1978)
The designer is shown arranging a frame similar to that of a crinoline.
1952

It is impossible to sum up, under the single heading of 'The Second World War', the peripatetic career of the man whom Balenciaga once claimed was the greatest designer of them all. Born in 1906, Charles James was a highly gifted individual whose life was punctuated by bankruptcies and schemes that were brilliant failures. He was constantly on the move, not just from one town to another, but from one continent to another. He left behind him a mass of rough drawings and sketches, which only his closest students have been able to assemble into a coherent body of work. He moved to New York in 1940 and there produced some of his finest designs, many anticipating the New Look. In models such as his quilted satin coat – a forerunner of the modern padded jacket – and his wraparound skirt, which wove a figure of eight around the wearer's legs, he demonstrated

a consistent originality that elevates his work to the rank of sculpture. An extremely talented and truly great American designer, he is today viewed as a cult figure.

Charles James died, ruined and more or less forgotten, at the Chelsea Hotel in New York, in 1978. Apart from a few young artists, drop-outs and remaining fans, the only people to visit him in his rooms were students, who came to imbibe the words of this passionate teacher, whom they regarded as some sort of guru. Yves Saint Laurent, Thierry Mugler, Azzedine Alaïa and many others have appreciated his architectural treatment of clothes and have frequently acknowledged their debt to him.

This page:

Balloon dress

In a brilliant pastiche
of historical styles,
combining an
Empire-line high
waist, a full skirt that
is straight from the
Second Empire
and an exaggerated
bustle from the late
eighteenth century,
James succeeds
against all odds in
creating a modern
dress with simple,
uncluttered lines.
1955

Left:

**Pagoda or
Egyptian tunic suit**
Photograph by
Lillian Bassman.
1954

American Ready-to-Wear

While Norman Norell, Jean Louis and James Galanos were striving to establish an American haute couture, the real innovations were being made in other fields.

Although the American ready-made clothes industry dates back to the second half of the nineteenth century, it concentrated largely on the manufacture of traditional clothes and had little in common with modern designer ready-to-wear. In parallel, there were dressmakers and tailors working on made-to-measure clothes for individual commissions. But it was French haute couture that women swooned over. Fine dresses from Paris could be bought at Bergdorf Goodman and, from 1925 onwards, from Hattie Carnegie in New York. These distributors would go to Paris and buy up dozens of items to sell on to their wealthy customers. Although fashion was generated in several different parts of the United States, notably Chicago and California, its home was New York's Seventh Avenue, where manufacturing was concentrated.

Between the wars, owing to the competitive state of the industry, which was well managed and receptive to new marketing techniques, ready-to-wear dramatically upped its share of the market. The first mail-order catalogues illustrated the latest fashions being modelled by film stars, such as Gloria Swanson and Joan Crawford, and the promise of twenty-four-hour delivery brought a spectacular increase in sales. American women welcomed

Sportswear ensemble in tweed, with a cape
Photograph for
Harper's Bazaar.
Autumn/Winter 1940

Hats
The New York
skyline, seen from
the roof of the Condé
Nast building on
Lexington Avenue.
1949

enthusiastically the French fashions of the Twenties, with their shorter skirts.
They liked their simplicity. They perceived the style, which was better suited
to their way of living, as more liberating and democratic. There was a large
following for Molyneux, Schiaparelli and Vionnet and great appreciation of
the evening suits shown by Chanel and Patou in 1930 in a variety of cottons.
Many states had long hot summers and these outfits were easy to copy.

With the Wall Street crash, the United States slapped a ninety per cent
tax on imported clothes. Material and dress patterns, on the other hand,
attracted no duty. This led to developing a technique of reproduction based
on toile models. Simplified prototypes were made up in different sizes and
were then copied in affordable materials, such as the newly developed
synthetic fabrics. The financial crisis and the shortages brought about
by the war accelerated an interest in more modest materials that had
previously been regarded as unworthy of couture.

Paris's isolated situation in 1940 enabled the Americans to exploit the creativity of their own designers. They, too, faced rationing during the war. In the end, the effect of the restrictions, which were finally lifted in 1946, was to stimulate ingenuity. One of the basics of the American style was the co-ordinated outfit, with interchangeable elements; it enabled the active woman to adapt her look for different times of the day and gave her the freedom to create her own ensembles.

During the Second World War, Vera Maxwell showed co-ordinates in plain, simply cut fabrics, which were particularly well suited to a period when rationing was in force and women's needs had changed. She also introduced innovations to men's work clothes.

Bonnie Cashin turned boots into a major fashion accessory and, in 1944, began to produce original and imaginative sportswear. Tina Leser, Anne Klein and, above all, Claire McCardell formed a remarkable trio of women who were to lay the foundations of American sportswear, ensuring that ready-to-wear was not considered second-best, but a comfortable and elegant way for modern women to dress. Although the Americans may not have invented sportswear, it was in their hands that it expanded and came of age, becoming the spearhead of American fashion.

Knitted bathing costume by Tina Leser
Specializing in sportswear, Tina Leser was one of the pioneers of the new wave of transatlantic designers. Photograph by Horst for *Vogue*. *April 1950*

Claire McCardell

After studying at Parsons School of Design in New York, Claire McCardell, the pioneer of American ready-to-wear, made her fashion debut in the Twenties. From 1940 onwards, she was to design under her own label for Townley Frocks.

In 1942, when the American War Production Board imposed rationing for certain textiles (notably wool and silk), she turned to cotton, using denim, cotton crêpe, mattress ticking and jersey to produce attractive easy-to-wear designs. These timeless creations demonstrate with panache how ingenuity could overcome the problems and shortages of war.

McCardell adapted and simplified the bias cut which she had seen in designs by Madeleine Vionnet. Her famous denim wraparound dress, which she launched in 1942, was produced for many years. She also designed jersey bloomers, which she teamed with cropped knits, introduced the leotard and brought ballet dancers' pumps out of the studio and on to the street. On top of all this, she anticipated the New Look of the reconstruction years, by abandoning shoulder pads and lowering the hemline of her full skirts. Since, in the casual elegance of her best work, she identified a typically American style, her influence on future fashion was considerable.

One-piece jersey bathing costume
Photograph by Louise Dahl-Wolfe.
1948

Claire McCardell
(1905-1958)

Menswear

During the war years, the shortages were particularly acutely felt by the male wardrobe, which relied heavily on textiles that were simply no longer available. The situation in France was made infinitely worse in 1942, when rationing was supplemented by the introduction of measures forbidding suits and overcoats to have gussets, box pleats, yokes, half belts, double-breasted waistcoats or plus fours. Stripped of their turn-ups, trousers could have only one inside pocket and the width of the trouser leg could not exceed 10 $^1/_2$ inches (26.5 centimetres) at the ankle.

With uniform still very much the dominant mode of dress, the zazou suit was born, a French version of the zoot suit of Afro-American origin. With its onomatopoeic musical echoes, the word sums up a look, a state of mind – and an adolescent crisis. This was the first time that youth, as such, had taken a stand to define its own codes against the prevailing trends. Over-long wide-shouldered jackets, brightly coloured materials, tapered trousers stopping four inches (ten centimetres) above the ankle, thick-soled shoes, white socks, narrow ties and brilliantined hair – later to be replaced by the quiff – were *the* look. Zazous loved jazz and American rhythms, like the jitterbug and swing. For the first time, music and fashion were associated in a movement that flourished simultaneously on both sides of the Atlantic. Impervious to parental disapproval, the birth of the zazou spelt the end of adult omnipotence. This was the beginning of youth fashion and what a phenomenon it was to become.

Liberation

On 25 August 1944, Paris celebrated its freedom. As the Allied troops continued progressing towards the frontiers of the Third Reich, a liberated Europe woke up to the rhythms of jazz and discovered the nylons that American GIs were carrying in their bags. The Americans, for their part, queued patiently outside the besieged Chanel boutique, so they could take a bottle of her famous perfume back home to their wives and girlfriends. Never before had there been such close personal contact between the people of Europe and the United States, or such an exposure to each other's cultures. It was to have a marked effect on fashion in the second half of the century.

Jacques Fath

**The model Bettina
in a white satin
battle-dress**
Army uniform
adapted for
womenswear.
*Autumn/Winter
1949–1950*

Jacques Fath
(1912–1954)

Born in 1912, he opened a salon in 1937 and died a hero in 1954. He is
remembered as an outstanding designer who embraced every aspect
of life. As France prepared to face one of the darkest periods of its history,
the handsome, laughing, young Fath, with his flowing blond hair, married
a gorgeous young woman called Geneviève, whose eccentricity encouraged
his own. In 1940, manipulating the media like a modern designer,
he promoted her image, linking it inextricably to his designs. Similarly,
after the Liberation, his parties, his perfumes and the celebrities he
counted among his friends became integral elements in his creations.

Rapidly diversifying, in 1948, he signed a contract with the famous
American store Lord & Taylor, setting up the distribution of garments
under the label Designed in America by Jacques Fath for Joseph Halpert,
and in 1950 he began publishing his patterns in *Vogue*. In 1953, he was
the first to enter into partnership with an industrialist,
Jean Prouvost, manufacturing ready-made skirts under the
label Jacques Fath – Université. Rising to prominence during
the war years, he had from the start exploited the concept
of youth. His wit and light-hearted subversion of good taste
were very much directed at an age range still unacknowledged
at the time. The unstuffy but highly sophisticated *style Fath*,
worn since 1946 by a generation of ravishingly beautiful
models, has left an indelible impression on fashion.

Evening gowns
Left to right: models by Schiaparelli, Balenciaga, Fath and Dessès. The Fath dress (modelled by Bettina) is in green satin acetate by Bianchini-Férier.
Photograph published in *L'Album du Figaro*, December 1951.
Autumn 1951

The Theatre of Fashion

'Théâtre de la Mode' was the title of an exhibition held in Paris at the Pavillon de Marsan in the Louvre, in 1945–1946. It merits a section to itself because of the extraordinary influence it had on the direction of Paris couture after the Second World War.

After the Liberation, France was stripped bare and the economy left in tatters; meanwhile fighting was still going on just beyond its frontiers. People were anxious to put the years of fear, humiliation and deprivation behind them and to rediscover how to enjoy life. Yet millions of men, women and children found themselves without the means to do so. Raoul Dautry, as Minister of Reconstruction and Urbanism, set up the Entraide Française, but faced the most appalling difficulties. A friend of his, Robert Ricci (co-founder with his mother Nina of the Ricci fashion house) came up with the idea of a huge public event. It would be organized by the Chambre Syndicale de la Couture Parisienne, where Ricci was in charge of international relations. Proceeds from the entrance tickets would go to support the national cause. It would provide an opportunity for all the professional branches of fashion to demonstrate the unquenchable vitality of their industries and to show that Paris could still produce beautiful clothes. Sadly, depite the enthusiasm of its human resources, in 1945, couture simply did not have the materials that it needed to create outfits for a major exhibition.

Ricci's deputy, General Paul Caldaguès, then came up with a brilliant solution to this impasse. The fashion houses' new designs would be shown on a range of dolls, thereby keeping the use of fabric, leather and trimmings to a minimum. But it had to be clear that these were not dolls' clothes.

A talented young illustrator called Eliane Bonabel was asked to come up with an original idea for the design of the miniature mannequin. This was then translated by the artist Jean Saint-Martin into a range of figures that were twenty-eight inches (seventy centimetres) tall. Each was given its own individual look, with the aid of a wire armature, and the heads, all different, were sculpted in white plaster by a Catalan refugee called Joan Rebull, who was a childhood friend of Picasso's. The painter and decorator Christian Bérard was brought in by Robert Ricci as artistic director of the project and Boris Kochno, who had worked with Serge Diaghilev at the time of the Ballets Russes, did the lighting for the various displays. The omnipresent Jean Cocteau waxed lyrical at considerable length, investing the project with his inimitable poetic touch. Painters André Dignimont, Georges Douking, Emilio Grau-Sala and Louis Touchagues, together with theatrical designers Georges Wakhevitch, Jean-Denis Malclès and André Beaurepaire, painted and built the miniature sets.

Dress by Pierre Balmain
The dress is modelled by a doll designed by Eliane Bonabel, in a set by Christian Bérard.
1946

From sportswear to ball gowns, each outfit was complemented by the full range of underwear and accessories, all produced with the same careful workmanship as would be required for the most exacting customer. The miniature buttonholes were handsewn and the tiny buttons really did do up. The hats were the size of a coin. The little shoes were fashioned by celebrated shoemakers, while furs, feathers and jewelry were the crowning touches to hair that had been cut and styled by hairdressers Antoine and Guillaume.

In thirteen miniature stage sets, 237 sumptuously attired dolls were presented, on 27 March 1945, to the accompaniment of music by Henri Sauguet, to a dazzled audience of Parisians. More than a hundred thousand people attended the Musée des Arts Décoratifs during the following weeks. Beyond the magic and wonder of the enchanted world of the 'Théâtre de la Mode' and beyond even the French passion for frivolity, this was a liberating and authentic breath of fresh air. And, more specifically, it advocated freedom of dress, without constraint. Quite apart from the large sums that were raised and the feeling of optimism it engendered, the exhibition had another unexpected spin-off.

The big American manufacturers had doubted whether Paris fashion would ever resurrect itself after five years of German Occupation. With the support of the American women's press, they believed they were in a position to take over where French haute couture had left off. But the exhibition moved on in triumph from Paris to London, then to Barcelona, Copenhagen, Stockholm and Vienna. Finally, in the following spring, it crossed the Atlantic. New mannequins were specially constructed before being submitted to the scrutiny of New York, in an all-or-nothing bid for success. On the morning of 2 March 1946, *Women's Wear Daily* pronounced itself well and truly stunned. The whole of America followed suit. France had demonstrated it was still a force to be reckoned with and, the following year, Dior launched his New Look. With the aid of a few rag dolls, haute couture had survived to fight another day.

The Fifties

Historical Review

Whether in the decorative arts in general or in the world of fashion in particular, throughout the Fifties there was a sharp division between those who wanted everything to stay the same, just as it had been in the old days, and those who wanted everything to change. In their hopes for a better future, people looked beyond a devastated Europe to both the United States and the Soviet Union. Although, in fact, the future was not to be as different as most people hoped or feared, it was during the Fifties that rules were devised for what was, in effect, an entirely new game. Fashion was not immune to this process. In the early 1900s, Paul Poiret introduced a more modern dress code, breaking with a centuries-old custom and claiming the right of the couturier to set the agenda, rather than the customer. Fifty years later, a further significant advance was made, this time on behalf of the people whom fashion had neglected, those whose limited means condemned their wardrobe to uniformity. Whether their clothing denoted their profession or trade, or the fact that they belonged to an inferior social class, it would always be bought off the peg. And all the pejorative connotations the expression carries were as applicable then as they are today.

Coming, as they did, from the land of democracy and belonging to a consumer society, the American conquerors were to accelerate the process of homogenization by imposing their own

Gruau
Advertisement for Rouge Baiser cosmetics.
1949

The college look in the United States
Circular skirts with stiff petticoats offer an alternative to jeans, sweater and slip-on shoes for young American devotees of the new craze of rock and roll.

practices on Europe. 'No need to envy American women their beauty any more' ran a headline in a supplement to *Le Figaro*. In fact, American good looks were the result not only of advances in cosmetics and of regular sporting activity, but also of a daily hygiene regime that was still way beyond most Frenchwomen's comprehension. The pioneering editor of *Elle* and fashion journalist Françoise Giroud wrote more recently: 'After the Liberation, *Elle*'s young women readers had first to be taught how to wash themselves, to change their underclothes and to smell nice.'

Technological developments, which are often accelerated by war, helped to further these aims. Progress in the domestic arts, better living conditions, improved communications and a taste for new ideas were also contributing factors. The textile industries, too, made advances, thanks to the introduction of synthetic fabrics. Nylon, use of which had previously been confined to making parachutes, entered the realms of rayon lingerie

English women discover the delights of the hairdryer.

and hosiery. Ladder-resistant stockings and hard-wearing, easy-to-wash socks were not only more economical, but rendered darning superfluous. A division arose between life before and life after nylon. A swimsuit – so skimpy it eventually became a bikini – could now dry in an instant, on beaches to which most of the population flocked to claim their right to holiday sunshine.

After years of invasion, death and deprivation, liberated France seemed to want to rediscover its roots. As it looked to the past, couture experienced a revival, which culminated in the launch of the New Look. Balls were held and polite society regrouped, closing its ranks. Far from being revolutionary, the styles promoted by Christian Dior and his confrères were reminiscent of the Restoration, in their use of opulent materials, superb accessories by Van Cleef & Arpels or Schlumberger, corsetted waists and swirling skirts to mid-calf.

Even though, after the Liberation, women had the right to vote, to work, and to drive their own cars, in practice, they chose to wear clothes that bore nostalgic echoes of the Belle Époque. Never better than in those extraordinary years did fashion demonstrate its ability to fly in the face of logic, continuity and erudite sociological predictions. It was the same in the cinema, where *Gone with the Wind* was the runaway success, and in the French theatre, where the big hit was *The Mad Woman of Chaillot*. A whole society which, in the Thirties, had believed in progress, was now more circumspect. War had imposed limitations and reconstruction, carried out in the name of progress, had made the everyday world look drab and monotonous. During those years, Messieurs Weill and Lempereur, owners of clothing businesses that bore their names, observed methods of production and distribution in the American ready-to-wear trade that was already well established in the States. This turned out to be a stroke of luck, since the new Parisienne had developed, having read all about them in magazines, an appetite for elegant clothes that were not necessarily within her means.

The women's press offered her patterns to copy and raised her expectations. All that was needed was for the textile manufacturers to respond. Throughout the Fifties – although it would be for the last time – European women continued to submit to the diktats of Parisian haute couture, as it was presented to them by word of mouth, in the press and by the models, patterns and copies that were available. Why should haute couture feel threatened, when, in ten years of renewed prosperity, it had spawned a myriad of star designers who benefited from the exponential growth of the media?

At the moment when the Hiroshima bomb exploded, haute couture announced the end of a period of hardship by lowering skirt hems. But behind its back, the phrase ready-to-wear was increasingly heard.

Cover of *Elle*
25 February 1952

Christian Dior

Christian Dior's meteoric rise to fame in 1947 is one of the major landmarks of twentieth-century fashion. It is significant that it was during the pivotal years leading up to the Fifties that his label made its mark, since Dior's world, although rooted firmly in the past, prefigures the paradoxical universe of an entirely new fashion system, such as was about to evolve.

How was it that this shy forty-year-old from the provinces, with a passion for the Belle Époque, came to be regarded as one the most famous international figures of our times? How was it that his designs, with their renewed emphasis on traditional female values, succeeded in conquering not only fashionable Europe but also a whole internationale of housewives who were desperate to resemble his models? How did a professional career that lasted only ten years leave behind it a fashion empire and a legacy of influence that would continue to grow from strength to strength? Merely to ask these questions, never mind answering them, is to acknowledge the unparalleled importance of the role that Christian Dior and his successors played at the head of a couture house whose fame has outstripped that of all others.

Celebrating its centenary in 1950, and yet still eternally youthful, couture capitalized on the new modes of communication to address an international audience – not just the privileged classes, but, literally, the whole planet. Elitist and deliberately ignoring the practical realities of life, Christian Dior's designs were

in no way intended as consumer products for the masses. But what they did provide was a spectacle for an entire society.

It was not unlike the miracle of transubstantiation, as everything Dior touched turned to gold (even his name ends in *or*, meaning 'gold'). From 1948 onwards, a whole range of products bearing his label were introduced, allowing a new type of consumer access to the rarefied designer world. Embracing stockings, lipsticks and many other accessories, this unparalleled diversification could not have occurred except as a spin-off from the prestigious collections designed between 1947 and 1957 by this visionary who hankered after past glories. Dior may not have loved the world he lived in, but he set out to conquer it, with a ruthlessness that, even today, makes Dior the flagship enterprise of the leading international luxury goods group Louis Vuitton-Moët Hennessy. A naturally anxious and superstitious person, Dior consulted astrologers. Could he possibly have foreseen his future success when still working as a designer for Lucien Lelong, with no other ambition than to earn a decent living and to do a conscientious day's work?

The Bar suit
Signature model for the New Look in Christian Dior's first haute couture collection.
1947

Born in 1905 in Granville, on the north coast of France, into a comfortable middle-class family, Dior revealed an early talent for creating fancy-dress costumes. After abandoning his studies at the École des Sciences Politiques, he opened an art gallery with a friend. Christian Bérard, Raoul Dufy, Giorgio de Chirico, Max Jacobs and Henri Sauguet were among those with whom he passed his time, until his father's bankruptcy in 1931 put an abrupt end to this dilettante existence. Several lean years followed, during which, in times of extreme hardship, he had to resort to his gift for sketching.

In 1938, Robert Piguet took him on as a designer and he then worked alongside his contemporary Pierre Balmain at the respected couture house of Lucien Lelong. He had already begun to transform the female silhouette when he was introduced to the textile magnate Marcel

The show
Dior's collections were so successful that close friends had to sit on the stairs.

Boussac. The latter was so impressed by the young man's determination that he decided to finance the couture house that Dior had dreamed of running. Housed in small premises on the Avenue Montaigne, the new house created a tidal wave with its first collection in February 1947. The waist was tiny and the bust majestic, with a full skirt swelling out beneath a small bodice. Such elegance incited Carmel Snow, the all-powerful editor of American *Vogue*, to exclaim 'This is a new look.'

The New Look was Christian Dior's passport to the American market and he was to capitalize on its success in all his subsequent collections. While remaining faithful to his style, he cleverly maintained an element of suspense by producing a whole host of new inventions in his twice-yearly shows. During the Fifties, the House of Dior was alone responsible for

A seamstress at work
Apprentices played
a vital role in
translating designs
into reality. Without
them, there would
have been no
dresses to show.

**Starkly simple coat
in fine grey wool**
This design
demonstrates how
Dior had learned
from Piguet
the lesson of
eliminating fussy
detail. Photograph by
Frances McLaughlin.
1952

half of all Paris's couture exports to the United States. The house created
its perfume division at the end of 1947, then opened a luxury ready-to-
wear operation in New York. In 1949, Dior signed his first licence for the
manufacture of stockings and ties by American firms. 1950 saw the creation
of a wholesale business to distribute accessories produced under the Dior
label. A 'boutique', as it was called, opened in London; a licence was issued
for the manufacture of lingerie in 1954; and further branches were set up in
Caracas, Australia, Chile, Mexico and Cuba. When he died suddenly in 1957,
the great designer employed more than a thousand people. His businesses
occupied five buildings and there were twenty-eight skilled ateliers for haute
couture alone. He left behind him a modern commercial enterprise, whose
power and influence had little in common with the craft operations that had
hitherto governed the world of fashion.

Pierre Balmain

Pierre Balmain

Born in St Jean de Maurienne, Balmain (1914–1982) studied architecture before opening his own salon in 1945. It was in a series of collections called Jolie Madame, after a perfume of the same name that he had launched in 1949, that this disciplined designer experienced his greatest success, from 1952 onwards. His image of the elegant woman was particularly Parisian and was typified by the tailored glamour of the New Look, with ample bust, narrow waist and full skirts, by mastery of cut and by cunning assemblies of fabrics in subtle colour combinations. His stylish clientele proved equally at home with simple tailoring, luxurious elegance and a more natural look. In tandem with his haute couture work, this talented businessman pioneered a ready-to-wear range called Florilège and launched a number of successful perfumes, among them Vent Vert.

Norman Norell

Norman Norell graduated from Parsons School of Design in 1921, before becoming assistant to Hattie Carnegie. In the history of American fashion, he represents the ideal designer, combining, as he did, prestige and luxury with a feeling for comfort, and subtlety and discretion with innovation. At the start of the Sixties, he was one of the first to present trousers for evening wear. The fluid lines and perfect finish of the seductive and beautiful dresses he produced throughout his career ensured this emblematic figure the enthusiastic patronage of New York's high society.

Norman Norell

Roger Vivier

Variations
Roger Vivier was the
master of the high-
heeled shoe, in all
its forms.

Roger Vivier
(1913–1998)
The celebrated
shoe designer in his
workshop at the end
of the Fifties.

Roger Vivier's talents elevated the handmade shoe to great heights,
earning him a well-deserved reputation as a leading figure of twentieth-
century fashion. From the time he opened his shop, in the Rue Royale
in 1937, to his retirement in 1972, he applied the principles of advanced
aerodynamics to footwear of every conceivable shape and form. The stiletto
of 1954 was succeeded by the inwardly curving *choc* heel of 1959. Then
came the Punchinello heel, the chisel toe, the square toe and even the
shoe covered in Rébé embroidery. It is not surprising, therefore, that
Vivier has been described as the Fragonard of the female foot.

From 1941 to 1947 he worked for the shoe manufacturer Delman, in
New York, and then as assistant to the photographer Hoyningen-Huene,
before opening a millinery business with Suzanne Rémy. Confirmation of

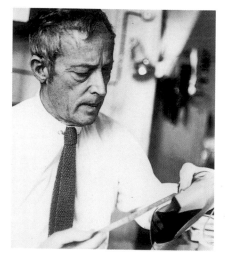

his success came on his return to France, when
he was chosen to design the shoes worn by Queen
Elizabeth II of England at her coronation. As one
brilliant innovation followed another, his designs
were snapped up by women of the post-war era.
It was during his collaboration with Christian Dior,
which began in 1953, that his work reached its peak
of elegance. Vivier also contributed to collections
by Pierre Balmain, Guy Laroche, Nina Ricci
and the young Yves Saint Laurent. For the latter,
he designed in 1967 a black patent pump with a
gold buckle and boot heel which sold in millions.

Balenciaga

If we were to stick rigidly to the chronological presentation adopted for this volume, Cristobal Balenciaga Esagari would appear under the heading of the late Thirties, which was when he made his debut. Yet it was during the post-war years that the full scale of his genius became apparent. He was born in the Spanish Basque country, in Guetaria, in 1895, but experienced a sort of rebirth at the age of thirteen when, as a shy adolescent, he was singled out by the Marquesa de Casa-Torrès, who gave him his start in life. Following a period with a tailor in Madrid, at the age of sixteen, he opened his first fashion house under his own name in San Sebastián; at the end of the Twenties he moved the business to Madrid. Then, after the fall of the Spanish monarchy, he transferred to Barcelona. In 1936, with the outbreak of the Spanish Civil War, he sought safety in Paris and opened his own fashion house in the following year at 10 Avenue Georges V.

Until shortly before the start of the Second World War, the man who even Christian Dior later acknowledged as his master, was still a nobody. And yet, without making any obvious effort, this supreme technician of the female wardrobe was already attracting the attention of the society women and famous actresses who set the trends.

With its perfect mastery of cut, its technical appreciation of construction and its ceaseless struggle to achieve a perfect balance between line, proportion,

Tunic dress in silk seersucker
Spring 1962

Cristobal Balenciaga
(1895–1972)
The designer as a young man in San Sebastián.
1927

Paletot in shantung
White shantung
with embroidered
navy spots worn
by Maggy, the
favourite subject of
Balenciaga's regular
photographer,
Kublin.
Summer 1960

style and palette, Balenciaga's art takes on architectural dimensions. In 1939, his emphasis was on the cut of the sleeve and square yokes. 1940 saw the first of the little black dresses that have ecome one of fashion's recurring themes. The longer-line jackets and tapered skirts of 1942 introduced the barrel line. In 1946, it was the first loose-fitting paletots and coats with kimono sleeves. Suits with cutaway basques

and full coats followed, in 1949, and then balloon dresses and collarless coats. Balenciaga excelled in puffball effects created by simple draping around the waist. In 1951, he transformed the silhouette completely, eliminating the waist and broadening the shoulders. Then, in 1955, came the tunic dress, which developed into the chemise dress of 1957. And finally, in 1959, his work culminated in the Empire line, with high-waisted dresses and coats cut like kimonos. His aficionados would hold their breath as, in each successive collection, his mastery of fabric design and creation continued to defy belief.

You may have thought you were looking at a Zurbarán, a Velazquez or a Goya, but it was always Balenciaga. Discouraging imitators, he created his aloof garments in an atmosphere of secrecy and calm for a small and elite number of wealthy beauties, who saw him as a cult figure. A frugal prince of luxury, Balenciaga was also one of the only couturiers who could use his own hands to design, cut and sew the models which represented the peak of his artistry. His timeless clothes have been described by Carmel Snow in *Harper's Bazaar* as the *ne plus ultra* of fashion.

Arum dress, made in two sections
Winter 1965

Sheath dress and black faille bow
Pale blue guipure over a matching faille underdress.
Spring 1951

Givenchy

Hubert James Taffin de Givenchy, whose grandfather ran a tapestry factory, was born in Beauvais in 1927 and opened his own couture house in 1952. He created a sensation with his *séparables*, or separates, which could be mixed and matched at will. Most famous was his Bettina blouse made of shirting, which was named after his top model who also handled his public relations. On the strength of this early success, boutiques were opened in Rome, Zurich and Buenos Aires. Givenchy received warm support from Cristobal Balenciaga and his designs, directed at the same distinguished international clientele, echoed those of his mentor, though pitched in a minor key.

Dress in
white organdie
Bettina is the
model for this dress
embroidered with
woollen flowers
and worn with a
shawl jacket.
January 1953

Hubert de Givenchy
(born 1927)
1953

One design alone, the little black dress worn by Audrey Hepburn in *Breakfast at Tiffany's* – still so popular today – would have been sufficient to assure Givenchy's posterity. An attractive and cultivated man of immense charm and distinction, he was, more than any other designer, an integral part of the world whose understated elegance he helped to define. His impeccable European style has been embraced with great enthusiasm on the other side of the Atlantic in the latter half of the twentieth century.

The Return of Chanel

Black suit with white satin lining
This simple design is one of Chanel's most elegant outfits.
1956

Two-tone high-heeled shoe
Chanel came up with the device of using two colours as a means of making the foot appear shorter. This famous shoe, made by Raymond Massaro, represents, with its many variations, the quintessence of Chanel style.
1958

Following the closure of her salons in 1939, Gabrielle Chanel maintained a frosty silence as she watched the public go overboard for the New Look, which she hated. In 1954, aged over seventy, she staged her comeback. On 5 February, in front of a sceptical audience, she presented a collection on which she had staked everything. Admittedly, she had already made her fortune, but failure would have jeopardized sales of the perfumes that were the source of such extravagant profits.

At an age when others were taking retirement, the fiery orphan was determined to have the last word. Returning to the first principles of her style, she showed her famous little braided suit with gold chains, silk blouses in colours that matched the suit linings, monogrammed buttons, shiny costume jewelry, flat black silk bows, sleek tweeds, her white fabric camellia, boaters, bows with which to tie your hair back at the nape of the neck, quilted bags on chains and beige shoes with a darker toe. She presented a whole raft of ideas that would be adopted and copied and adapted by millions of women all over the world, although no copy could ever hope to re-create the flair of the original. In addition Chanel produced evening dresses and furs that were marvels of simplicity. Benefiting from the success of a whole new range of perfumes, accessories and cosmetics, by the time its founder died, the House of Chanel was, once again and against all expectations, among the most powerful and influential houses in Paris. It was a unique destiny for a label that had demonstrated remarkable flexibility and an instinct for adapting its fixed aesthetic principles to changing tastes.

And Also

Guy Laroche
(1921–1989)
Photograph by
Jean-Philippe
Charbonnier.
1958

**Ball gown by
Jacques Griffe**
Photograph by
Frances McLaughlin.
1952

During the Fifties, a number of minor houses grew up on the fringes of Parisian haute couture. Among them were Jacques Griffe and Jacques Esterel, who, in 1959, made Brigitte Bardot's famous gingham wedding dress. Other names have survived because of their association with perfumes that are still on the market. This is true of Guy Laroche (1921–1989), who was taken on as a designer by Jean Dessès in 1949 and opened his own couture house on the Avenue Montaigne in 1961. He simultaneously opened a boutique and launched a ready-to-wear label called Guy Laroche Femme. The simplicity and practicality of his designs assured their rapid success.

Her name was Carmen, but she became Carven. A tiny little woman, born in 1909, she opened her own couture house in 1944. Her aim was to provide clothes for those who, like herself, were petite, whether plump or slim, and could never find a style to suit them at the big houses. From this basic principle flowed a whole new look. It was both classic and fresh, modest and well-bred, directed at the demure young woman. Later, Madame Carven was to specialize in air hostesses' uniforms.

Line Vautrin, the daughter of a metal-founder and herself a sculptor, opened a tiny boutique in the Rue de Berry in 1937. There she sold exquisite accessories, jewelled buttons, buckles, clasps, hooks, necklaces and earrings. Her speciality was silvered or gilded bronze, embellished with

ceramic, mother-of-pearl and spun glass. The resultant limited editions combined wit with esoteric charm. Having made an original and poetic contribution to fashion and decoration, the unfailingly charming Madame Vautrin has left a gap that is still to be filled today.

The same is true of Lola Prusac who also set up a small couture business in 1937; it was based on high-quality craftsmanship, employing weaving and hand embroidery of exceptional virtuosity. In the subtlety and originality of their designs, her knits, jerseys, jewelry, scarves, swimsuits and turbans succeeded in combining made-to-measure quality with the spirit of the boutique, enabling her label to leave a modest but distinctive imprint on fashion during the years of change.

A Greek from Alexandria, born in 1904 and established as a couturier in 1937, Jean Dessès retained from his Mediterranean youth a taste for lightweight materials, which he liked to drape with his own hands. A specialist in exquisite ball gowns, this virtuoso of chiffon and mousseline, which he combined, sculpted, pleated and pinned together with love and an instinctive sense of elegance, was also sufficiently forward-looking to join the Couturiers Associés: Paquin, Carven, Piguet and Fath. From 1950 onwards, the group of five had links with seven manufacturers, each of which was contracted to produce seven models every season, to be distributed by selected shops in the provinces. This was one of Parisian haute couture's first ventures into the mass market. As we shall see in later chapters, every progressive movement in fashion would henceforth involve establishing a new equilibrium between made-to-measure and ready-to-wear to reflect the social changes. The move away from total elitism in fashion towards a wider market base did not take place in a uniform and continuous manner, but as a result of individual acts of innovation. From 1955 onwards, the label Jean Dessès – Diffusion manufactured mass-produced dresses to be sold in selected stores in France and

Saute-mouton **(Leap-frog or, literally, Leap-sheep) necklace by Line Vautrin** Musée des Arts Décoratifs, Paris. c. 1950

North Africa. At the same time, the couturier opened a boutique in the Galeries Lafayette and set up what he called a 'bazaar' on the ground floor of his couture operation, where he sold a variety of novelty accessories. By the time Dessès retired in 1963, the most radical shake-up in twentieth-century fashion was already well under way.

**Evening gown
by Jean Dessès**
The dress is entirely
covered with
embroidery
by Lesage.
1952

1 **Lauren Bacall, Humphrey Bogart and Marilyn Monroe** at the première *of How to Marry a Millionaire*, 1953. Hollywood's designers invented a particular style of glamour for the mythic stars of American cinema.

2 **Brigitte Bardot**. Sex kitten of the Fifties, her fashions, hairstyle and approach to life were copied around the world.

3 **Rita Hayworth** in *Gilda*, 1946. The actress immortalized the black sheath dress designed by Jean Louis.

4 **Cover of *Harper's Bazaar*** by Louise Dahl-Wolfe, March 1950. The magazine enjoyed a peak of success during Alexey Brodovitch's reign as artistic director, from 1934 to 1958.

5 **Grace Kelly** carrying the famous handbag which Hermès named after her.

3

Harper's
BAZAAR
Incorporating Junior Bazaar

American
Spring Fashions
Shoes and
Accessories

March 4st. 1950

5

From Couture to Mass Manufacturing

Mass manufacturing, as such, did not really take off until the second half of the twentieth century. Meanwhile, the arbiters of couture continued to see themselves as having inherited from the royal courts the responsibility of determining how people should look. Couture was a source of wealth and a large employer, and it took two world wars, with the social upheavals they left in their wake, for the greatest change in clothing history to get under way, in the Fifties. It would eventually grant the masses unprecedented access to clothes that matched the spirit of their times.

Echoing wider developments in the industrial society, the clothing industry concentrated its efforts on the male wardrobe, at first, on jackets and trousers that were so much more difficult to make than skirts and dresses, which mothers and daughters could run up at home in the evenings. For labourers and farm workers, the lowest strata of society, daily life had not changed enough to necessitate much variation in their clothing. This was true, at least, until the commercial dynamism of the big department stores shifted the emphasis to the mass market. Fashion then became one of their most profitable lines. À La Belle Jardinière, a store right in the centre of Paris by the Pont Neuf, would soon attract a new kind of female customer. With the disappearance of crinolines and bulky bustles, she wanted the sort of well-cut coat that the rag trade were expert at producing in large quantities – in particular, firms like Maison Weill, the oldest established business in the French clothing industry.

During the Thirties, with the Depression affecting people at every level of society, demand for mass manufacturing increased. With better wages

Department store in the United States
A typical display of women's fashion in the early Fifties.

for workers encouraging the growth of the industrial sector, mass-produced garments were being bought by twenty-five per cent of French women by the end of the decade. But the shortages that followed the defeat of 1940 and the anti-Jewish measures that hit the clothing trade disproportionately hard were to slow down this expansion. From 80,000 workers in 1938, the French clothing industry dwindled to a mere 25,000 employees in 1943. However, with the Liberation, a whole new ball game came into being and subsequently things progressed very quickly indeed. Contemporary images produced by the Popular Front in 1936 show crowds discovering the seaside on their first paid holidays. Men and women were photographed rushing towards the water with their town clothes rolled up to their knees. It was to them and their children that a new high-quality industrial product, made by a skilled workforce, would be directed. It reflected the feeling of optimism that had resulted from freedom being restored in France. This freedom would later be expressed in fashion and on the streets and, most notably, via a category of society which the commercial world had hitherto ignored:

Stockings on the production line, in the United States

youth. That young people might have a distinctive sensibility, exert an influence or constitute a market and that their fashions need no longer emerge from designer salons were ideas that slowly began to surface during the Fifties.

In the generation that followed, these concepts exploded, as the large numbers of children born in the Liberation years developed their own music, their own way of life and their own look, characterized by spontaneity. In the meantime, although few were yet prepared to admit it, most couturiers were anxious about the financial stability of their houses and planned to diversify along the lines pioneered by Christian Dior. With the exception of Chanel and Balenciaga, every major house developed a subsidiary range during the Sixties. Although marketed under a couture label, its manufacture was generally entrusted to an industrial company, from which the couturier had to distance himself. Did not the statutes of the Chambre Syndicale de la Couture forbid the major houses even to use a sewing machine? Although they had set out from the same starting point in the 1850s, couture and manufacturing now found themselves on opposite sides of the fence, which was particularly unfortunate at a time when new markets, avid for fashionable clothes, were opening up.

On the couture side, the regular sensations contrived by Christian Dior at his collections and the resulting benefits for the whole profession, together with the rediscovered patronage of monarchs, film stars and international heiresses, helped to maintain the prestige of Parisian luxury fashions. Their mystique encouraged a number of spin-offs. Contracts and licences enabled couturiers to use their names on shoes, leather goods, eyewear, jewelry and watches – items that were well outside their own area of expertise. The more rigorous designers – and in the long run the more credible – would ensure that they only exported goods that were guaranteed to have been 'made in France' and that were of a quality that corresponded to the label under which they were marketed.

If there was one product where diversification offered obvious benefits, it was the designer perfume. Its success depended on its ability to sum up the essence of a style, so that the originality, glamour and fame of the clothes would then reflect on the fragrance. Many of the scents launched in the Fifties still testify to the houses that created them, whose long-term survival they help to ensure. But here, too, it is necessary to distinguish between the houses that have retained control of their perfumes as they have of their couture ranges; those who have released their capital to the big cosmetic groups; and those whose perfumes are manufactured under licence.

A magazine, anxious to bring the new trends in consumer goods to a wider audience, was founded to reflect these changes in lifestyle. Established in 1945, the weekly magazine *Elle*, under the editorship of Hélène Lazareff, served as an intermediary between the Parisian producers and their potential customers. In its February 1955 issue, *Jardin des modes* devoted several pages to the summer ready-to-wear collections. The following August, the prestigious monthly magazine *Vogue* devoted a whole issue to these collections. Something had definitely changed within the realm of fashion.

Lempereur and the Pioneer Stylists

**Embroidered dress
by Lempereur**
One of the first
French pret-à-porter
designs.
1955

Famous for producing industrial garments that still had much in common with the processes of couture, Albert Lempereur, born in 1902, was the head of a business, established in 1929, to manufacture clothes for children and teenagers. He was one of the first to address the needs of his young customers as they grew up.

'Lempereur dresses young women with style' announced one of the advertisements he used so effectively. He employed the budding talent of Brigitte Bardot, then still a model, to promote his casual, easy-to-wear youth fashion. It proved so successful that, in a reversal of the usual situation, mothers soon began to copy their daughters, wanting the same clothes for themselves. Having discovered ready-to-wear in the United States, Lempereur, the great co-ordinator of the French clothing industry, launched prêt-à-porter in France. Grammatically speaking, it should have been 'prêt-à-être-porté', but if the neologism was intended to indicate modern speed and efficiency, it was not far wrong.

After a miraculous escape from the Warsaw ghettoes, Zyga Pianko journeyed from the Russian camps of Archangel to Tehran and from Pakistan to Uganda, before his odyssey finally ended in Paris. Because it seemed so quintessentially French, he adopted the name Pierre d'Alby in the Fifties and set up a small business making reversible gabardine coats. His love of taking risks attracted him to the talents of some of the young stylists who were beginning to make a name for themselves in 1958. The first he took on was Daniel Hechter, who designed a very simple coat that proved so successful that its creator left to set up his own business.

Pierre d'Alby
These two designs
are by Emmanuelle
Khanh, then working
for Pierre d'Alby.
*Autumn/Winter
1964–1965*

Emmanuelle Khanh replaced him and she, too, became famous. She was replaced in 1967 by Michèle Rosier, then Jean-Charles de Castelbajac. Subsequently it was the young Agnès B., whose fruitful collaboration with D'Alby lasted until 1976.

At around this time, an entrepreneur of Armenian origin called Georges Vaskène bought up an old paper factory in Sologne. There he was to turn out as many as 100,000 little poplin dresses every year. Maxime de la Falaise, Gérard Pipart (later a designer with Nina Ricci) and then Karl Lagerfeld were the creative talents who cemented this historic alliance of style and industry. Two others major groups played an equally influential part: J.-D. (a subsidiary of Belleteste) and Indreco, today run by Léon Cligman. Although it occupies an entirely different position in the market, the House of Chloé, launched by Gaby Aghion in 1952, completes this panorama. Amid popular acclaim, it took couture on at its own game.

Like freelance butterflies, stylists such as Christiane Bailly, Tan Giudicelli, Graziella Fontana and Jacques Delahaye would flit, with youthful unconcern, from one manufacturer to another. It was through its ability to hang on to the versatile talents of Karl Lagerfeld that a prêt-à-porter label like Chloé was able to match the media appeal of the star designers of the Sixties, such as Cardin, Courrèges and the king of them all, Saint Laurent.

Pierre Cardin

Pierre Cardin, doyen of a new wave of fashion, straddled the world of the past and that of the future, which was so ardently desired by the young. Already well on his way to success, this visionary, ambitious and supremely egotistical man chose to identify with the modern France that Jacques Tati condemned and that decision-makers like Georges Pompidou remodelled. In a country where it seems that everything has to change in order to remain the same, Cardin appeared, for a time, to be the man of the hour. Half-society man and half-cosmonaut, multi-talented and a believer in change, he promised widespread access to contemporary luxury, especially as he would be the one to facilitate it and the first to reap the profits.

The son of Italian farmers who emigrated to the Loire in 1926, the young Cardin had no inclination to work the land and, at fourteen, became

Haute couture
Spring/Summer 1960

Pierre Cardin
(born 1922)
Photograph of the
visionary designer.
1960

apprenticed to a leading tailor in St Étienne. He worked hard and, by 1944, had found employment with Paquin in the Rue de la Paix. There he perfected his craft, demonstrating a natural ability that landed him the job of *premier tailleur* (leading tailor) at Dior. In the meantime, he had met Christian Bérard, the painter and set designer commissioned by Jean Cocteau to create the fabulous costumes for his film *Beauty and the Beast*. It became Pierre's ambition to open his own costume business, which would give him the opportunity to vent his prolific imagination. This he did, in 1949, with the support of Dior himself. The latter directed society women and

1 **Etamine dress**
Dress with draped
front in pale
blue mohair.
*Autumn/Winter
1958–1959*

2 **Three coats**
1958

3 **Jacket with
fur-trimmed hood**
*Sunday Times
1967*

theatre producers – anyone Dior could not accommodate himself whenever there was a ball, a ballet or a show – to his protégé. Apart from these one-off costume designs, Pierre Cardin showed remarkable flair in early ranges of coats and suits, whose cuts already attracted buyers. In 1957, helped by his tirelessly loyal friend André Olivier, he made the transition from costumes to couture and presented a full collection of 150 models for town and evening wear. His creative energy also spilled over into other activities. Aware that haute couture could no longer survive on its own, Cardin opened the boutique Eve, and later Adam, whose ready-to-wear collections were produced in his own workshops. At the same time, inspired by the example of Dior, this keen businessman negotiated his first licences. In the Printemps department store, on the Boulevard Haussmann, he soon had his own 'corner' (the name given in France to an area of a store exclusively reserved for, and decorated by, a designer).

Supported in everything he did not only by *Elle* magazine, but by most of the daily newspapers as well, the media-conscious Cardin began to add his signature to all sorts of products which, before long, had little to do with fashion. It became increasingly difficult to keep track of the heterogeneous assembly of articles that propagated the Cardin label, the Cardin style and the Cardin look throughout the world. By the beginning of the Eighties, Cardin held a grand total of some 540 licences. The size of his fortune must be considerable, but it is difficult to estimate because he handles all business transactions himself, keeping them strictly private. All decisions remain entirely in the hands of this unique businessman, who is one of the few couturiers who knows how to sketch, cut and sew a garment himself.

Menswear

1 **Young Teddy boy in Tottenham, London**

2 **Catwalk fashion for men**
The Brioni show at the Pitti Palace.
1952

3 **James Dean**
Under his influence, jeans and a T-shirt became the uniform for an entire generation.

The Allied victory confirmed the success of the American look for men in post-war Europe: broad shoulders, straight-legged trousers, floral ties and shirts with long pointed collars, often in bright colours for summer, that – most daringly – were worn hanging out instead of tucked in. The widespread installation of central heating led to the introduction of lighter textiles and, eventually, to synthetics. It was the age of minimum-care garments.

Alongside a classical wardrobe with a strong influence on sportswear, Anglo-Saxon Teddy boys and Hell's Angels made distinctive contributions to fashion. The zoot suit and its French equivalent, the zazou, took on a new lease of life, while, on screens all over the world, James Dean and Marlon Brando had already begun to popularize the new uniform of jeans and black leather jacket. Against the prevailing trend, certain London manufacturers succumbed to nostalgia and ushered in a revival of Edwardian elegance, a tight-fitting retro look calculated to appeal to traditionalists. Paradoxically, a style that was originally aimed at the respectable young man about town was translated into popular fashion as the Teddy boy look.

Further south, on their Vespas, the Latins were already staking their claim as the leaders of style. With Caraceni, Cifonelli and Brioni, transalpine design and manufacture were expanding at great speed; it would not be long before they offered an alternative to London's fashion scene. On both sides of the Atlantic, the Italian look was to be taken up by a whole generation of handsome young lovers.

CHAPTER 2

1960–2000

**Yves Saint
Laurent at Dior**
(born 1936)
As a young man
of twenty-one,
Saint Laurent was
greeted by the glare
of flashbulbs when
he appeared on the
balcony of the Dior
building, following
the triumph of
his first collection
Trapeze. He opened
his own couture
house three
years later.
1958

The Sixties

Historical Review

Twiggy
The young English
model who hit the
headlines in 1965 is
treated as a star in
the United States.

*Qui êtes-vous
Polly Maggoo?*
**(Who are you
Polly Maggoo?)**
Poster for William
Klein's film.
1966

Haute couture was kept alive during the Fifties by Paris and its Parisiennes, a group of perhaps no more than four thousand elegantly dressed women, not necessarily all of whom were French but who were all part of the same social scene. Parisian design was considered the touchstone of fashion throughout the world. Then, between 1960 and 1970, a radical shake-up occurred, not so much to the form as to the fundamental structures of European fashion. Thereafter, there would be no one single trend, no one fashion, but a kaleidoscope of possibilities, inextricably linked to all the various influences in other areas of people's lives.

America had restored peace and prosperity to the free West. It also offered the enticing prospect of mass-produced goods which it excelled in manufacturing. Images of another world arrived – in a stream of illustrations in women's magazines, often in colour, and via transistor radios and television sets which were becoming increasingly common – to stir the imagination of a woman whom the transatlantic media treated like royalty, in these boom years.

Happiness was going to be everyone's prerogative in the future. The stars gave cosy interviews and passed on their favourite recipes and beauty tips. Photographers took advantage of technological advances in their equipment and transported their models far from their anonymous studios

to real locations in the town or countryside. Increasingly often, they photographed them on beaches that represented the housewife's new Shangri-La, the reward that awaited her when her tasks were done.

The economic growth that smoothed the progress of life in the Sixties was not the only major transformation. Young people, with a power and culture of their own, were a force to be reckoned with. Baby boomers, now of an age to speak out, were the anonymous heroes of this saga. It began in the cellars of Saint-Germain-des-Prés, before moving to the London clubs, to the beat of pop rhythms rooted in bebop, rock and roll and the blues. It encompassed the American teenagers' 'rebellion without a cause' and stills from *Blow Up*, the Roman *La Dolce vita* and the Parisian sentiment of *The Four Hundred Blows*.

It was the first time that there had been an independent youth fashion that was not based on the prevailing conventions of an older age group. The latter were duly shocked and the generation gap, which lasted approximately twenty years, was born. Conversations in those days tended to revolve not so much around Brigitte Bardot's films, but her behaviour in them. No fashion mentor could claim to have influenced this free spirit. Her shamelessly flaunted body symbolized the distance that had been travelled since the New Look. In the past, failure to follow fashion simply meant that you were poor. From the Sixties onwards, it was just as much a statement of personal freedom. Changes in appearance were now instigated by people working on the margins of society. 'It's the fringe that sets the pace,' said Jean-Luc Godard, pioneer of the *nouvelle vague* of subversive films. Actresses as different as Jean Seberg, Natalie Wood, Sue Lyon, Audrey Hepburn, Anouk Aimée, Anna Karina and Anita

Marianne Faithfull
Symbol of a generation for whom London was the centre of the world, the singer helped to popularize the Chelsea look.
June 1965

Anna Karina and Jean-Luc Godard
The actress and film director were the presiding geniuses of the French *nouvelle vague*. July 1966

Ekberg; models like Twiggy, Jean Shrimpton, Veruschka and Nicole de Lamargé; and singers such as Juliette Gréco, Zizi Jeanmaire, Joan Baez, Marianne Faithfull and Françoise Hardy all, in their various ways, exemplified a new type of look. A sign of the times, women were now referred to as 'chicks', or addressed in love songs as 'baby'. It was the apotheosis of the child-woman, half-goody-goody, half-rebel.

In 1965, what the press called the Courrèges revolution acclimatized the rarefied world of Parisian haute couture to changes that were already under way at every level of society. A few months later, Chanel mounted her rearguard action against the exposure of the knee, while Yves Saint Laurent responded with his legendary Mondrian dress. Mary Quant's skirts were already short in 1963, but three years later they had risen to mid-thigh. Much to the sorrow of devotees of the suspender belt, tights became widely available, in a range of colours, which introduced a new level of feminine comfort. They ensured modesty even in the shortest skirts, whether a woman was curled up on one of the new designer sofas or dancing the twist. No longer in her partner's arms, she stood independently, looking him straight in the face. In all this, the poor male was very much the victim of events, even though the women's liberation movement had barely begun. The mini skirt was followed by the maxi coat, shorts, blousons and knee- and thigh-high boots, setting off a massive revolution in appearance. Meanwhile, the contraceptive pill was barely tolerated in a society where women still tended to be given the more menial tasks and earned much lower wages for doing the same work as men.

The epicentre of the movement of student protest that emerged in several countries at about this time was the University of Nanterre in the suburbs of Paris. Here, in May 1968, events began that were to spread to the rest of France and then to Europe and to the United States. It is indicative of the level of freedom that people were enjoying at the time that the original incident that sparked off this student revolution was a ban on boys visiting girls in their rooms. Whether the girls demanded equal freedom in that respect remains unclear.

And yet, in the mid-Sixties, because of the strength of the English music scene, a trip to London became the more or less obligatory rite of passage for the young foreigner, providing a chance to follow in the steps of the Beatles and to observe the liberated English dolly birds. Carnaby Street was the home of a new unisex style of dressing, a specifically English eccentricity that coincided with the loss of the Empire. As the decade progressed, small independent boutiques moved west to the Kings Road. The culmination of the London style was Biba, a boutique whose romantic decadence chimed perfectly with the birth of the hippy culture. At the end of a decade of radical change, London style, paradoxically, flew in the face of everything the Sixties had stood for: technical advances, simplified lines, lack of ornament, beauty through utility and practicality. But in fashion, everything has its moment, both good and bad. The pendulum swings one way and then the other.

Ensembles by Louis Féraud
At this time, Féraud liked to combine simple lines with graphic detail. 1966

Laced leather trousers by Stephen Burrows
The trousers are worn, Forties style, with a blouse.

Yves Saint Laurent

**Yves Saint Laurent
and Victoire**
After they met
at Dior in 1958,
Victoire became
Yves Saint Laurent's
favourite model.
1962

Pop Art collection
Photograph by
Jean-Claude Sauer.
1966

'The little prince of couture' was how an enthusiastic press described the young man whose timid exterior could not conceal, even at the dawn of the Sixties, a superstar in the making. Four decades on, Yves Saint Laurent has lost none of his mystery, none of the magnetism which continues to enthral the world of fashion. In the timelessness of his designs, he resembles Chanel, whose influence he acknowledges. But his work also retains that aura of aloofness of the Dior years, whose magic he has somehow kept alive. It is his ability to synthesize these two worlds – opposed in their day – adding to them a breath of youth and his extra-sensory perception of the needs and wants of his contemporaries, that has led to the YSL monogram leaving its stamp on a whole era.

Dior updated the grammar of haute couture that Worth had devised a century earlier, while Chanel assembled a practical vocabulary for her contemporaries. Drawing on both their achievements, Yves Saint Laurent invented a whole new language that incorporated both the evening dress and the safari jacket, the formal train and the fisherman's oilskin, sequins and the Perfecto jacket. Its vocabulary could be adapted to any circumstance and virtually any kind of customer – even if only indirectly, through the products it inspired.

In the future, it may well be difficult to explain exactly what was so utterly new, indeed revolutionary, about female fashion appropriating the reefer jacket, the dress suit, the trench coat or the double-breasted jacket. People will no doubt be amused by references to Cocteau, the Ballets Russes, Christian Bérard and Matisse, but they will not remember the aura of scandal that so often clung to these fashion shows, from which audiences emerged in a state of shock.

After the sudden death of Dior in 1957, Yves Saint Laurent was chosen as his successor. However, constant disagreements with the owners of the business led he and his friend Pierre Bergé to join forces and open their own house in 1961. Embarking on a period of inspirational creativity, Yves rallied to his cause the most progressive journalists and the most illustrious clients, routing the old couture and laying the foundations for ready-to-wear. 1965 saw the launch of the Mondrian collection and January 1966, the first 'smoking' or dress suit. In July, the Pop Art collection was presented and, in the same year, the first Saint Laurent Rive Gauche boutique opened, a subject to which we shall return in due course.

Mondrian collection
In homage to the painter Mondrian, Yves Saint Laurent featured reproductions of his works on straight jersey dresses.
Winter 1965

Bare-backed dress
Crêpe dress with lace back from the provocative Forties collection. A classic of fashion photography by Jeanloup Sieff.
1971

Besides the exclusivity of his haute couture, ready-to-wear, shoes, accessories, furs, perfumes and cosmetics, a remarkable homogeneity existed across the whole range. As not only the creator but also the orchestrator of all the products that bore his name, Yves Saint Laurent remained the master of his own destiny, frequently retaining control even of the manufacturing processes.

Since, on a formal level, his work was not particularly innovative, he escaped the ridicule that, with the passage of time, was the fate of some of his more futuristic colleagues. And yet, in constantly ringing the changes, reinventing – albeit with the keenest sensibility – the most beautiful fashions of the century, he was not immune to the modern evil of melancholy. Convinced that he was the last of a dying breed, and yet unanimously hailed as the leader of a new world, Yves Saint Laurent marks the transition between yesterday's fashion and today's.

André Courrèges

Zip-fronted bolero jacket
Gabardine bolero jacket with hipster trousers. Photograph by Peter Knapp. 1968

Ensemble with horizontal stripes
Dress and jacket in wool satin with white panama hat. *Spring/Summer 1965*

Born in Pau in 1923, Courrèges was a qualified civil engineer with a passion for architecture, design and style. At the start of the Fifties, he went to work for Balenciaga and remained with him for eleven years. When he set up on his own, his former employer sent him a number of clients prepared to try something more adventurous. With his combined technical and artistic background, Courrèges was perfectly placed to capitalize on couture's embryonic overtures towards industry. Turning his back on the licensing system and calculating that his uncluttered lines would lend themselves to mass production, he decided to design, manufacture and distribute everything himself. With a factory in Pau and an exclusive distribution network, he enjoyed a large measure of autonomy, which was only cut short by the economic downturn and – rather paradoxically, given his visionary reputation – by his blindness to changes in taste during the Seventies.

The sensation caused by his white collection of 1965 has left an indelible mark in the history books of fashion; its effect on haute couture is only really comparable to that of the New Look in 1947. Anticipating the woman of the year 2000 (as only the age of plastic could have imagined her), Courrèges ushered in the reign of the mini skirt in France. He also set the trend for trousers, co-ordinated outfits in clinging knits and garments with stark minimalist lines. It was a style that made no reference to the past, unless perhaps to certain ideas of the Russian Constructivists or to the Bauhaus. Today Courrèges enjoys an almost mythical status, as well as being remembered as a great designer.

Paco Rabanne

Hooded dress
Plastic discs,
coloured or
transparent, were
a regular feature
of the couturier's
designs from
1967 onwards.
c. 1967

Paco Rabanne
(born 1934)
The great avant-
garde designer
is past master of
the art of using
unconventional
materials, such as
iron, plastic and
leather.

The son of a former head seamstress at Balenciaga, Francisco Rabaneda Cuervo was born in 1934 in San Sebastián. He opened his own couture house in 1966 and, from the start, produced resolutely modern designs. Instead of using traditional dress materials, he created garments from aluminium, Rhodoïd (a rigid plastic) and pieces of scrap metal, which caused a sensation when presented in the course of his 'manifesto' shows, to the accompaniment of concrete music. No less disciplined for being provocative, Paco Rabanne's designs, as well as being experimental, were also closely in tune with what modern open-minded young women wanted to wear. They have continued to be popular, winning this likeable and original designer the respect of the more adventurous customer. Among his innovations are the low-budget disposable dress made of paper and nylon thread, which he launched in 1967, and the seamless dress made, after much experiment, by spraying vinyl chloride on to a mould. He was

also, in 1966, the first designer to use black models, which almost resulted in his dismissal from the Chambre Syndicale de la Couture Parisienne. Fortunately, the considerable success of his perfume Calandre has helped support the less profitable areas of his work, while his utopianism has assured him a unique position in the conservative world of couture.

Emilio Pucci

Emilio Pucci

Emilio Pucci was nearing his forties when, having spent his younger years studying art and social sciences, he embarked on a career in ready-to-wear. In the early Fifties, this Florentine aristocrat's first sportswear designs and prints influenced by Op art and by psychedelia earnt him a reputation that extended well beyond the circles of high society. His clothes were simple in form, often tubular. His sleek shift dresses, tunics and beachwear, for sunbathing in Capri or on the deck of a yacht, unleashed a Puccimania that was all part of a movement to liberate the female body. With styles that have changed very little over the years, the label has retained its elitist feel, which is tinged today with an element of retro.

Rudi Gernreich

Along with Charles James, he was probably America's most original designer, one of those rare avant-garde geniuses who carried about him the authentic aura of scandal. This culminated in the mid-Sixties when Gernreich launched the first monokini – regarded as a symbol of sexual liberation, although it was, in fact, designed principally to allow the body greater freedom and mobility. As a former dancer, born in Vienna in 1922 and based on the West Coast, Gernreich always opted for forms and textiles that offered women maximum ease of movement. With most of his contributions being a good decade ahead of their time, it was inevitable that Gernreich and his futuristic designs would eventually come to seem old-fashioned.

Rudi Gernreich

And Also

The Sixties saw the opening of a small number of new houses in Paris. A final wave of young designers were duly admitted to the Chambre Syndicale, although with little prospect of ever being able to defray in full the heavy costs of haute couture.

Louis Féraud and Jacques Esterel were originally partners running a dynamic boutique, before they opened their own houses in 1958. Ted Lapidus, whose cuts were unrivalled, set up his couture business at around the same time. He also opened a boutique called Tedd, one of the first to offer de-luxe ready-to-wear for men, aimed specifically at the younger, more upmarket customer. His sister Rosette adopted the pseudonym Torrente when she launched her own label at the age of twenty-three. By the time she was admitted to the ranks of couture in 1971, she had already successfully established, two years previously, a ready-to-wear range called Miss Torrente that was perfectly in tune with the times. She occupied premises on the Rond-Point of the Champs Élysées and her suits and coats, at which she excelled, attracted a discreet clientele that included the wives of many senior businessmen and politicians.

After nine years with Givenchy, Philippe Venet set up a small house of his own in 1962, which won him a reputation for simple refined designs and superbly crafted coats. Another modest venture was that of Serge Lepage, whose discreet good taste was combined with a concern for the highest possible quality. It seems that his loyal customers, who were not in the least anxious to draw attention to themselves, enabled Lepage to run a number of enterprises that offered, essentially, high standards and traditional expertise.

Giorgio di Sant'Angelo
(born 1936)
The model Elsa Peretti was the Italian designer's inspiration for this Scheherazade outfit.

Jean-Louis Scherrer was a former assistant of Yves Saint Laurent at Dior, who set up on his own in 1963. Patronized by a quintessentially Parisian clientele, who appreciated the freshness and floral prettiness of his uncluttered designs, he reached the apex of his career when he was appointed official couturier to the wife of President Giscard d'Estaing. The finale of many of his collections featured original embroideries by the Maison Lesage, superb examples of the contribution that this great house has made to the prestige of haute couture.

Of all the couture houses born out of the economic euphoria of the Sixties, we should single out that of Emanuel Ungaro, who remains a powerful influence today. He was born in Aix-en-Provence in 1933, the son of a tailor who had emigrated from Italy. His father taught him all the secrets of his craft; the rest he learned in the shadow of the great Balenciaga

**Flared catsuit by
Emanuel Ungaro**
Photograph by Peter
Knapp.
1970

Carita hairstyle
Maria and Rosy
Carita were famous
for their Spanish-
style chignons for
evening; extravagant
wigs for dinner
parties; bows worn at
the nape of the neck;
and sleek helmets of
hair coming down
over the eyes.

and then with Courrèges. In 1965, with virtually no money, he showed his first collection. Its success enabled him to move to the Avenue Montaigne four years later. Ungaro's Italian roots led him away from Balenciaga's classicism in the direction of bold baroque contrasts, expressed through drapery and virtuoso layering. This proud yet modest craftsman found his niche by creating a body of work aimed at a particular sort of woman. Not restricted to the catwalks, his dresses, with their imaginative use of colour, were worn at the most prestigious events in Parisian life. His select and varied clientele were always enthusiastic about his designs, their loyalty betraying an affection that Emanuel himself reserved for his work. This is something now so rare that it is worth pointing out.

In the United States, Oleg Cassini was a talented businessman and, as a designer of seductive dresses, he was greatly influenced by the Hollywood interpretation of Parisian fashion. In the Fifties and Sixties, his popularity extended from the East Coast to the West. Bill Blass injected Thirties glamour into classic styles, while Anne Klein offered sophisticated sportswear for the active modern woman. Pauline Trigère's ready-to-wear was always beautifully cut, in discreetly feminine styles and she was known for her original use of wool in evening wear.

For a younger clientele, Giorgio di Sant'Angelo offered a style of revealing hippy chic that flattered the female body, while Betsey Johnson's cheerful, brightly coloured clothes were very much in tune with the spirit of the Paris boutiques in that era. Hattie Carnegie started to produce her own designs and Oscar de la Renta took his first steps on the road to success.

In Rome, meanwhile, in 1959, Valentino Garavani opened a couture house which he called simply Valentino. It rapidly won favour with the aristocracy of the city who, ever since the release of the film, seemed to embody the

Federico Fellini
La Dolce vita
Federico Fellini, accompanied by a *Vogue* model wearing a coat by Simonetta, is photographed by William Klein at about the time of the release of his controversial film. *1960*

Valentino
On the rooftops of Rome, Veruschka wears a kaftan of ottoman silk over chiffon pyjamas. *Spring/Summer 1967*

image of *dolce vita*. His style relied on a superb made-to-measure technique. Glamorous and elegant rather than innovative, it perfectly complemented the sensuality of women who enjoyed being the centre of attention. The jet set loved him and international celebrities, such as Jackie Kennedy and the Empress Farah Dibah, assured his social and commercial success, which has never dwindled. At the end of the century, he has 560 points of sale to his name in countries all over the world. He owns sixty boutiques devoted exclusively to his designs, selling eight ranges of ready-to-wear, which are just some of the many variations that this Italian master has composed on the theme of the eternal feminine.

Also in Rome, capital of *alta moda*, the beautiful evening dresses of Simonetta Visconti and the varied and imaginative sculptural designs of Roberto Capucci enjoyed continuing success.

Twiggy

Biba

Swinging London

While young ready-to-wear designers known as stylists were attempting to spread their wings in Paris, England was experiencing the musical rebellion of Swinging London. During the mid-Sixties, to the beat of pop music, a teenage culture took hold in Carnaby Street and the Kings Road which was to have a radical influence on future behaviour. Long hair was all the rage for boys, with short cuts by Vidal Sassoon and mini skirts for the girls. It was a spontaneous movement, summed up by the personality of Mary Quant, who, along with André Courrèges, launched the mini skirt. The style was propagated in boutiques that were as pulsating as they were ephemeral. In a matter of months, the trend had spread throughout Europe, attracting to London hordes of exuberant adolescents caught up in the excitement of one of the most extraordinary moments in the history of fashion. Among the many profoundly original designers were Foale & Tuffin, John Bates, Thea Porter, Gina Fratini, Zandra Rhodes, Anthony Price and Ossie Clark, who worked for Quorum and whose chiffon dresses, printed with his wife Celia Birtwell's designs, were the runaway success of the Kings Road. The contributions of all these designers were reproduced in photos by David Bailey and launched to the rhythms of the Beatles and the Rolling Stones, themselves promotors of a style of dress that stood in direct opposition to the British tradition. Transitory and lacking a solid economic base it may have been, yet this dazzling outburst of creativity has helped to sustain London's continuing appeal for fans of the Sixties.

The Beatles

QUANT BY QUANT

Mary Quant

Mary Quant

The Empire of Style

Ski suit by Michèle Rosier
The French sportswear pioneer used new materials, such as vinyl and nylon padding.
November 1968

Cacharel shirts
Founded in 1962 by Jean Bousquet, Cacharel achieved early success with its seersucker shirts, later made in Liberty prints.
1962

The house of Emanuel Ungaro – independent, rooted in the highest traditions of couture and founded by a designer who had been reared within its closed world – was the last of its kind. Its opening brought to a close a century of haute couture that had been inaugurated by Worth. The prestige of couture remained unrivalled, but that on its own, as we have seen, was no longer sufficient to ensure the survival of a label. Gradually, as each house tried to find its own way of diversifying, the practice of selling models for foreign buyers to reproduce was abandoned, in favour of the substantial revenues that could be gained from an exclusive ready-to-wear operation. As many struggled to set up such an enterprise, between 1966 and 1967, the number of houses enrolled with the Chambre Syndicale des Couturiers Parisiens fell from thirty-nine to seventeen. The couture side of their businesses continued to decline.

Well aware of commercial realities, Yves Saint Laurent and Pierre Bergé set up an organization that has subsequently served as an example for the whole profession. Trading under the name Saint Laurent Rive Gauche, its first venture was to open a boutique in Saint-Germain-des-Prés, well away from the fashionable part of town and in an area then considered resolutely alternative. It sold, at accessible prices, clothes manufactured to the highest standards by the skilled seamstresses of the Mendès factory. Far from considering this first attempt at diversification as an inferior form of couture, Saint Laurent created a distinct type of fashion, with its own

set of rules. A flood of customers rushed to the new fashion Mecca, which spilled out on to the street. The formula was exported throughout the world to dozens of similar boutiques, as part of a strictly controlled franchise operation that was subject to the same terms and conditions worldwide. In an effect that was almost comparable to the miracle of the loaves and fishes, the original product multiplied, under the strict control of its creator, into a myriad of articles, all designed by the master himself and his team and marketed under his label.

Through partnerships and acquisitions shrewdly masterminded by Pierre Bergé, the house ended up controlling the entire production chain. The business's success relied on the talent of its founder, of course, but, beyond that, it owed everything to its homogeneity. As haute couture was forced down from its pedestal, manufacturing began to buck up its ideas, aware that a change in the market had opened up new avenues. In order to meet the demand for novelty, it employed its own creative workforce. In France, these designers were known as stylists, the dictionary definition of style being 'a particular manner of treating form and content in the production of an item'.

Prisunic dresses
Long dresses
in cotton jersey
designed in-house
by Prisunic.
Summer 1967

Maïmé Arnodin, the great pioneer of styling, was one of the first Frenchwomen to be awarded a diploma by the École Centrale des Arts et Manufactures. From the late Fifties onwards, acting as a consultant to major industrialists, she worked on ways of organizing the production process into a coherent whole, from manufacture right through to distribution. Having set a precedent, any consumer product could subsequently be styled in this manner. She was particularly good at discovering new talent and, when she took over at *Jardin des modes*, she helped to familiarize the public with the faces behind the labels, with those who performed this new creative role. Generic articles were transformed into branded

products and anonymous objects into lines that became identified with the
famous young stylists whose names were the talk of the town. Many of them
had no background whatsoever in couture. They included, among others, the
three amazons of style – Emmanuelle Khanh, Christiane Bailly and Michèle
Rosier – leading one paper to remark that 'Ready-to-wear is now in the hands
of women.'

In other words, a minor revolution had taken place in the macho world
of textiles. Madame Arnodin, with her charisma and unfailing charm, was
precisely the right person to advise the big industrialists on the changes
they needed to make. A committed European, determined that French
fashion needed to expand to an international scale, and a great believer in
combining beauty with utility, in 1961 she opened her own style consultancy.

This was something entirely new and acted as a catalyst for the trends, talents and specialist skills available to the decision-makers.

Daniel Hechter, a prolific stylist during these hectic years, was barely twenty-two years old when he decided to break away and set up on his own. Meanwhile, Jean Bousquet, recently graduated from technical college, installed a few sewing machines in premises in the Marais and, using a bolt of coloured crepon, launched the famous Cacharel shirt that became almost a uniform for an entire generation.

A new sort of boutique began to appear at around this time, operating as part of a small chain. The first was opened by Elie Jacobson to sell original designs by his wife Jacqueline. Their commercial/design partnership traded as Dorothée Bis, a name which dominated the headlines for ten years. Their clothes had a strong influence on the fashion of the day and sold in huge numbers. A similar set-up was adopted by Sonia Rykiel. It was the unusual sweaters that she sold in her tiny shop on the outskirts of Paris that first attracted the attention of the fashion gurus. By 1968, she had moved to 6, rue de Grenelle and from there, she developed the style that made her so popular with the big American stores and with the many young women who appreciated her relaxed and individual style.

Mixed separates by Dorothée Bis
These non-matching separates, cleverly designed to create interesting contrasts, are only for the young. The label was founded by the Jacobsons in 1962. *September 1970*

Maïmé Arnodin and Denis Fayolle
joiend forces in 1968 to set up the design consultancy Mafia (Maïmé Arnodin Fayolle International Associés).

Also a boutique called Victoire opened up in 1964 on the Place des Victoires. Its aim was to promote new talent and it was one of the first to establish the successful formula of stocking a variety of different labels.

Amid this whirlwind of activity, the fashion editors seemed to develop amnesia as far as couture was concerned. All they were interested in were these new stylists that their readers were so crazy about. The clothing industry waited with bated breath to see what they would produce next, hoping the magic would rub off and that they could pick up some ideas for themselves. Since Chanel, copying was nothing

new, but everyone's life was made a great deal easier in 1966, as the result of an initiative by a woman called Françoise Vincent, who originally trained as an engineer. She turned her hand to producing a series of source books listing current trends, all carefully identified and itemized by her company Promostyl. It meant that every season, all the different sectors of textile production – often based in the provinces and therefore relatively cut off from the latest developments in fashion – had access, for a fee, to these invaluable tools that brought together the broad trends in fashion, classified by theme, form, material and colour. The formula was extended to all domestic products, such as china, household linen and furnishings, until eventually companies in more than thirty countries were gleaning their ideas from these detailed breakdowns.

Another important figure concerned with large-scale distribution was Denise Fayolle of Prisunic, who made it her mission to inject new life into the 460 sales outlets controlled by the popular chain store. Her credo, 'ugliness doesn't sell', echoes that of the great Franco-American designer Raymond Loewy. A determined woman, Denise wanted the largest possible number of people to have access to attractive, well-conceived products that would not break the bank. In 1960 to 1961 she launched the Prisu label, which was intended to achieve precisely these objectives. Following American prototypes, it took off immediately. The refurbished sales areas, redesigned shops and more youthful packaging helped promote sportswear that was enthusiastically received by a new clientele, a fact reflected in a steeply rising sales curve. People began to go to Prisunic not just because of its low prices, but out of curiosity. And they tended to find what they wanted, cheaply.

The experiment extended from clothes and accessories to furnishings and objects for the home. Many of these were designed by a young Englishman called Terence Conran, who later launched the Habitat chain. Her mission accomplished, Denise Fayolle left Prisunic in 1967, determined to tackle another of the dinosaurs, selling by mail order. As product consultant at Les 3 Suisses, she

Coloured tights by Dim
The suspender belt was replaced by the panty girdle, then briefly by tights with a demarcated panty top, before all-in-one tights took over.

**Lingerie by
the illustrator
Antonio Lopez**

Lopez dominated
fashion illustration,
injecting energy into
a discipline that had
been going downhill
since the Fifties.

began to introduce fashion garments for the younger generation. Together
with Maïmé Arnodin, she also co-founded Mafia, a style consultancy and
advertising agency combined, which remained, right up until the Eighties,
one of the most creative forces in a mushrooming advertising sector.

That such progress was made so rapidly proves that developments in
fashion closely mirrored the economic fortunes of the period. A younger
population, an increase in purchasing power, a new optimism after the years
of war and shortages and profound social upheavals all helped to make the
Sixties one of the most decisive eras in the long history of human behaviour.

1 **Jean Shrimpton**, 1968. Her hair is styled by Carita to look like the sun.

2 **Jean Seberg**, 1960. Carita created this famous short haircut especially for Jean Seberg's role in Jean-Luc Godard's film *Breathless*.

3 **Audrey Hepburn**, 1961. In the film *Breakfast at Tiffany's* by Blake Edwards. At a time when clothing was being revolutionized, the actress opted for haute couture and Givenchy.

4 **Catherine Deneuve**, March 1966. With her husband, photographer David Bailey, arriving at the royal première of the film *Born Free*.

5 **Jackie Kennedy**, May 1960. Wearing a red wool Oleg Cassini suit inspired by the uniform of the Canadian Mounties.

6 **Donyale Luna**, 1966. One of the first black models to become famous. Seen here posing for the magazine *Twen*.

Menswear

1 Mods in the streets of London

2 Brioni jacket
Jacquard-weave double-breasted jacket with decorative topstitching.
1967

3 Mao suit by Testa-Taroni
Famous opera director Pier Luigi Pizzi, photographed by Ugo Mulas.
1968

Following pages:
Op art fashion
Fashion echoes the optical effects of Op art. Jean Shrimpton compères the popular television show *Dim Dam Dom*.

The rapidly developing menswear sector was dominated by the youthful yet classic lines of the Italian look, the *ragazzo* style. In France, as a result, the local tailor became a dying breed. Paris had its *minets* and England its Mods, with their waisted jackets and boots. A few futuristic rumblings were set off by Pierre Cardin, and then Courrèges, but the three-piece suit survived intact. The principal change was in the weight of the fabric. The choice of materials, often synthetic, and the method of manufacture produced a suit that, because it was lighter in weight, had a completely different look. The line was closer to the natural shape of the body, causing men to look at their figures more critically. Shirts gained darts, while the new low-waisted trousers lost their tucks and trouser legs began to taper. Young men grew their hair down to their collars and Cacharel added a touch of colour, and even floral motifs, to their shirts. The polo neck never quite succeeded in replacing the tie, but the adoption of the workman's jacket in rough corduroy, and especially the Mao jacket, by artists and psychoanalysts, proved to be more than merely a political statement. The spread of jeans – and of protest movements – served to accelerate a radical change in the male wardobe. Men would, in the future, find it less difficult to admit to taking an interest in their appearance, since it would no longer call into question their virility. However, they were still far less ready than women to pick up the fashion gauntlet.

Street Fashion and Anti-Fashion | 1968–1972

In 1960, in his sixth collection for Dior, Yves Saint Laurent presented a black leather jacket. Admittedly it was made of crocodile and trimmed with black mink, but, nevertheless, it was unmistakably inspired by *The Wild One*, a film starring Marlon Brando that had caused a scandal when it was released in 1954. The style it promoted had since been adopted by the young working classes, but this was the first time that life had erupted off the streets and into a Paris salon. The jacket received a lukewarm reception, which may have contributed to the dispute that arose between the young designer and the management of the house that he then resolved to leave.

As Mary Quant said, neither she nor Courrèges invented the mini skirt, it was born on the streets. No one told the short-skirted Londoners, with their pert schoolgirl looks, their trousers and their boots, what they were supposed to wear. The boutiques that fed their frenzy for dolly-bird clothes were merely climbing on the bandwagon, responding to demand. For the boys, too, everything was now in flux. Clothes emphasized sex appeal, anticipating the notion of men as objects of desire, in the image of the male pin-up. Generally, love was on everybody's mind. Not sentimental love, but the act of love, now demanded by right, as the obligatory rite of passage for the young, who, in their words and music at least, wanted nothing more to do with the past.

As part of this counter-culture, counter-couture was just one of many phenomena that took hold in the crossover years between the Sixties and

Embroidered shirt by Levi Strauss & Co. The shirt is embroidered by Pat Haines. The rustic imagery and celestial symbols reflect the pacifism and back-to-nature beliefs of hippy culture. Oakland Museum, Oakland.
1973

Hippy gathering
The Road Hog,
El Rito Parade,
California.
4 July 1968

Seventies. Homosexuals, for example, came out, determined to express their identity, especially in the Anglo-Saxon world where they were less liable to persecution. The anti-fashion trend summed up the aspirations of a whole section of society who wanted more flexible attitudes and more scope for their imagination. As a general rule, the seismic upheavals in fashion were no longer perceived during these two decades as inevitable swings of the pendulum of taste, but rather as progress, as concrete achievements, even revolutions. With hindsight it is clear that their impact was relative, but, nevertheless, ten years of radical rethinking left its mark. A thriving anti-fashion developed alongside the new structures that had been set up to cope with the requirements of the international clothing trade. Even today, anti-fashion remains a powerful force, offering a libertarian alternative. No contemporary creator can afford to ignore its spontaneous innovations or fail to incorporate them into their work at regular intervals.

When Yves Saint Laurent launched garments such as the reefer jacket, the safari suit and, above all, trousers (the wearing of which was forbidden to women in any formal environment and even in the workplace), all he was doing was transporting trends that had long been visible on the streets of London and Paris into the boutique. 'Haute couture is dead,' announced Emmanuelle Khanh in 1964. 'I want to reach the woman in the street.'

The baton passed from swinging London to San Francisco as flower power developed a momentum and pop gave way to the hippy culture. This time the revolution was purely cultural and it spawned its own particular kind of anti-fashion. Guaranteed to help recover lost youth, it was enthusiastically espoused all over the Western world. Having once tasted freedom, fashion shed its inhibitions. It rediscovered garments that had formerly been the exclusive preserve of the working class and the peasantry. American blue jeans, for example, were worn, in a daring combination, with the Mao jacket. Traditional fashion was viewed as a mark of petit bourgeois individualism and kept a low profile, betraying a rather touching desire to please as it struggled to adapt. The smarter parts of town saw an influx of afghans, Indian scarves, curly hair, flower-print tunics and an abundance of cheap tat, all the accessories of an artificial paradise.

Denim boots by Golo
Boots, in leather and printed denim, designed by Leila Larmon and Stephen Bruce. Metropolitan Museum of Art, New York.
1973

Yet people were sufficiently down to earth to develop alternative industries – in those days everything was 'alternative'.

'Is it a girl or is it a boy/A boy with long hair or a girl in trousers,' was the gist of a song by that knowing Lolita, France Gall. The fashion for unisex mushroomed, with young couples wanting to share everything. As secondhand tat fought it out with homemade clothes, a crude sort of fashion evolved, a mishmash of traditional craft techniques and ethnic influences. A generation of backpackers developed a taste for travel and suddenly various world cultures – the remoter the better – found themselves represented in districts inhabited by students and by dissident minorities dreaming of a happier tomorrow.

At the same time, these years of change witnessed a return to images of the recent past. Many of the young people who were interested in foreign culture were also film buffs. In

Sonny and Cher

Angela Davis

The Jackson Five

Jim Morrison

Paris, the Musée de l'Homme is virtually next door to the Cinémathèque. Be that as it may, the Seventies were as much about retro as they were hippy. The cast-offs of the Hollywood stars were combined with the subversive paraphernalia of Kathmandu's finest, to create a look that defied all argument. 'Please yourself' was the catchword of the 'me' decade. Many saw it, without much regret, as the end of good taste.

Coming hard on the heels of the hippy culture, soul music from the United States and a vast movement claiming civil rights for blacks created a sensibility that combined nostalgia for Africa with the norms of American culture. A radical chic emerged, influenced by Angela Davis, James Brown, Diana Ross and the Black Panthers, in everything from the rock scene to political demonstrations, from afro hairstyles to platform soles. There were fashions for glitz, with Elton John providing a prime example of the white, gay version. Black stylists such as Stephen Burrows and Scott Barrie played a decisive part in all this. And yet, here too, the genesis was spontaneous, rooted essentially in levels of society that had little purchasing power. Stars like Isaac Hayes, David Bowie and the Rolling Stones were all on the alert for the latest new sound to emerge from the increasingly cross-cultural anonymous masses.

One of the practical and commercial landmarks of anti-fashion was the opening of the Elio Fiorucci shop in Milan in 1967. The Italian designer had set up his own label in 1962, attracting attention with his brightly coloured rubber boots and plastic daisy sandals. When he acquired his new shop right in the pulsating heart of the city, he filled it with every conceivable object that stood in opposition to the traditional practices of fashion. Before long, he added his own ranges

Live action Barbie
Barbie wears a flared printed trouser suit with broad fringed sash and tasselled bracelets.
1971

Diana Ross
The Madonna of soul
music is as imperial
as she is elegant.

of accessories and, from 1969 onwards, inexpensive clothes that were
designed to be worn and then discarded, just like the guiding principles
of the day, kitsch, retro and pop. The chic and shocking image of the
Fiorucci galaxy, together with its irony and adept consumerism, went
hand in hand with display and merchandizing strategies that in those days
were still novel. A whole section of the counter-culture could not stop itself
from walking straight into the arms of the consumer society it despised. It
was a reconciliation which was to produce, in the advertising-led generation

that followed, the flashing neon illuminations of hyperrealism, glam rock and fake fur.

In a violent reaction to such delicious indulgences, the Seventies also saw the emergence of punk. It was born out of the unemployment that hit the British proletariat harder than the rest of Europe and, once again, it spread through protest music. However, this time, the songs were the vehicle for a hatred that was more visceral than political. With their ripped T-shirts, Dr Martens, Red Indian hairstyles, bondage trousers and chains, the punks exported a general feeling of disgust around the globe. Fashion, never discouraged and never tiring of being ripped off, dipped its toe even in these dangerous waters, seeking new sources of inspiration. Because of punk, London retained a considerable degree of influence over fashion, most notably in the boutiques of the Kings Road, where Vivienne Westwood's shop, opened in 1971, blew with the prevailing wind. Originally it sold Fifties clothes secondhand, as well as clothes inspired by that era, under the name Let It Rock. Before long, however, this temple of English iconoclasm concentrated on fetishistic accessories and ranges of clothing in which black rubber and steel studs were the outward

Fiorucci's neon sign

**Jerry Hall
and Antonio**
Ocho Rios, Jamaica.
1975

signs of an underlying sadism. It was on exactly the right wavelength for a youth dedicated to the cult of the safety pin. At that time, the boutique was called Sex. As punk declined, it took the name World's End; it was indeed the end of a world that had been defined by those years of anti-fashion.

Jean Bouquin

Anti-Fashion
Becomes Big Business

Mainstream fashion has always been remarkably good at assimilating new trends, including those that see themselves as operating outside the system. In the sphere of anti-fashion, Frenchman Jean Bouquin and Englishwoman Laura Ashley illustrate this fruitful paradox with particular force.

The former was a window dresser before opening a de-luxe souk for the rich hippies of the Côte d'Azur in St Tropez in 1964. Brigitte Bardot was one of the first fans of this Oriental style, with its lightweight, easy-to-manufacture garments. Four years later, Bouquin had progressed to Saint-Germain-des-Prés in Paris. His psychedelia, floaty fabrics, embroideries and afghans were a triumphant success. In 1971, true to his beliefs, he retired having made his fortune.

Laura Ashley and her husband ran a small business in Wales. Sensitive to the romantic charms of the surrounding countryside, their designs were resolutely unmodern in spirit. The vision of a Pre-Raphaelite maiden, in a wide-brimmed hat decorated with flowers, began to translate, in 1966, into coherent ranges. With an emphasis on mauves and purples, a touch pretty-pretty, floral, modest and rustic, Laura Ashley proved a huge hit in town. Converts to this rural lifestyle – with their long dresses trimmed with broderie anglaise, their furnishing fabrics and their big straw shopping bags – looked as if they had nothing more urgent to do than tend their cottages and drive their cart to market.

The company continued to expand until the accidental death of its founder in 1985. By turning to more humble sources rather than to haute couture for inspiration, Laura Ashley discovered a recipe for fashion that was not only highly successful but also very profitable.

Laura Ashley

The Seventies

Historical Review

The pace of change in fashion accelerated during the Seventies, as the flood of inventions and new ideas that had emerged during the previous decade were assimilated. Everything altered, from people's appearance in the street to the way they thought, from the notion of what was chic to what was considered to be the right look. In other words, what really changed, in the Western world, was people's relationship with their clothes. The East observed this development with interest, but were still denied access to fashion of this kind. The designed product was as different from the generic product as architecture was from building or cuisine from cooking. Parisian couture needed new strategies to guarantee its commercial viability in the face of competition from mass-produced designer goods, if it was to maintain the primacy that it had enjoyed for more than a century.

In the meantime, ready-to-wear was on a roll, creating its own names, those who in the Sixties had been christened the stylists. Styling was everything. It was a global concept, a sort of spice you added to the recipe to bring out the flavour and enhance the product. Yet, even though magazines like *Elle*, *Marie Claire* and the American *Women's Wear Daily* (the only daily magazine in the world) publicized the names, personalities and faces of those working on the industrial product, the stylists of the Sixties were almost always

Platform shoes by Fiorucci
Plastic shoes in bright colours were a big hit with the young.

Flower power

For a substantial section of the younger generation, the rejection of the conventions of modern industrial society was reflected in a conspicuous lack of interest in fashion and in the adoption of clothes from places far afield (Afghan jackets, Indian shirts, etc.) Their floral motifs corresponded to an ideal of peace and liberty.

freelance. They were paid by employers who, in practice, tended to be general manufacturers like Mendès, Rodier, Léonard, Biki, Pierre d'Alby and Weinberg. What became clear during the Seventies was that this anonymous talent needed to proclaim its identity. Along with generalists, you also had to have specialists, particularly in fashion, where each creative individual is unique. Out of this realization emerged the phenomenon of the *jeunes créateurs*, or young designers. Young, in this context, refers not so much to the age of the prodigies themselves as to the youthfulness of their creations. It was by placing the emphasis on individuals, each with their own distinctive approach, that Paris, in the Seventies, managed, in the eyes of the rest of the world, to keep control of an increasingly explosive situation. Not everyone saw it the same way. The press publicized the elegant image of Claude Pompidou, wife of the president of the French Republic, who wore the designs of all the leading couturiers, from Chanel to Courrèges, with a certain degree of style. Meanwhile, her husband announced, in a phrase that still sends shivers down the spines of everyone working in the luxury goods industries: 'We don't want to be the France of couture and perfumes.'

The naturally conservative disposition of the right; the left's confusing imaginations with frivolity; the old-established industrialists' inability to understand the *jeunes créateurs*; and the majority of the French populations' yearning for the Concorde, motorways and new towns (Pierre Cardin was all they knew about fashion and only because he posed as a cosmonaut) were among the many factors that contributed to a shift towards foreign goods. As a result, brands from abroad greatly increased their share of the market

Katmandu
Rajah suit in silk with a floral design embellished with gold. Trousers, waistcoat over a chiffon blouse, hat trimmed with a band of fox fur and velvet boots.

Floral fashion
Rustic dress photographed by Peter Knapp.
December 1970

during the Seventies. In France, Italy and the United States, many of the new trendsetters no longer emerged by a process of natural selection from the closed world of the Parisian couture ateliers. In the future, there would be no single idea. No one fashion, but fashions. Creativity during the Seventies was multifarious and often contradictory. Bursting with the energy of a fast river that sometimes overflowed its banks, it resisted the efforts of anyone who tried to regulate its course. It must be said, however, that 'the France of couture and perfumes' was not particularly good at exploiting this new libertarian mood. Yet, at the end of the century, fashion, essentially, still revolves around the axis established by Paris during the late Seventies.

France

As the French fashion industry took steps to bring itself up to date during the Seventies, it made efficiency its goal, enabling couturiers willing to take up the challenge to play the ready-to-wear card. In 1966, Courrèges opened his first boutiques, in Paris and then in two major stores in New York and Houston. Under the impetus of his managing director, François Baufumé, twenty-eight boutiques were to open in the United States between 1970 and 1976.

The other leader in this process of democratization was, of course, Yves Saint Laurent. Under the direction of Anne-Marie Muñoz and working in collaboration with the Mendès factories and its studio, Saint Laurent Rive Gauche added a new dimension to the manufactured article. Able to be bought off the peg and more freely inventive than couture, Rive Gauche, from the outset, anticipated what was required for a clientele that, although still traditional, wanted something a little bit different. Over the next twenty years and working in regular cycles, Yves Saint Laurent would continue to develop his style, always producing something new but never contradicting himself. At the same time, uniquely, he retained control of both his haute couture and highly successful ready-to-wear operations.

Marc Bohan, another of Dior's assistants, took over from Yves Saint Laurent at Christian

Safari jacket by Yves Saint Laurent
Veruschka poses in the legendary lace-up safari jacket in beige cotton, with bronze ring belt, worn over black cotton Bermuda shorts. A classic from the collections of Yves Saint Laurent.
1968

Kenzo (centre) with friends

Dior, where he continued along established lines. Philippe Guibourgé was given the responsibility of launching the secondary line, Miss Dior, but its lack of success led to the designer's departure in 1975. He then went to Chanel and set up its first ready-to-wear range, at a time when the house was still struggling to recover from the death of its founder. The head seamstresses were continuing to produce two couture collections every year with no one at the helm. The hard-wearing braided suit that was considered such a good investment by rich customers of a certain age was seized upon with enthusiasm, during those years of transition, by women ministers (still rare) and by the wives of heads of state. Of course, they did not then have access to the range of clothes for the executive woman that was soon to be perfected by Armani. And, following Armani, came all those others who, mostly without knowing it, were distant successors of Redfern, who, even before the turn of the twentieth century, was designing tailored unisex styles for Queen Victoria.

Guibourgé remained at Chanel for seven years, and his designs –
the first black leather suit, a more youthful line, shorter skirts – brought
the long-established house a success that prepared the way for its
comeback, that would be masterminded by Karl Lagerfeld in 1983.

Sonia Rykiel
(born 1930)
The undisputed
queen of knitwear,
her designs are
sophisticated and
luxurious enough
to be worn in the
evening as well as
during the day.

In the meantime, it was Sonia Rykiel who, in
the eyes of America at least, proved herself to be
Chanel's true successor. Having moved her shop
to the Rue de Grenelle in 1968, this free-thinking
woman went on to achieve considerable success
by addressing women like herself as sisters.
The queen of figure-hugging knits, in 1974,
she designed her first pullovers with reversed
seams. But more than that, she designed a whole
range of clothes that were highly individual
and yet could be worn anywhere, allowing the
attractive and sophisticated young woman of
those exciting years to inhabit a more liberal
society without losing any of her femininity.
The Rykiel style has since been dominated by
fluid knitted garments, dark blacks, rhinestones,
little crocheted hats and long boa-like scarves.
A strong-willed, powerful and creative woman,
Sonia Rykiel is also a sensualist. Not only has she conquered and retained
the respect of the American market, but she has also demonstrated that,
in a male-dominated world, she is one of the rare women with the
confidence to express her opinions.

The other undisputed star of Parisian fashion in the Seventies was
Kenzo, the colourful, floral counterpart of the more restrained Rykiel. Fate
led this young Japanese, whose surname was Takada, to Paris in 1965 and
he held his first show at the Galerie Vivienne behind the Place des Victoires
in 1970. With the help of a few friends, he took out a lease on an old shop
and repainted it with tropical forests in the style of Douanier Rousseau.

In doing so, he created Jungle Jap, the cornerstone of an empire on which the sun has not yet set. Kenzo is not really a Japanese designer but more an authentic Parisian, irrepressibly youthful with his upbeat attitude and permanent smile. Born in 1939 in Japan, he now lives, works and has his manufacturing base in France. He draws his inspiration from all over the world, combining Oriental and Western folk influences with a wonderful *joie de vivre* and an intuitive sense of what his young customers want. No one has matched him in bringing all the colours of the rainbow on to the grey streets.

With his unusual prints, fluid lines, clever accessories and finery that was hitherto unprecedented in ready-to-wear, he literally turned fashion upside down. With the doll-like figure – half-femme fatale, half-hippy chick – that he designed and then gave life to, he created the ripples of a sexual revolution. Life before and life after Kenzo are separated by the opening of his first big store on the Place des Victoires in 1976.

Karl Lagerfeld was born in 1938, into a rich family of German industrialists, and arrived in Paris in 1952. Jointly with Yves Saint Laurent, he won first prize in a competition run by the International Wool Secretariat. For three years he worked as assistant to the couturier Pierre Balmain, before moving in 1958 to Patou as head of couture. He had achieved all of this before embarking, in the early Sixties, on one of the most brilliant careers as a designer of ready-to-wear in the history of contemporary fashion. A protean talent, he rang the changes with many different labels, among them, Timwear, Krizia, Ballantine, Cadette, Carel, Charles Jourdan, Valentino and Fendi. But it was under the Chloé label, from 1964 to 1984, that Lagerfeld reached the peak of his creativity. There is no one Lagerfeld style, but a thousand. The originality of his work consisted in his ability to anticipate, often from a considerable distance, the image the world had of a particular label. Always hidden behind his dark glasses, Karl affected the cultivated air of a dandy. Like a theatre director, he constantly interrupted at every stage, from the first sketches for a collection to the final press release, maintaining at an even temperature all the different ingredients that go into the production process of a fashion design.

The underlying structures of fashion have never changed as much or as quickly as between 1965 and 1975, with the introduction of new boutiques, freelance stylists, fashion stores, ranges of de-luxe ready-to-wear and designer pret-à-porter. It was a reflection of what was happening in the rest of society, as the appearance of everyday life was totally transformed.

One of the major developments in French fashion in the Seventies centred around the phenomenon of Créateurs et Industriels, an alliance

Ensemble by Kenzo
Loose-fitting wool and mohair coat over a floral dress with matching scarf.
Autumn/Winter 1984–1985

Coats by Kenzo
Photograph by Peter Knapp.

of interests founded by Didier Grumbach, a background figure who was heir to a line of clothing industrialists. In 1970, he was managing director of the C. Mendès group, which manufactured, among others, Saint Laurent Rive Gauche, Givenchy Nouvelle Boutique and ranges by Philippe Venet, Valentino and Chanel. Not only had he the foresight to modernize his equipment, unlike most French industrialists, but the young entrepreneur was also in close touch with the young mercenaries, the stylists. He came to the conclusion that they ought to enjoy the same privileges as the

The tennis look by Karl Lagerfeld
V-necked pullover with white pleated skirt or trousers: the crisp lines and easy-to-wear elegance of the tennis look at its simplest.

Silk dress by Karl Lagerfeld
Photograph by Sarah Moon.
1976

couturiers, in other words, that they should put their name to a product or a line, or indeed to an exclusive range, that would then be merchandized under their label. In future, the specialist industrialist would do no more than provide a service, albeit on an exclusive basis, and would have no direct influence on the artistic content of the label. The fruitful association of Mendès with Saint Laurent Rive Gauche served both as an example and a stimulus to Grumbach's plan. The term *créateur* emerged and was subsequently applied to the designers who represented the avant-garde of ready-to-wear. Créateurs et Industriels was set up, on a fee-paying basis, to promote a group of stylists assembled over a period of five years, a task that had been accomplished with unparalleled commitment and inventiveness. A utopian scheme, the initiative injected new life into ready-to-wear and constituted an investment in the future of a distinctively Parisian brand of fashion.

The first to join were Emmanuelle Khanh and Ossie Clark, the most famous London designer of the time. He was then followed by his compatriot Jean Muir, much prized for her long jersey sheath dresses, then Fernando Sanchez, who specialized in glamorous homewear, and Roland Chakkal, a meteoric talent considered one of the most brilliant of his day. They were joined by Issey Miyake and, eventually, Jean-Charles de

Castelbajac, Thierry Mugler, Claude Montana, Angelo Tarlazzi, Michel Klein, Jean-Paul Gaultier, for his first knitwear collection, and the Argentines Pablo and Delia. In addition there was a whole group of newcomers for whom this represented their first break.

It was to promote this array of youthful talent that Créateurs et

Industriels held the spectacular catwalk shows organized by Didier Grumbach's muse and right-hand woman, Andrée Putman. The first of their kind, they were full-scale performances, with proper direction, lighting and music. In a clean break with convention, they were often held at venues chosen for their novelty value. Between 1971 and 1973, the type of fashion produced by these *créateurs*, in effect, sealed their divorce from couture and also distanced them from the various traditional salons that sold ready-to-wear. Nothing would ever be the same again and this time Paris was at the forefront.

Jean-Charles de Castelbajac's first catwalk show
It was held at the Musée Galliera in Paris and organized by Créateurs et Industriels.
1972

Constructible clothes by Issey Miyake
1969

At the end of the Seventies, the opposite poles of couture and designer ready-to-wear were to regroup, pooling their forces. United by the Chambre Syndicale des Couturiers et Créateurs de Mode, they would prove the perfect complement to each other's activities. Working to a common calendar, the joint organization was to preside over a packed week of catwalk shows every October and March. As, twice a year, thousands of journalists and buyers poured into Paris to see over a hundred shows, the model of fashion that Paris had striven to implement during the Seventies became an accepted institution in the Eighties.

London

1 Mr Freedom (Tommy Roberts). Continually flirting with bad taste, he sometimes used Hollywood symbols, such as Mickey Mouse and Donald Duck, in his irreverent designs.

2 Ossie Clark catwalk show, 1970. For many years the designer showed under the Quorum label, founded by Alice Pollock.

3 Zandra Rhodes. With her brilliantly coloured motifs and exaggerated make-up, she aims for a look of timeless exoticism.

4 Anthony Price, 1972. His stunning basque-style evening dresses appear on many of Roxy Music's record sleeves.

5 Sex, 1974. The interior of the boutique at 430 Kings Road, with its padded pink plastic sign, was spray painted with graffiti.

6 David Bowie, 1973. For the Ziggy Stardust tour, the singer wore a spangly costume typical of the glam rock movement.

4

Roxy Music

5

6

Italy

'There is no such thing as Italian fashion. Not in furniture, not in decoration, not in clothes. We can create it and we must.' Thus spoke Benito Mussolini in the Thirties. The response must surely have exceeded his expectations.

Before the Second World War, Italian fashion simply did not exist. Then, slowly but surely, it took an increasing share of the international market during the Fifties. This was in large measure due to orders from America, which were placed to help a country ravaged by war.

The knitwear industry was particularly dynamic. Backed by a strong craft tradition and concentrated in the foothills of the Alps, within easy reach of wool centres – such as Florence, Prato and Valdagno, capital of the Marzotto empire – it rapidly acquired a new lease of life. Lombardy, north of Milan, was the centre of cotton production. It was this industrial infrastructure, fired with new enthusiasm and developing exponentially, that financed a major clothes-manufacturing operation during the Sixties. The Italians' remarkable receptiveness to all forms of creativity; their ability to spot trends as they swept through post-war Europe; and the speed and flexibility of a production process that was so dependent on the ephemeral mood of the day were all factors that attracted many European brand names. Minimal social security contributions and a policy of low salaries helped produce a competitively priced article for export. Advertising techniques were already well advanced and new methods of distribution in operation.

As a result of all these developments, the first salons specializing in male or female ready-to-wear were opened. In the course of the Seventies, as a result of its ready-to-wear industry, Milan confirmed its position as

**Italian designers
by the pool at
La Mondadori**
Left to right:
Gianfranco Ferre,
Luciano Soprani,
Aldo Ferrante,
Giorgio Armani,
Walter Albini and
Mariuccia Mandelli.
1978

second only to Paris as a centre of international fashion. The *alta moda* preferred Rome, where couture clothes were presented by Valentino, Capucci and Schön to audiences of divas, princesses and actresses.

In 1965, the Fendi sisters took on the young Karl Lagerfield as a designer for their small family firm, founded in 1925, which sold furs and Roman leather goods. Together they transformed it into the far-sighted concern it remains today. Their fur designs in particular were of unparalleled virtuosity.

The American fashion writer Eugenia Sheppard once remarked that if you want to be chic you need to look like everybody else. This was the basis of the Italians' success. Capitalizing on the prevailing trend of anti-fashion, with all its contradictions, Italy offered a glamour that had nothing to do with the diktats of haute couture. While benefiting from a clearly defined style, Italian fashion was luxurious and easy to wear. As *Women's Wear Daily* noted, in an article comparing the democratic and casual American ready-to-wear product with that produced in Milan, Italian textiles were the best. The two styles were not dissimilar, but the latter conveyed a sense of European luxury. It was a form of chic that appealed to a clientele still geared towards couture. Significantly, the man who was to become a master at producing clothes that were casual yet inventive, discreet yet distinguished, began his career designing men's clothes. When he turned his attention to women's fashions, he applied the same basic principles.

Giorgio Armani was born in Piacenza in 1934. Having founded his own business in 1974, he embarked on a radical reassessment of the male suit jacket. He re-examined it in terms of structure, weight, the way the different elements were assembled and the materials of which it was made. This return to first principles lay at the heart of the very individual style he developed, one that was also well suited to mass production by the high-tech Italian industries. In 1975, he produced his first collection for women. From the outset, the line was urban, dynamic and understated, androgynous in inspiration. For a whole population of women who now had access to the world of work and occupied

Ensembles by Armani
Autumn/Winter
1977–1978

**Suit and dress
by Krizia**
Mariuccia Mandelli
diversified into
a number of
different ranges,
each characterized
by its originality and
flair. Italian *Vogue*.
October 1971

increasingly senior positions within it, Armani offered a restrained style that gave them a sense of security. And also authority. This was only the start of a remarkable career, which came to fruition in 1981 when Emporio Armani – the budget label of a style that could be adapted to suit every class of society and every generation – was launched.

Krizia was founded in 1954 by Mariuccia Mandelli, whose vision and determination steered the enterprise from its first knitwear collections to the position it enjoys today, as a group offering twenty-five separate ranges of ready-to-wear.

It was in 1881 that the three Cerruti brothers opened a factory just outside Biella and that date remains the company's lucky number. Grandson of one of the founders, Nino Cerruti took over the management of the firm in 1950.

Seven years later, he opened the menswear boutique Hitman in Milan. A man of taste and discrimination, Cerruti employed Giorgio Armani as his assistant, passing on to him all the fundamentals of his craft. In 1976, he presented his first collection for women. Two years later, he launched his first perfume. By the start of the Nineties, the company controlled more than twenty-five ranges, distributing them worldwide. As well as the three Cerruti boutiques, one of which is in the Place de la Madeleine in Paris, there were exclusive franchising arrangements with some seventy other boutiques. In combining the career of a successful industrialist with that of a high-quality designer, Cerruti occupies a unique position in Milanese ready-to-wear.

In 1972, Gianfranco Ferre produced his first designs as pat of the Ketch line for the Genoese house San Giorgio. Gianni Versace moved to Milan and began work as a designer for Genny, Callaghan and Complice. Walter Albini, having started out with Krizia in 1962, found himself ten years later working for five Milan houses simultaneously, producing for each of them a full-scale collection with its own distinct identity. When he started his own label in 1973, he established the principle of the secondary or budget range, providing a prototype for designer ready-to-wear that is still current in Milan today.

Ken Scott was born in the United States in 1918 and moved to Europe in 1946. In the Sixties and Seventies he produced simple flowing garments in Impressionist-style prints. The visual impact of flower power, as seen in the boutiques, had a powerful influence on the fashion and decor of the day.

The luxury good firm Gucci, founded in Florence in 1922, benefited during this period from the passion for all things Italian that suddenly sprang up all over the world. This highly successful label became the toast of New York and before long controlled an international chain of boutiques. Following its introduction in 1957, the bamboo bag was eagerly snapped up by the darling of the jet set, while the famous Gucci loafer, with its horseshoe buckle, was popular with fashion-conscious males.

Cerruti
Both male and female model wear matt vinyl trousers, accompanied in his case by a black fake-fur bomber jacket, in hers by a hooded blouson.

Such hits were followed by luggage, scarves and a variety of canvas and leather goods that have gone on to become classics.

Laura Biagiotti was born in Rome in 1943. She produced and exported ready-to-wear by various Italian designers, before launching her first collection in 1972. It showed sophisticated materials, such as linen, taffeta and cashmere, in simple, classic, easy-to-wear shapes, clothes that immediately attracted customers of elegance and standing who appreciated their understated chic.

In 1958, Maria Carmen Nutrizio Schön set up her own ready-to-wear business. Born in 1919, she was an aristocrat from Dalmatia and one of the first to suggest a new direction for Roman couture, which was still very much based on the Parisian model. Simplicity was the key to everything she produced, whether for day or evening wear, and her bold use of pure colour was reminiscent of synthetic abstraction and Op art. Mila Schön also ran her own silk factory. During the Seventies, she successfully marketed evening tunics and kaftans that combined an imaginative use of colour with embroidery.

Essentially knitwear specialists, in 1953, Rosita and Ottavio Missoni developed the original family firm, based in Varese, into their own ready-to-wear business. It was immediately successful, impressive both for the originality of its designs and for its streamlined production process, and it has subsequently demonstrated its ability to maintain that appeal over the years. Situated at the heart of the small village of Legnano, with the design studio adjacent to the factory, the company rapidly developed a distinctive style that stood out from the rest. With Rosita producing the designs and Ottavio developing the colour ranges, the couple worked in unison to create a series of brilliant and light-hearted collections, in which quality of fabric was consistently complemented by inventive colour schemes. Missoni pullovers, produced in short runs, are small-scale works of art. A model enterprise, the company provides employment for a large number of the local villagers, often many generations of the same family.

Missoni
The Italian couple enjoy a reputation for originality of design and subtle colour combinations.
1969

United States

By 1970, women in the United States had already had the vote for fifty years. Generally speaking, they were way ahead of their contemporaries in respect of the resources, influence and independence they enjoyed. That fact had not escaped the couture world. Since the Fifties and the effect of Dior's New Look, American journalists and buyers were handled with kid gloves on their visits to Paris. Success or failure hinged on what they thought.

In the United States, the overall trend in fashion was towards simplification and longer skirts, despite many women reacting negatively to the midi length, which they felt was ageing. Trousers, on the other hand, won unanimous approval. All the big American designers, such as Bill Blass, John Anthony and Oscar de la Renta, included them in their collections, all the more readily given the precedent that had already been set way back in the Thirties by actresses like Greta Garbo, Marlene Dietrich and Katharine Hepburn. Jeans benefited the most from becoming an accepted part of the American fashion scene in the Seventies, their new-found respectability deriving from their inclusion in the collections under the heading of sportswear.

Generally speaking, it was the principle of equality – the foundation stone of Anglo-Saxon democracy – that inspired the behaviour and lifestyle of a whole generation, including the clothes they wore. Nevertheless, the notion of equality that was invoked so passionately on the other side of the Atlantic – as part of the utopian ideas that blazed through university campuses and of the associated phenomena of the counter-culture –

Halston and his models

Photograph by Duane Michals for American *Vogue*, at a time when the designer was at the peak of his popularity and his designs were acclaimed as timeless masterpieces of understatement. *1972*

did not mitigate the American citizen's desire for success. If, to the people of Europe, post-war America seemed like the new Eldorado, it was due to its ability to reconcile directly opposed philosophies, allowing it to consolidate its prestige, even while under attack from the protest movements of the Seventies. The burning of a few American flags around the globe did not stop Levi Strauss, Coca-Cola or McDonald's from penetrating new markets. Pop art infiltrated the elites through music and art galleries, with Andy Warhol playing the Jean Cocteau role during those brilliant and paradoxical years. Not only was the average American finally able to shed his complexes about his superior European ancestor, he now had his own avant-gardes as well. New York acted as the catalyst for major artistic trends in the Seventies, in the same way as Florence had done for the Renaissance and Paris for modern art at the turn of the twentieth century. At the same time, the New York rag trade staked its own claims to aesthetic independence.

**Evening dress by
Oscar de la Renta**
The American is
known for his elegant
and flattering dresses
in delicate materials,
inspired by European
notions of glamour.
January 1971

**Woollen dress by
James Galanos**
In his luxury ready-to-
wear, the designer
emphasizes quality
of materials and
sophistication of cut,
notwithstanding a
deceptively simple
appearance.
1973

The new stars of ready-to-wear, at the head of successful companies,
adapted the best of what they had learned from Europe to the vast American
clothing industry. Ralph Lauren and Calvin Klein emerged from anonymity
more or less simultaneously to tackle the question of designing clothes
specifically for the men and women of the new world. They and a few others
founded the major 'concept' labels that twenty years later would establish
their hegemony over the middle-of-the-range market. In the meantime,
two competing tendencies dominated fashion in the United States during
the Seventies. On the one hand, there was the tailored, unisex look; on the
other, fluid, unstructured garments with a distinct hint of Thirties Hollywood
glamour. Halston, the undisputed star of his day, belonged to the second
category. When he expanded his couture business in 1972 to include a ready-
to-wear budget department, which he installed in his basement, he gained

celebrity status on the New York scene. His particular skill was in reconciling the made-to-measure garment for the special occasion with the notions of naturalness, comfort and relaxation, to which most American women adhered. Sport was an important part of their routine, long before the practice was adopted to any significant extent in Europe.

With his kaftans, djellabas, ultra-lightweight shift dresses – sometimes hippy chic, even tie-dye – shirtwaisters, tunics worn over shorts and wide-legged trousers, Halston was the modern caliph of a thousand and one New York nights and a regular visitor at the VIP room of Club 54 after its opening in 1977. Sadly, he was not to survive the short but intense era of which he remains an icon. Born Roy Halston Frowick in Des Moines, Iowa, in 1932, he started life selling hats in Chicago, before going to New York to join the department store Bergdorf Goodman as a designer in 1958. He gradually lost control of his business before his death in 1990.

It was through working with Halston that the former model Elsa Peretti, born in Italy in 1940, achieved her reputation as one of the most original designers of contemporary jewelry. In the early Seventies, she concentrated on sensual, organic forms, usually in silver, and, in the Eighties, became Tiffany's most accomplished designer. While her simple, sculptural style set off individual stones perfectly, she also integrated materials as different as diamonds, driftwood and pieces of glass worn smooth by the sea.

The initial success that Geoffrey Beene achieved when he set up his own company in 1963 was to continue throughout the Seventies. Praised for his sophisticated cuts, which he combined with the baby-doll look, and for his use of black and white, he was at his best in the radically simplified designs at which he excelled. With his smart little dresses and well-cut suits of wool, jersey and flannel, he was instrumental in discouraging American women from over-accessorizing, to which so many of them were prey. In the same way as Rudi Gernreich's unique talent had singled him out from other American designers during the Sixties, Geoffrey Beene was proclaimed the undisputed leader of his profession in the following decade.

Evening dress in silk chiffon by Geoffrey Beene
Synonymous with stripped-down elegance, the American designer's garments are comfortable to wear.
Autumn 1974

Bill Blass moved to New York in 1941 to work in fashion and launched his own range in 1962. In 1970, he bought the company he worked for and renamed it Bill Blass. A likeable man, he developed the habit of travelling all over the United States in order to hear for himself what his customers wanted. Over the decades he has perhaps been almost too successful in fulfilling their wishes. One of the country's most popular designers, he is particularly favoured by businesswomen and the wives of senior executives, who admire his disciplined style and workmanship.

Adolfo, Stephen Burrows, James Galanos, Anne Klein, Pauline Trigère and Ben Zuckerman are among the other stylistically less distinct names who were popular in a society that found itself still torn between a reverence for Paris couture, often translated into a more provincial style, and the good value of the mass-produced article. Betsey Johnson changed all that. She started out designing for Paraphernalia, a boutique that was reminiscent of those in Carnaby Street in the Sixties. Using vinyl and metallic fabrics

and putting the emphasis on independence, imagination and wit,
she brought a then-unprecedented spirit of irreverence to Seventies
New York. In a similar vein, Norma Kamali opened an unpretentious and
highly original boutique which brought a breath of Swinging London into
the heart of Manhattan. Yet it would be another ten years before New York
fully developed its own individual style.

Burberry

T-shirt

Lacoste

Converse

Perfecto

Dr Martens

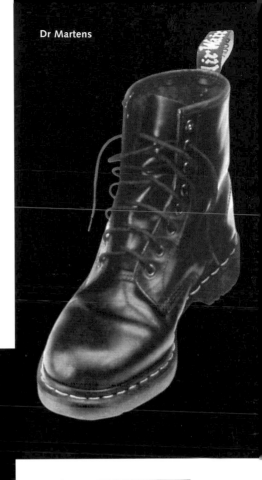

Basics

The term 'basics' refers to the basis of a wardrobe,
those items that never date and that constitute, if
not a fashion in themselves, then certainly a distinct
style. Often inspired by military uniforms and work
clothes, these everyday garments are born of chance
as much as of necessity. Their popularity in the
Seventies signalled a return to classical styles,
a phenomenon that would be repeated at regular
intervals in the future, in lulls between movements
in fashion. But their defining feature is that basics
are casual and comfortable garments, destined
more for leisure time and for holidays, than for
city life. Sporting them in town, on the other hand,
indicates that the wearer who has chosen them,
often to the exclusion of any other form of fashion,
is proclaiming an indifference to social formality.
The great ladies of the press – less prone to
overstatement than fashion's more outspoken
critics – never fail to come up with an article
once or twice a year in praise of the basic good
buys that are indispensable to a balanced wardrobe.

Levi's

Agnès B.

Above right:
**The first
Agnès B. boutique**
3 Rue du Jour, Paris.
1975

Below right:
Sketch by Agnès B.
The famous cardigan
with press-stud
fastenings.
1979

Below:
Agnès B.
(born 1941)

Agnès Troublé, who founded Agnès B., has never claimed to belong to the world of fashion. She defies categorization and yet her company has enjoyed considerable success both in Europe and in the United States for more than twenty years. Although she may have come from a background in anti-fashion and shared the revolutionary ideals of a generation that liked to keep its distance from the consumer society, this extremely pretty and essentially modest, youthful and vulnerable woman has nevertheless became one of the most influential figures in the rag trade. And yet one hesitates, in her case, to talk of a style, with respect to the garments that appear under the Agnès B. label, since that would imply a certain degree of authority. She never imposes things or lays claims; she merely makes tentative suggestions, proposing a possible alternative to the fashion system and its diktats. Her boutiques are bazaars which contain a little of everything. But all the items which form the basis of a practical modern wardrobe have undergone imperceptible and judicious modifications under the watchful eye of Agnès and her team. These little changes somehow make all the difference and, without it being easy to see quite why, transform the generic garment into a designer product. Many of the men, women and children who are Agnès B.'s customers would never shop elsewhere and yet they would be astonished to hear that her clothes are considered high fashion. Or would they?

1

2

american-look issue

what
ou
ear with
hat
a put the great
eparates together

aper new accessories
make everything work—
to the

!
tful skirts are back

ur makeup
r hair
you'll want to look this fall

health, good skin,
ation, vigor—all in the bath

d your own
t looks
ur surprise
nd-flip-the-pages game

e most out of your summer:
om famous trend-setters

3

4

1 Serge Gainsbourg and Jane Birkin, 1969. Thanks to them, 1969 was known as the year of eroticism.

2 Beverly Johnson, 1974. The first black model to make the cover of American *Vogue*.

3 Margaux Hemingway. Overnight the novelist's granddaughter became the new face of American fashion, appearing on the cover of virtually every magazine.

4 Lauren Hutton, 1970. The American model made the cover of *Vogue* twenty-five times and was the first to sign a lucrative cosmetics contract, with Revlon.

5 Jane Fonda, 1970. Vadim's former muse got involved in politics and became a spokeswoman for the younger generation.

6 Roman Polanski and Sharon Tate. A couple who were never out of the headlines.

7 Diane Von Fürstenberg, 1976. In the age of disco, she designed relaxed, sexy dresses that would not date.

Menswear

Fur coats by
Le Gardien
Fur was now being
used in the younger
generation's
wardrobe.
Photograph by
Oliviero Toscani.
Autumn/Winter 1970

There was also a new generation of menswear boutiques. Like their counterparts for women, they aimed to change the rituals, decor and customer base of a traditionally 'difficult' trade. To sell fashionable clothes to a young man at the end of the Sixties was still, in some circles, tantamount to questioning his virility. In this highly sensitive area, it took the authority of the pop stars of the day to set new precedents. The great revolution of the Seventies was not really in the clothes men wore but in the length of their hair, which young men simply refused to cut. Once it was only hooligans who adopted the subversive look of sideburns and Brylcreemed quiff. Yet, from 1965 and for about ten years, in intellectual circles, among students and artists, in the coteries of the Left Bank in Paris and of Chelsea in London and on the leading American campuses, hair would often be worn halfway down the back, or back-combed, afro-style. Hair was an endless cause of scandal; there were rows, people lost their jobs, others were ostracized – until the following generation came along and practically shaved their heads bare. Men's appearance changed more in this ten years than it had done in an entire century.

One of the great made-to-measure specialists was Gilbert Feruch, a formidable technician of tailoring and inventor of the Mao collar. Many of the designers who revolutionized the male look owed a lot of their innovations to Pierre Cardin: tight-fitting lines, narrow shoulders, no interfacing, no tie, sometimes no shirt, waisted jackets or tunics, zip-up boiler suits, etc. Even in fashion's exalted circles, workclothes provided the

1 Jacques Dutronc
The French singer
used his acerbic
humour to attack the
frivolity of trendy
Parisian *minets*.
Photograph by
Jean-Marie Périer.
September 1966

2 Mao
Mao never decreed
the wearing of
uniform, but the suit
that bears his name
was widely adopted
during the cultural
revolution of 1966
and copied in the
West by pro-Chinese
students.

3 Mick Jagger
The famous rock star
invented for himself
an ambiguous stage
personality with
homosexual
overtones.
January 1971

inspiration for young men to dress less formally, to look beyond the traditional suit and, for example, adopt a unisex style or investigate the inexhaustible supply of secondhand clothes. Sometimes this type of male dressing-down, often stigmatized as 'hippy', gained formal recognition as a deliberate look. At other times, as part of a retro movement, flea market bargains ushered in a revival of Thirties elegance. Many young men, clearly still undecided whether to identify with the new rock stars or to stick with their love of old films, opted instead for improbable combinations – mass of curly hair, double-breasted white linen jacket, flared jeans and American boots or Weston shoes – with perhaps a few carefully chosen accessories, such as a suede cap, a Hawaiian shirt, or socks printed with the American flag. Peace logos, pro-Chinese pins and Bakelite badges were hoarded like precious jewels. The exhumation of old military clothing, preferably khaki and from the US; Oxford shirts; English-style shoes; impeccable T-shirts; the reincarnation of the age-old vest as the tank top (the male version of innerwear as outerwear); little rucksacks; tweed jackets with padded shoulders; brightly coloured V-neck sweaters; and cashmere-printed scarves draped around the neck all imposed a certain uniformity on the casual beatnik look of the male wardrobe at the end of the Seventies.

The Eighties

Historical Review

Ready-to-wear
Left to right: designs
by Emmanuelle
Khanh, Karl Lagerfeld
for Chloé, Angelo
Tarlazzi and Fournier.
Photograph by
Helmut Newton.
November 1981

John Travolta
The American film
star disco-dancing in
Saturday Night Fever.
1977

It was in 1985 that everyone suddenly started talking about the Eighties. This was not a concerted action but a spontaneous phenomenon, as, almost overnight, articles, analyses and exhibitions dedicated to exploring the image of the decade began to appear. This self-consciousness was good for fashion, which had never been so à la mode, a defining feature of a society that was no longer criticized as consumer, but was, instead, interested in 'the spectacle'.

In France, the decade can be seen to have begun with the discomania of 1978 and to have finished with the bicentenary of the French Revolution in 1989. It was as though the century was in such a hurry that it ended ten years early. Economic recession did not help, cutting short the rather forced euphoria of the decade.

Appearance was allied to performance, which was of paramount importance to a generation of yuppies, or young urban professionals. Their need to look the part related to a desire for power that, after twenty years of utopian dreaming, was a source of inspiration for the upwardly mobile. The rag trade became a social phenomenon in its own right, along with its associated activities. Just twenty years before the end of the millennium, fashion

came full circle, re-creating the carefreeness of the years when Paul Poiret had held sway. In his image, the young designer of the Eighties was now treated as a demigod, the natural successor of the rock star. Top models were more famous than actresses and catwalk shows were transformed into spectaculars.

These media-saturated occasions laid on by the major houses were prestigious affairs and frequently televised, taking high priority in the social calendar. It was no longer a question of jeans for all, but of the right look for a chosen few. Tribes reassembled into sub-groups, each with its own clearly visible identifying features. The way in which women and an increasing number of men related to the latest fashions was no longer a matter of passive submission but one of active choice. Those less charitable would claim this only made it worse. But what did the new consumers care? For an adult age group which enjoyed a comfortable salary and was hell-bent on success, shopping was a sport and fashion a competition, with immediate gratification its universal and absolute goal.

Work clothes had been the inspiration for the Sixties. In the Eighties, it was party clothes, and the vogue for flea markets and retro was clearly influenced by the reappearance of evening dress and long gowns. Where the previous generation had reappropriated the Twenties and Thirties, the Eighties, at least as far as the younger element was concerned, witnessed a return to the styles of the Fifties and Sixties. For the baby boom generation, now in their forties, there was literally nothing to make them feel a day older. They looked on in amazement as the accessories of their own youth were sold off at auction. Everything was moving so fast. Fashion was in constant evolution, submitted to the merciless six-monthly schedule of the collections. Where design had once seemed more like a game, it had now entered a fiercely competitive arena. With a pack of imitators at

Betty Lago
After the Chanel couture catwalk show. Photograph by Roxanne Lowit.
July 1988

Thierry Mugler catwalk show
Showing a collection has become a full-scale theatrical performance, a creative expression of the Zeitgeist.
Spring/Summer 1986

their heels, designers had to rack their brains to be ever more ingenious if they were to stay ahead. Either you were in or you were out. It was impossible to fathom why, but you knew at once.

To enter the spirit of the Eighties fully, you needed to keep your distance. Of course, there was consensus fashion, which had been perfected, not without difficulty, by two generations of ready-to-wear designers and industrialists. The press, department stores and well-established distribution networks disseminated the trends shown in their collections to a mass audience. Their power was therefore considerable. But alongside all this unanimity, there were marginal designers, with alternative roots, who wielded an underground influence. Their non-mainstream styles attracted derision, but competitors nevertheless kept a watchful eye on them, cautiously tried them out and eventually adopted them wholesale. The two sides spent ten long years accusing each other of daylight robbery. Then, once a truce had been signed in the Nineties, everyone agreed to make and wear the same things at the same time. The fringe had had its day.

For fashion victims of the Eighties, it was a case of flattering neutrals and the egalitarian notion of 'beauty for all'. But once these ideas had been taken on board by the major distributors, the pioneers were on the lookout for something new and distinctive. In their efforts to venture from the well-trodden paths of fashion, many revisited the classics and the endangered masterpieces of haute couture. While new operators rushed to buy up old firms, a young public colonized the past. People talked once more of made-to-measure, ball gowns and past splendours. A long-forgotten word resurfaced: baroque.

In this context – and completing a picture already teeming with contradictions – it comes as no surprise that a section of society thought to have vanished for ever in the Sixties should once again make its presence felt, a full twenty years later. Between 1980 and 1990, high society rose from the ashes of the protest movement, dazzling as ever, with all its spending power that was so vital to the luxury goods industries. The rich and their hangers-on were not extinct after all, they had simply been in hibernation.

**Sketches by
Christian Lacroix**
Storyboard for
Christian Lacroix's
first haute
couture show,
Autumn/Winter
collection 1987–1988.
July 1987

Balls at Versailles and a houseful of servants were replaced by holidays in the sun and Swiss bank accounts. For them, as for everyone else, jeans had replaced jewels. And, in the light of a socialist/communist coalition coming to power in France in 1981, they seem to have chosen wisely. But neither fashion nor Parisians are frightened of the occasional paradox. That is their charm. While America kept its distance and the banks, luxury goods firms and couture houses remained distinctly aloof, some of the younger Parisian designers, who themselves held idealistic beliefs (albeit of a fairly vague nature), were determined to make the most of the change in atmosphere. They were keen to establish a rapport with the new government, which was not such a bad idea given that, in France, ever since the seventeenth century, artistic policy has always been determined at the highest levels of state.

In 1983, it was announced that a museum of fashion, the Musée des Arts de la Mode, was soon to open in Paris, situated in the wing of the Louvre adjacent to the Rue de Rivoli. The leading couturiers and ready-to-wear designers were fêted publicly and were now best of friends with the president of the French Republic, François Mitterrand. In the salons of the Élysée Palace, the latter delivered an eloquent eulogy on fashion, ending with a phrase that, although not strictly true, united all sides at the time: 'Countries without fashion are countries in uniform.'

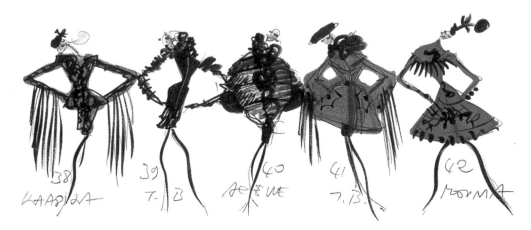

Azzedine Alaïa

Dress by
Azzedine Alaïa
Groninger Museum,
Groningen.
1984

Azzedine Alaïa
Working on the
fringes of couture,
the virtuoso designer
help dress the top
models who
patronize his studio
workshop in the
Marais, Paris.

In the Eighties, stars, top models, pretty girls, the rich, the famous, the anonymous and women of every generation identified with the exemplary simplicity, finish and sheer sexiness of Azzedine Alaïa's style. Past master of all sorts of techniques that had previously been the preserve of haute couture, he experimented with new and underused materials, such as viscose, and artificial fibres, such s Lycra. Known for his breathtaking combination (leather and lace, silk jersey and tweed) and a total perfectionist, this sculptor of fabrics profoundly influenced the silhouette of the modern woman, controlling all the stages in the construction of a garment, as well as dictating the manner in which it should be worn.

Alaïa first came to Paris from his native Tunisia in the Fifties. He was an

independent spirit who created a recognizable label of his own and won great respect at every level of the fashion milieu. Seldom leaving his magnificent home in the heart of the Marais, he gave advice and retouched clothes in strict confidentiality for an astonishing number of celebrities. After producing no more than the occasional collection of strictly limited editions and a few exquisite made-to-measure gowns for private commission in the Eighties, Azzedine Alaïa eventually went into partnership with Prada in the Nineties, where he now supervises regular collections, to the delight of his many fans.

Models in the wings
Final preparations
before the the
Azzedine Alaïa
catwalk show.
Summer 1992

Thierry Mugler

Born in Strasbourg in 1948 and a former dancer in the corps de ballet at the Opéra du Rhin, Thierry Mugler was profoundly influenced by both his native Rhineland culture and his early theatrical experience. Since launching his own house in 1974, he has produced designs which mix futurism with Hollywood retro. This explosive combination engendered a series of catwalk shows of devastating impact, in which, assisted by lighting and music, each model 'acted out' the dress she was wearing. With her sharply accentuated shoulders and rounded hips, and just a hint of the spacewoman, his diva represented the final routing of the flower child of the hippy era and the acceptance of a more structured silhouette. A supremely confident designer, Mugler dresses the superwoman who is not afraid to hold centre stage.

In 1978, he indulged his passion for photography as the first designer to execute his own publicity campaign. Despite a repertoire that encompasses glamorous dresses and studded leather, with both Barbarella and gypsy influences, it is nevertheless at the elegant couture suit that Thierry Mugler excels. At the outset, he created his own vocabulary and he is rare in remaining entirely true to himself over a period of more than twenty years.

Launched in 1996, the perfume Angel proved a remarkable success for his company. It is still one of the few in France to control the whole chain of production, from atelier to boutique, including all stages of manufacture and distribution.

Countryside near Volgograd
Angela Wilde and Stepanek photographed by Thierry Mugler for his book *Thierry Mugler: Photographer*.
July 1986

Thierry Mugler
(born 1948)
Photograph by Dominique Isserman.

Stephen Jones

Born in a country where no official occasion or private party was complete without its complement of eccentric hats, Stephen Jones established his place in the grand tradition of English millinery. During the early Eighties, he was one of the key designers of the New Romantic movement, led by figures such as Boy George and Steve Strange. As well as creating many highly individual designs of his own, he also worked with internationally acclaimed designers, such as Claude Montana, Thierry Mugler and Jean-Paul Gaultier, helping to revive interest in an accessory that had largely become obsolete.

Claude Montana

Among the most talented young designers of Parisian ready-to-wear at the end of the Seventies was Claude Montana, whose aggressive silhouettes would have been at home in Thierry Mugler's futuristic universe. His refined, figure-hugging designs, in lightweight materials or heavy leather, were created for a galactic heroine, with broad shoulders, narrow hips and robotic gestures. They may look a touch old-fashioned today and seem of somewhat specialist taste, but Montana nevertheless demonstrated, when he took charge of couture at the Maison Lanvin from 1990 to 1992, that he, too, was of the stuff of which true couturiers are made.

Claude Montana

Jean-Paul Gaultier

From the beginning, Jean-Paul Gaultier has enjoyed a reputation as the *enfant terrible* of fashion. It is a subversive and yet strangely innocent image that he has always been keen to live up to. Of all the top designers, he is the most marginal, but also the best at incarnating the aesthetics, attitudes, desires and ambiguities of a whole generation of young people, not only in France but on an international level. The high level of recognition that Gaultier has achieved in London and New York is reinforced by the success of his perfume.

La Concierge est dans L'Escalier
The invitation card for this collection was inspired by pre-war French film posters.
Spring/Summer 1988

Jean-Paul Gaultier
(born 1952)
The *enfant terrible* of fashion. Photograph by David Seidner.

This passion for the image rather than the reality of fashion is reminiscent of the type of hero-worship that the rock stars of the previous generation – people who, incidentally, were Gaultier's friends – induced in their fans. But the success of his image has always been underpinned

by detailed workmanship and remarkable imaginative flair, accompanied by a total mastery of technique and by his knowledge of fashion history. In his mission to reinterpret the entire male and female wardrobes – mixing genres, mingling influences, dates and functions, adopting clichés in order to subvert them and categorically refusing to show his designs for women separately from his collections for men – Gaultier has, ever since the late Eighties, reigned supreme.

LA CONCIERGE EST DANS L'ESCALIER

Giorgio Armani

It can confidently be said that, not only the streets, but also the contemporary wardrobe, would look radically different had Giorgio Armani, the great deconstructor of garments, never lived and worked. Having first redefined the sacrosanct concept of the male suit, by introducing new fabrics and novel combinations of neutral colours, he went on to revolutionize, with similar success, the wardrobe of the active and liberated young Italian woman.

A trained tailor, this virtuoso of unisex has subsequently produced infinite variations on his formula of perfect cut, careful finishing and form governed by function. He applies his simple but extremely rigorous principles to garments that contrive to be luxurious without ever lapsing into ostentation, which is the essence of the Armani style. In a world where the office, corporate activities, business travel and working lunches occupy an increasingly large part of life, the Armani style has become if not a uniform then certainly a mark of identity on both sides of the Atlantic. It not only offers reassurance and a guarantee of good taste, but also lends young businessmen and their female counterparts a touch of glamour and sexiness, something that was all too often lacking in garments for everyday wear. Armani's success can be measured by the extent to which that situation has changed. If his label did not exist, there would certainly be a gaping hole in the market. Which is no doubt exactly what was in the minds of Calvin Klein, Jil Sander, Donna

Giorgio Armani
(born 1934)
Having made his name by dressing Richard Gere in *American Gigolo*, in 1981 he launched the Emporio Armani range and proceeded to dominate male fashion for the next decade, introducing the trend for crumpled fabrics.

The active woman as seen by Armani
The master of unisex design, Giorgio Armani adapts his Eighties look for the wardrobe of the modern, active woman. *Autumn/Winter 1984–1985*

Karan and all the others who drew inspiration from Giorgio Armani's pioneering venture, when they launched their labels. They have achieved their own success in his wake, promoting an image of sophistication that is integral to the clothes themselves.

Emporio Armani was launched in 1981 and introduced an even more unisex garment that was also younger, sportier, more casual and, of course, cheaper. This time success was international. 1991 saw the launch in the United States of the Armani Exchange shops, offering well-designed basics at moderate prices. The business now has a total of five separate divisions, all under the artistic and commercial control of the original founder. To this day, Armani remains the sole proprietor and is one of the most powerful company directors in Europe.

Ralph Lauren

Ralph Lauren

Ralph Lipschitz was born in 1939. First
he was a salesman, then a buyer and
finally a designer for a range of neckties
which brought him early success. In
1968, he founded Polo Fashions, which
produced men's clothes. Three years
later, he opened a boutique for men
and women in Beverly Hills. In 1978,
he launched Polo, his first male
fragrance, and Lauren, a perfume
for women. The Eighties saw him
expanding into other areas – among
them, sportswear, luggage, eyewear,
leather, shoes, linen and rugs – always
applying his basic principle of good old
Anglo-Saxon chic. Aristocratic good
looks at prices the average American
could afford caused a sensation.

The quality of his garments was
faultless, in respect of both the supple,
patinated luxury of the materials and of
the care taken to perfect even the tiniest
details. His shops, that were equally
careful reconstructions of the image,
helped to propagate a whole way of life –
the copy, for once, proving better than
the original. In Europe, his style was,
ironically, adopted by the very people
who had inspired it in the first place.
For an elite faced with all sorts of avant-
garde fashions, it represented a rallying
point, promoting, as it did, a classic
look that had been adapted for an
active life. The number one of American
ready-to-wear, Ralph Lauren was a true
social phenomenon. He was equally
successful with his sportswear and
jeans, which enabled him to reach the
widest possible range of social classes
and age groups. Ralph Lauren is a label
whose immense success stands in
inverse proportion to its originality.

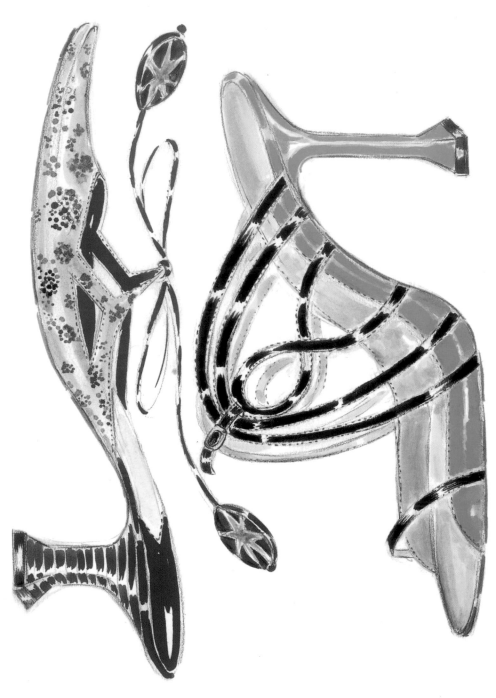

Manolo Blahnik

Manolo Blahnik, the most famous
of contemporary shoe designers,
has, for the last thirty years,
demonstrated his skill and
virtuosity in shoes of infinite variety.
Their unashamed luxuriousness
and exquisite workmanship are
unmatched in present-day fashion.
Blahnik was born in the Canary
Islands in 1943 and laid the
foundations of his early success
in a tiny boutique in Chelsea,
London. The world's prettiest
girls were quick to beat a path to
the door of a cobbler whose divine
mules, high heels and majestic
boots were unsurpassed in their
ability to set off a leg, a figure
and a personality. His customers
adore him and he repays them
a hundredfold.

Adidas

In 1986, the hip hop group Run DMC
released 'My Adidas', an ultimate
celebration of the streetwear that
was all the rage in Manhattan and,
before long, in big cities throughout
the world. Adi Dassler, born in
Germany in 1900, could never
have predicted such success for
the business he founded in 1948.
Having been appointed official
supplier to the Olympic Games in
1972, the label went on to achieve a
level of street cred that is second to
none, opening up many new markets
that, even today, are hotly contested
by American competitors.

Adidas

Zoran

Ladicorbic Zoran was born in Yugoslavia
in 1947. During the Eighties and using
methods that were reminiscent of his
European counterparts, he proved to be
one of the most unusual of the New York
designers. A committed minimalist, he
eliminated all detail, developing a few
basic shapes into garments that were often
seamless and lacked a defined waistline.
His comfortable designs in sober colours
were, variously, knotted, draped, unrolled
or pulled over the head like a T-shirt. Their
simplicity was deceptive: not only did he
use luxurious fabrics, but the architecture
was highly complex, making the garments
almost as enigmatic and unfathomable as
the man who designed them.

Lagerfeld at Chanel

For the doyenne of the surviving couture
houses, Karl Lagerfeld's appointment as
design director, in 1983, represented the
chance for a fresh start. As designer of
the haute couture, ready-to-wear and
accessories collections, he rapidly
demonstrated his ability to reconcile the
aesthetic codes developed by Chanel herself
with the best of contemporary influences.
Having originally worked freelance, moving
from one ready-to-wear manufacturer to
another, when Lagerfeld assumed the
mantle of a major couturier, he aroused
universal curiosity. His imperturbability,
humour and protean talent won him a
level of popularity that has never dwindled.
Nor has that of his collections, which have
helped to maintain Chanel's position as one
the leading contemporary fashion houses.

Chanel

Chanel

Sybilla

Film, photography, design, fashion and interiors all benefited from the sense of freedom that swept through Madrid after its liberation from Franco's rule in 1975. The movement was baptized Movida and captured the imagination of Europe. One of its leading icons was Sybilla, who showed her first collection of made-to-measure clothes in Madrid in 1983. By the end of the Eighties, she had expanded into women's ready-to-wear, shoes, accessories and home ranges. By then, her empire was sufficient to furnish and equip an entire private house, in which she displayed her designs. A perfume, deals with Japan, a solid base in Madrid and a network of loyal friends enabled Sybilla, a discreet, charming and original woman, to survive outside the traditional fashion system.

Romeo Gigli

When Romeo Gigli set up his own house in 1983, he immediately established an independent style. Surrounded by the functionalism of the slick ready-to-wear collections at which Milan excelled, he preferred to design for the flower child rather than the career woman, concentrating on fluid shapes, naturally unstructured garments, harmonious colours and exquisite materials. Chaste and yet sexy, intimate and timeless, Gigli's collections combine literary influences and ethnic decoration to illustrate the diversity of trends that constitute the contemporary look.

Christian Lacroix

**Dress and pinafore
in chartreuse
duchesse satin**
Lacroix's vision of the
Parisian woman is
photographed by
Javier Vallhonrat
to publicize the
designer's first haute
couture collection.
July 1987

Christian Lacroix
(born 1951)
Photograph by
Jean-François Gaté.

When Christian Lacroix arrived on the scene in 1987, he sent shock waves through the world of haute couture. Born in Arles, in 1951, he was not only the youngest of the couturiers, but a true original, with a passionate enthusiasm for the history of costume and international folklore. He took the American press by storm, filling their pages for a year. During this magical interlude, Paris and New York's Madison Avenue were translated into the Provence of chirruping crickets and Arlesian beauties. As the price of farmhouses in the Bouches-du-Rhône rocketed, women experimented with flouncing skirts, polka-dotted crinolines and embroidered corselets. Bustles reappeared, shawls were draped modestly over bosoms and nightclubs, packed with Carmen lookalikes and Sevillian maidens, echoed to the rhythms of flamenco.

Drawing on his encyclopedic knowledge of the history of theatre and opera, Lacroix also designed costumes for a number of productions, including Mikhail Baryshnikov's *Gaieté Parisienne* at the Metropolitan Opera in New York and a production of *Carmen* staged in the amphitheatre in Nîmes in July 1989. At the end of the decade on which he had left such an indelible mark, Christian Lacroix launched a fragrance in the most baroque bottle imaginable. Whether as a gesture of defiance or of resignation, it was called C'est la Vie!

Marithé &
François Girbaud

Marithé & François Girbaud

Working as a joint team, Marithé &
François Girbaud produced designs
that were never mainstream. After
several attempts at creating their own
collections under a variety of labels, these
two pioneers of sportswear finally made
their breakthrough in the late Eighties
under their own names. They are famous
for transforming jeans into a designer
product, introducing a series of variations
in collections whose aggressively casual
styles were quickly adopted by other
designers and copied on a grand scale.
Enthusiasts for all things American, in
the Sixties, they opened a small boutique
called Western House, near the Étoile
in Paris. It became a magnet for young
people who were desperate to acquire
the American imports that were so
essential to the look of the period.

Jean-Charles de Castelbajac

The Limousin-based ready-to-wear
designer Jean-Charles de Castelbajac
was an influential member of the *jeunes
créateurs* movement in the early Seventies.
Among his subsequent innovations was
his use of materials not normally found
in fashion. He produced coats cut from
blankets, dresses made of sacking, two-
person ponchos and garments made
of quilting, dusters, jute and oilcloth.
A provocative dandy and a collector of
contemporary art, he liked to draw parallels
between his designs and avant-garde
movements in the arts. His style is built
on the amusing paradox of integrating
historical elements into clothes that
are frozen moments in time.

And Also

Parisian fashion flourished between 1978 and 1988, boosted by the international recognition of a number of its designers whose powers of imagination were matched only by the media hype that surrounded them. There were many success stories, not only of promising newcomers but of designers triumphantly confirming their reputations, most of them specialists in their own particular spheres. Of course, they shared the same influences and were aware of what each other was doing, sometimes vying at the same game, yet, each career, each designer profile and each product was different and distinctive. A multiplicity of trends blossomed in a series of truly glorious seasons, before being curtailed by the economic recession that set in at the beginning of the Nineties. It was to have a devastating impact on fashion companies that were often already precariously balanced. This awakening was made all the ruder by the fact that sexually transmitted diseases were simultaneously beginning to take their toll on the design professions. In so doing, they destroyed the optimistic mood that is so conducive to the fashion industry.

Among all the many new ideas that flourished in this era, who can forget the highly original concept of Angelo Tarlazzi's dresses? A remarkable technician who once worked in haute couture at Patou, he dazzled the press and his customers with his 'handkerchief' dresses. Made of squares of fabric, they proved, when you came

Coat by Anne-Marie Beretta
Loose asymmetric lines with an Oriental influence in a design that subverts the very notion of what a coat should be. Photograph by Peter Knapp.

Pareo dresses by Angelo Tarlazzi
These dresses in sequinned cotton jersey are all variations on a shiny and brightly coloured theme.
1979

to put them on, to be far more complicated than they at first appeared. Many a Parisian soirée of the Eighties was enlivened by his designs, all in a fluid and ingenious style, in which cutting and sewing were kept to a minimum.

For the city dweller looking for classical elegance without seeming too conventional, Myrène de Prémonville, from 1983, produced beautifully constructed suits using unexpected colour combinations and demonstrating a strong sense of detail. In 1986, the precociously talented Michel Klein opened his own house, subsequently giving free rein to a creativity that found expression in a variety of different forms, typical of the very best of contemporary design. The high priestess of lace and sexy stockings,

Chantal Thomass won a devoted following for her provocative underwear and for evening gowns that looked like nightdresses and vice versa.

At the end of the Seventies, Guy Paulin was one of the first to promote a severely plain and uncluttered style. His garments were classical in their proportions and designed for comfort and simplicity, with their harmonious lines enhanced by a subtle palette of colours and fine materials. Although, sadly, his career was cut short by his premature death, his influence continues to be felt today.

Under his own name, Joseph designed luxury knitwear along classic lines, creating loose, sexy garments in neutral colours. In his luxury London boutiques, he was the arbiter of the latest fashions, giving his imprimatur to the best of the new designers by allowing them space in his state-of-the-art shops.

Anne-Marie Beretta, having worked for Pierre d'Alby in the Sixties, opened her first boutique in 1974. There she specialized in outfits for city wear, of Oriental inspiration and simplicity. Her clean-lined, functional garments, stripped of all incidental detail, were frequently innovatory in their use of new materials or of original manufacturing techniques.

Marc Audibet was both a fashion and an industrial designer, who carried out extensive research on materials, notably on the development of elasticated versions of classic fabrics. In particular, he worked on stretch nylon for Du Pont. Jean-Rémy Daumas mounted a brave campaign against conventionality, lighting up the catwalks, until 1990, with collections that were full of exuberance, wit and inspired invention. The memory of his powerful visions still lingers on. Equally creative, Jean Colonna initially designed jewelry and accessories for Jean-Paul Gaultier, Claude Montana and Thierry Mugler. In 1985, heavily influenced by the club scene, he began producing reasonably priced deconstructed clothes in deliberately cheap-looking fabrics.

Back in 1974, Kansai Yamamoto was one of the first Japanese designers to try his luck with the Paris collections, presenting a series of bold, dynamic and brightly coloured designs. His compatriot Junko Koshino followed him

Norma Kamali's Sweatshirt collection
With her short skirts made of sweatshirting, headbands, leotards and leg warmers, she made jogging look fashionable.
Spring/Summer 1980

in 1977, opening her own boutique in 1989. Another Far-Eastern talent, Junko Shimada established her own business in Paris in 1981, therein confirming the ability of French fashion to attract and integrate the most diverse trends.

Walter Steiger was a shoe designer of Swiss origin who worked for a number of different labels, among them Karl Lagerfeld, Chloé, Claude Montana, Oscar de la Renta and Nina Ricci. He opened his first Paris boutique in 1973, designing shoes that combined sophistication with comfort.

In the Sixties and Seventies, some of world's most famous and best-dressed women had their hair done by Alexandre. In the following decade, he went on to create hairstyles for Claude Montana's and Thierry Mugler's catwalk presentations. More recently, in 1997, Jean-Paul Gaultier asked him to work on his first haute couture show.

Carolina Herrera was born in Caracas in 1939 and was long regarded as one of the most elegant members of the jet set. In 1981, she launched a series of collections targeted at women like herself, featuring impeccably cut clothes of extremely high quality and exceptionally attractive evening gowns. Similarly, Carolyne Roehm was a member of New York's high society who, in 1984, began designing formal dresses which combined luxury with practicality, aimed at rich and famous women like herself.

Central to the success of a new wave of American sportswear was the Perry Ellis label, established in 1978, which used colour and natural fibres to great advantage in its sophisticated variations on the basics. It was right at the end of the Eighties that Isaac Mizrahi, the wild child of the New York fashion scene, sent a breath of fresh air coursing through Seventh Avenue, as he produced, over the next few seasons, designs full of imagination and colour. He executed reinterpretations of the classic forms of American sportswear in new materials, employing bold and unusual colour schemes.

The Japanese Phenomenon

In the Spring/Summer ready-to-wear collections of 1983, two Japanese contributors induced cold sweats, perplexity and enthusiasm in more or less equal proportions among an audience of international fashion experts.

Both Yohji Yamamoto and Rei Kawakubo offered a look which marked a complete break with the prevailing fashion image of the lacquered and painted femme fatale with accentuated waist, broad shoulders and high heels. Some sought to find justification – in the apocalypse, in Hiroshima or in the influence of punk – in an attempt to explain these tattered rags of such ostentatious poverty. And yet, beyond the provocation, there was an undeniable poetry in the way that Yamamoto and Kawakubo proclaimed their difference. Flat shoes, no make-up, modesty, reserve and secrecy – theirs was a resolutely modern look. Gradually it began to incorporate details from styles of the past, as Europe's ancient sites were revisited, with curiosity, by these anarchists of fashion, whose influence on the shape of clothes and clothing, at the end of the century, has become legendary.

Yohji Yamamoto

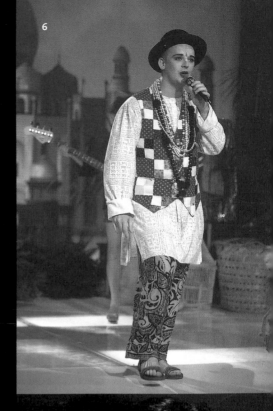

6

1. Loulou de la Falaise. Muse and close colleague of Yves Saint Laurent for over thirty years, she also designs knitwear collections and extravagant jewerly. In 2003, she opened her own top-of-the-range fashion and accessories shop.

2. Bianca Jagger. Star of the New York social scene and ex-wife of the Rolling Stones singer.

3. Edwige. Queen of punk, singer and model, she was a huge star of the nightlife in Paris and New York.

4. Inès de la Fressange, 1986. Chanel's top model, hers was the face that launched the perfume Coco. Even now, she represents a particular vision of Paris. Photographed here by Karl Lagerfeld for the haute couture collection, Autumn/Winter 1986–1987.

5. Paloma Picasso, 1980. Daughter of the artist.

6. Boy George. The ambitious, subversive style of the British singer set the tone for the decade.

7. Tina Chow. The most elegant woman in New York in the Eighties, her collection of twentieth-century dresses is legendary.

5

7

The Nineties

Historical Review

As the Nineties bring to a close a century of fashion, it is fascinating to speculate on whether the last hundred years has perhaps been the exception rather than the rule in the long history of costume. After all, fashion has not always existed. It is conceivable that it might disappear again tomorrow, to be replaced by some new fad, some alternative form of self-expression, some entirely different way of keeping the body warm and proclaiming one's identity. Already there are many designers who, smitten with the new technology, regularly produce outfits that are dictated purely by functionalism, not by fashion. Even if you do not go that far and even if you ignore the Fifties prediction that by the year 2000 everyone would be wearing astronaut suits, you still cannot help but notice how the various looks have become increasingly universalized. They are adopted everywhere, from Oriental souks to Japanese nightclubs and from the avenues of Manhattan to markets in Provence. Once there were clothes for the court, outfits for society events, work wear and both military and religious uniforms. As far as the teenager in his Nikes and T-shirt, the executive in his grey suit and white shirt and the pensioner in his tracksuit bottoms are concerned, the situation is largely the same today. Only the context has changed; a different set of rules is now in play and we have an unprecedented degree of technical know-how at our disposal.

It was entirely predictable that fashion, having been hugely à la mode in the Seventies and Eighties, would become less so in the following decade.

Today it is no longer the done thing to follow fashion slavishly. Calvin Klein advertisements proclaim 'Be Yourself' and yet the company's huge success lies in selling identical T-shirts to the same social groups all over the world. The old fear of being underdressed was superseded a few years ago by the fear of overdressing. By a process of progressive elimination, simplification and revision, fashion in the Nineties has united around a new standard, minimalism. A term borrowed from the vocabulary of the artistic avant-

gardes of the Seventies, minimalism has been the justification for styles of stark simplicity (although not perhaps for the look of the poverty-stricken waif). Similarly, black has always been present in the collections, from Chanel to Yamamoto and from Rykiel to Alaïa, but is now ubiquitous. Fashion shows are swamped in it, probably more so in the audience than on the catwalk. In the early Nineties, the big American fashion store Barney's had its interior decorated in the style of Jean-Michel Frank (one of the fathers of minimalism from the decorative arts movement of the Thirties) and devoted five whole floors to displays of uniformly black garments by all the top designers, displayed against beige walls. The effect was elegant

Photograph and concept by Oliviero Toscani for United Colours of Benetton The Italian firm with an international reputation has discovered the art of selling fashion basics through controversial advertising campagns that are often more striking than its designs. *February 1999*

and striking, but threatened to be a touch monotonous in the longer term.

Despite the efforts of a few designers who continue to fly the flag for pretty dresses with all the trimmings, the concept of elaborate finery has virtually disappeared. Today's average woman in the street is not that much better dressed than in previous generations. Although the general quality of her basic garments may have increased steadily over the last thirty years, her efforts now go into improving her body, by practising sport and through beauty treatments. Not since ancient Greece have people placed such emphasis on their physique, toning and displaying an anatomy that has become increasingly clinical in its quest for perfection. Top fashion models are today's equivalent of the pin-ups of the Fifties, compensating perhaps

for a lack of larger-than-life glamour among actresses, but they are presented to us as remote goddesses, 'models', in the literal sense of word.

Whatever their differences, the designer labels that have survived the Nineties and confirmed their reputation all target a particular consumer elite, a clientele for whom looks are paramount and who are normally of the same generation as the designer they patronize. It is unusual for a daughter to shop at the same places as her mother. Fashion houses tend now to die with their founders, except in exceptional cases where the label acquires an upmarket luxury image that raises it above the U-turns of fashion. Chanel is one of the most compelling examples of this rare breed.

At the opposite end of the spectrum from the experimental designers dedicated to exploring new trends are the big international companies, whose mass-produced garments have in some sense replaced those of the ready-to-wear manufacturers of the pre-war era. The main difference

lies in the fact that most of their factories have now relocated to third-world countries where labour costs are lower. In both Europe and the United States, these labels are often masterminded by a star designer and geared to the development of a global concept and to the creation of a whole universe centred around the label. They tend to target a specific section of the market, with saturation publicity. As well as the styling of the product, its promotion in the media is now crucial to its success and its image. Where once the major houses spent approximately two per cent of their budget on publicity, nowadays the advertising expenditure is more in the region of twenty-five per cent. Most designers operate more like artistic directors, less concerned with design proper than with co-ordinating all the different elements in the production and distribution chain. They all know what each other is doing, use the same research and have the same style, marketing and PR consultants. The risk is that, before long, they will become so formulaic that their customers will tire of them.

In the past, fashion was a celebration; at the dawn of the twenty-first century, it has become big business. This idol has feet of clay – *pace* the international investors – because the stuff of which fashion is made is intangible. It adopts the form of its receptacle before evaporating or being transferred into other moulds, each as impossible to predict as the one before. Increasing financial pressures over the last ten years have had a disastrous effect on the development of new talent and weakened the autonomy enjoyed by more established designers.

Protected by a screen of double glazing, the bankers peer out uneasily at the weathervane of fashion to see which way the wind will blow tomorrow.

Yohji Yamamoto

Dress by Yohji Yamamoto
Spring/Summer 1999

Yohji Yamamoto
(born 1943)
This master of cutting approaches clothes like architecture.
He explores their structure and questions conventional ideas of beauty with every new collection.

At the end of the century, Yamamoto was an acclaimed and established designer working at the height of his powers, perfecting his vision in avant-garde designs which have assimilated references to the high style of Parisian couture. From the moment that the artistry and distinctive style of the Japanese master were introduced to the European fashion world, he made his position clear. He distanced himself firmly but not aggressively from the prevailing sexy styles aimed at the glamorous femme fatale of the Eighties. Women, according to Yamamoto, are chaste and reticent, presenting a neutral façade, and are slow to reveal themselves, like time bombs waiting to explode. It takes a while to appreciate fully their loosely

wrapped clothes, flat shoes and scrubbed faces devoid of make-up. Yet Yamamoto's vision of women has had a devastating impact on a whole branch of fashion. Secure in his highly distinctive and original approach to clothes, Yohji likes to explore the classical garments of his heritage, presenting a perfectly integrated synthesis of the past and a prospective view of fashion. Visionary but consistently elegant, his work reconciles the grand opposites: eccentricity and functionality, seduction and reticence, eroticism and modesty. At the end of the century, perhaps it was Yamamoto, more than anyone else, who represented the essence of couture.

Gianni Versace

The phenomenal success of Versace and his tribe; their high-octane relationships; the discreet aura of scandal that surrounded the Milanese designer; and, of course, his tragic death have sometimes obscured the distinctive style of Gianni Versace. With his brilliance, sexiness and love of colour – the absolute opposite of the purist vision of the sober-minded Yamamoto – the designer to the stars was very much in tune with the sensibility of the Nineties. His clothes are fluid, sensual, often provocative and, however upmarket they may be, they always seem to hint at the erotic promise of the naked bodies beneath. Anyone wearing a Versace label is made to feel the equal of Madonna, Sting or Princess Diana, of those exceptional beings who instinctively gravitate towards the limelight. Impeccable physique and a will of steel are almost mandatory attributes in the Versace world. By the end, his empire included not only couture but several ranges of ready-to-wear, accessories and home designs. Today it is his loyal little sister Donatella who has taken over from a prematurely extinguished shooting star. She is no more sober or restrained than her brother and the atmosphere of a Versace show continues to resemble that of a fiesta. Such extravagance was quite commonplace in the Eighties, but the relentless party spirit is disconcerting at the end of the century, when fashion is generally seen in a more serious vein.

Elton John with Kristen McMenamy and Nadja Auermann Gianni Versace dressed stars and top models to perfection. Photograph by Richard Avedon. 1996

Gianni Versace (1946–1997) Photograph by Rodriguez Duarte.

Comme des Garçons

Red sequinned dress
Photograph by Paolo Roversi.
Autumn/Winter 1999–2000

Hong Kong Kids
Publicity shot for the Transcending Gender collection.
Spring/Summer 1995

Rei Kawakubo has operated under this curious name since she first began to carve out her highly individual career in Tokyo in 1973. Within ten years, the label had become synonymous with a particular avant-garde look, of torn and tattered garments. Her clothes were deliberately designed to look unfinished and worn, defying common sense and challenging notions of perfection (she would happily remove screws from the machines to ensure that the textures were not too uniform or perfect). At first she was regarded with revulsion, but this eventually gave way to amazement and admiration. The logic of her work is impeccable, if not always easy to follow, and her pioneering influence has been felt by the whole of the fashion industry. She is an architect of the dress, deconstructing garments in order to build them anew, always adding innovations. Rei never speaks out in public but expresses herself forcefully through her work, communicating emotion and a sense of wonder and dark desire that is absent from the collections of many of today's young designers.

Where Yamamoto is a master of cut, a veteran craftsman transmuting the artistic traditions of Japan into images of Western fashion, his compatriot Rei Kawakubo states her aims more plainly. Her garments, above and beyond their need to pay their way, are intended to be conceptual acts, works of art that are designed to be worn. You have to go back as far as Balenciaga to discover a sculptor of fabric working at a similar level of abstraction.

Martine Sitbon

A Frenchwoman born in Casablanca in 1951, Martine Sitbon arrived in Paris when she was ten. She started her own ready-to-wear label in 1985 and, today, she is one of the rare women who have created a sophisticated, personal and highly original style of their own. Working as a freelance designer at first, she lived for a while in the United States, did a stint in the Australian rag trade and also produced some designs for firms in London.

Dress by Martine Sitbon Photograph by Nick Knight.

Martine Sitbon (born 1951) Photograph by Christophe Riher.

From her frequent visits to Great Britain, she retains a love of the Swinging London of the Sixties, which provides the inspiration for many of her basic silhouettes. The look is unisex, dandyish and emancipated, with long jacket, flared trousers, neat waist and dark colours or fluid dresses in layers of thin fabric or dévoré velvet. The fragile, clean-lined, elongated silhouettes are always variations on the same androgynous themes. Enjoying a high profile in Japan, Martine Sitbon launched a second label in 1989, Martine Sitbon Fantaisie. For nine consecutive seasons, starting in 1988, she also designed collections for the ready-to-wear label Chloé. In addition, in partnership with her husband, artistic director Marc Ascoli, Martine was one of the first in France to come up with the idea of an upmarket catalogue to complement and publicize her clothes. Contributors include photographers as eminent as Nick Knight and Javier Vallhonrat.

Vivienne Westwood

Formidable mother of punk during the mid-Seventies, over twenty years later Vivienne Westwood is still running a boutique in London, leading a scarcely less frenetic life. Her partnership with punk rock promoter Malcolm McLaren ended in 1984. As she began to work full-time as a designer, Vivienne started to present regularly in Paris, with collections that deliberately set out to challenge British conventions. Her shows contained many influential ideas that were taken up in the early Nineties by young people in love with decadence. With their salutary invitation to anarchy, Westwood's references to eighteenth-century courtesans and to the Marquis de Sade – rounded hips, corsets and platform soles – ruffled quite a few feathers in the somewhat staid world of ready-to-wear. The intrepid Englishwoman often had very little in the way of resources, yet her innovations were

Anglomania collection
Linda Evangelista wears a Highlander ensemble in mixed tartans. Photograph by Roxanne Lowit. *Autumn/Winter 1993*

Cover of *Tatler*
Vivienne Westwood parodies Margaret Thatcher for the society magazine. *1989*

highly influential. Her Pirate collection of 1981 sparked the wave of New Romanticism, then came her Buffalo collection, based on the conquest of the Wild West, and Vive la Cocotte which was loosely inspired by eighteenth-century France. Bustles and corsets abounded, amid over-large trains, curly wigs and excessive costume jewelry, as outrageous fetishistic accessories combined historical references with humour and preciosity with provocation. Westwood was awarded an OBE in 1992.

Gucci

The House of Gucci, founded in 1922, was originally the flagship of the Italian luxury leather goods industry, before the label expanded in the Sixties to include a variety of products of eminently Latin glamour. Gucci scarves, bamboo bags and loafers with horseshoe buckles were considered objects to die for among the jet set and their successors. That enthusiasm had largely evaporated when, in 1989, the Gucci heirs surrendered control to Invest Corp., who planned to turn the business around. The resurrection surpassed all expectations and is often quoted as an example by long-established companies dreaming that they, too, might enjoy a Gucci-style revival. To put it more accurately, Invest Corp. cleverly transformed a de-luxe house, essentially committed to traditional products, into a new fashion label, with all the lateral diversification that implies. Because the successful updating of the Gucci image had been carried out by the design consultancy formerly run by the American Dawn Mello, it was on her advice that managing director Domenico De Solé asked Tom Ford to be his design

Publicity photograph
This photograph by Mario Testino illustrates how Gucci updated its image under the direction of Tom Ford.
1999

Loafers with metal bars
Guccio Gucci designed this timeless classic in 1932.

director in 1994. This unknown from Santa Fe in Texas, was to trigger an earthquake. Ford co-ordinated the whole thing – chic and shocking collections; product ranges that had fashion victims drooling; perfumes for men   and women; revamped boutiques and advertising campaigns. In 1995, Gucci was floated on the stock exchange and the group merged with Pinault-Printemps-Redoute to create a giant consortium in 1999. In 2004, Tom Ford and Domenico De Solé finally left Gucci to seek other opportunities.

Prada

Corset top and hipster skirt
The straps of the nylon waffle top cross at the back.
Autumn/Winter 1999–2000

Mules and high-heeled shoes in patent leather and suede
Autumn/Winter 1999–2000

Given the Milanese label's immense popularity with the press and the younger generation today, many people outside Italy believe it to be a new company. In fact, Prada is a long-established firm.

From 1923 onwards, it used to sell high-quality shoes and leather and it was not until the end of the Seventies that the management was taken over by Miuccia Prada, the founder's niece. She began by making bags which made elegant use of waterproof fabrics produced by a new technical process. These were followed in 1985 by a range of women's shoes and then ready-to-wear sportswear of discreet, streamlined, and yet unmistakable, luxury. Without ever claiming that what she was doing should be considered fashion and always opting for the subtle rather than the obvious solutions, this influential designer became a real creative force during the Eighties. Prada provides yet another compelling example of how a long-established firm will simply wither on the vine unless it can reinvent itself to produce designs that are in tune with the times. The woman Miuccia caters for is no rebel. Although overtly bourgeois, she is not conventional and likes to play with the stereotypes of a social class that has long been a fashion outcast. Her standards are neither those of a top model nor those of a provincial housewife. With discreet charm, she pretends to be like any other woman. Like the many privileged young customers who shop in her boutiques, Miuccia knows that real power consists in concealing the fact that you have it.

The Life of a De-Luxe Label

Hermès
Long reversible coat and double-breasted jacket, semi-fitted, in natural camel, with a reversible round-necked sweater in beige cashmere.
Autumn/Winter 1998–1999

Céline
A new take on an old look by Michael Kors.
Spring/Summer 1999

Fashion labels are born, flourish and then fade with the generation on whose back they rose to success. High-quality de-luxe labels, on the other hand, improve with age. They are the true inheritors of the great designers who were the court suppliers of the nineteenth century. Those rare few which have survived, because they were flexible enough to adapt, are today branching out into fashion, although it will often account for no more than perhaps twenty per cent of their turnover. Fashion is a means of attracting media publicity to these older labels, rendering them newsworthy. It is far easier to photograph a cashmere coat on a top model than it is to photograph a range of luggage, however fine its saddle-stitching. Several seasons ago, many of the big traditional names, such as Hermès, Céline,

Vuitton and Loewe, branched out into the realms of youth fashion, following the example of Gucci and Prada. Vuitton signed Marc Jacobs; Céline, Michael Kors; and Loewe, Narciso Rodriguez. But it was Jean-Louis Dumas who caused the greatest stir by acquiring for Hermès, that temple of classicism, the skills of inspired extremist Martin Margiela. Successful though the exercise has been, it remains fraught with peril. Once installed at the heart of these great bastions of luxury, if fashion becomes more important than the other lines, eventually, when it falls from grace, there is the risk of a knock-on effect on the other ranges, whose value depends on craftsmanship not passing trends.

1 **Vuitton**. Monogram Vernis collection, 1999.
The famous Louis Vuitton monogram has already
outlived the century and Marc Jacobs continues to
produce impeccable modern variations on the design.

2 **Trussardi**, Autumn/Winter 1999–2000. The house
founded in 1910 is famous for its skill in treating
high-quality skins like fabrics.

3 **Loewe**. In 1997, Narciso Rodriguez was brought in
to modernize the de-luxe leather goods manufacturer
established in 1846.

Jil Sander

Doubly unusual in the world of fashion for being both a woman and of German nationality, Jil Sander launched her ready-to-wear career in Hamburg in 1973. The collections often incorporate clever detailing into designs of masculine severity. She is known for her use of materials, old and new, her perfect cut and her neutral palette. With no subsidiary lines, her superbly restrained designs, including some discreetly luxurious evening dresses, have brought her considerable commercial success.

Martin Margiela

The origins of this enigmatic and disturbing designer are rooted in the movements of the avant-garde. He was born in Belgium in 1957 and studied at the Royal Academy of Fine Art in Antwerp. In 1984, he set up his own label, which immediately attracted attention, and he also worked for Jean-Paul Gaultier. A theoretician and experimentalist, he has developed his own distinctively downbeat style. With their exposed seams, unfinished hems and their systematic deconstruction and reinvention, his silhouettes seem to point towards a new future for clothes, revealing one of the great talents of this generation.

Martin Margiela

Paul Smith

Philip Treacy

Paul Smith, Philip Treacy and Patrick Cox

During the Nineties, London has produced a number of original talents. Paul Smith is synonymous with menswear of relaxed elegance, combining the tradition of the great London tailors with the originality that the young demand. Having opened his first boutique in 1979, he now has six shops in London, forty-three in Japan, one in New York and one in Paris. Philip Treacy's light and airy constructions of irresistible fantasy have injected new life into the art of millinery and hat-wearing, in a country where the practice still lives on. Meanwhile, shoe designer Patrick Cox has, since 1987, created new models of footwear. Famous for his shoes for both men and women, Cox combines a modernist sensibility with Anglo-Saxon classicism.

Patrick Cox

Helmut Lang

Born in Vienna in 1956, Helmut
Lang opened his own boutique in
1979 and showed collections in
France from 1986 onwards. His
almost perversely sober palette
appeals to the disenchanted
younger generation. A designer
of influence, in 1998 he moved
to New York, where the originality
of his style stands out from the
prevailing consensus fashions.
The stark look he favours may
perhaps derive less from the
minimalist art of the Sixties,
as is usually claimed, and more
from the recurrent tradition of
romantic poverty.

Dolce & Gabbana

Domenico Dolce was born in
Sicily in 1958, the son of a tailor.
Stefano Gabbana was born in
Milan in 1962. After studies at,
respectively, university and a
design school, they met in 1980,
when they were working for
the same designer. Five years
later they formed a partnership.
With their superfeminine
style – that is witty and fresh
and enlivened by flowers,
leopardskin prints, corsets
and lingerie – they achieved
considerable success by the
end of the Eighties. Beneath the
guise of Mediterranean fantasy,
their collections are coherent
bodies of work in tune with the
prevailing mood.

Dolce & Gabbana

Marc Jacobs

Born in 1963 and graduated from Parsons School of Design in 1984, the New Yorker Marc Jacobs belongs to the new generation of American designers that have emerged in the Nineties. Unlike their predecessors, they are not so much co-ordinators of a mass-produced garment as designers in the European sense of the word. On the far side of the Atlantic, that fact alone was enough to win the newcomer a reputation as one of the most promising talents in a resurgent fashion industry. The LVMH (Louis Vuitton-Moet Hennessy) group confirmed that verdict by offering Jacobs the job of designing a line of ready-to-wear to complement the de-luxe products of luggage specialist Louis Vuitton.

Michael Kors

Michael Kors was born in the United States in 1959. In New York, he worked as a salesman for a fashion label before being promoted to merchandising manager and ultimately, designer. He set up his own business in 1980. Right from the start, his knowledge and awareness of trends enabled him to create a simple well-cut product, whose sophistication appealed to a whole new breed of wealthy American customers attracted to the new fashion for minimalist chic. In 1998, when he was invited by Céline to design a line of ready-to-wear in parallel with his own, he made the transition with triumphant ease. In 2005, he parted company with the group to concentrate on his personal brand.

Michael Kors

Dries Van Noten

Dries Van Noten

Dries was born into a family of textile
manufacturers, in 1958, and naturally
gravitated towards the fashion
department of the Royal Academy
of Fine Arts in his home town of
Antwerp. He chose menswear for his
first collection, which was executed
and presented in London in 1985.
Subsequently, he progressed to
women's ready-to-wear and a line
of shoes. His work is founded on a
solid mastery of the art of tailoring,
to which the young designer adds
discreet touches of fantasy in a highly
personal style. His work manages to
be both classical and original, all in
half-tones, and appeals to those that
like to express their individuality rather
than slavishly following fashion.

Ann Demeulemeester

Since its inception in 1987, Ann
Demeulemeester has rapidly won
for itself a reputation as one of the
most original of the Belgian labels
which have recently caused such a
stir. Since 1991, when she first showed
at the Paris collections, Ann has
demonstrated talent, confidence and
powerful invention. While naturally
inclined to understatement, she
builds her designs on contradictions,
introducing contrasting elements into
her fluid, streamlined forms. It is a
genuinely original approach, which
points the way ahead to a new sort
of fashion. With tact and eloquence,
Ann Demeulemeester appeals to
women who dress, above all, to
please themselves.

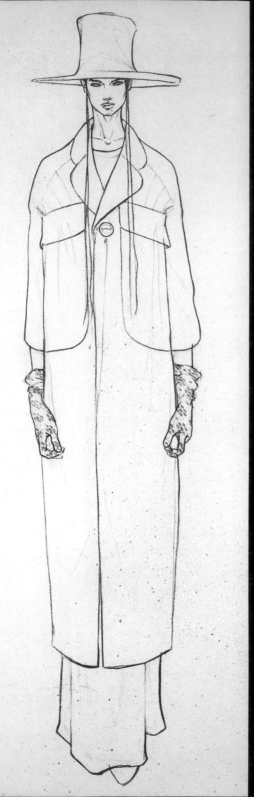

John Galliano

John Galliano began working in Paris in the early Nineties, using his meagre resources to put together small collections of evening wear that were in every respect worthy of haute couture. His name has become known to a wider public since Dior asked him to take over as head of its couture and ready-to-wear operations. In London, he has enjoyed a reputation for originality and talent ever since he left Central St Martin's College of Art and Design in 1984, renowned for his complex cutting and master of fabric. His work is often historically inspired – drawing on eighteenth-century France, the Belle Epoque and Paul Poiret – its glamour matched only by the immaculacy of its cut.

Alexander McQueen

An iconoclast and a son of the people and proud of it, McQueen was one of the stars to emerge from the prestigious St Martin's College in London, from which John Galliano had graduated a few years earlier. Youthful rebel he may have been, but he also passed through the workshops of the famous Savile Row tailors and possesses a perfect mastery of the techniques of cutting. The aggressive eccentricity that is still very much the currency of youth fashion in London, combined with the highly respected tradition of Made in England tailoring and the forceful personality of the young designer himself, have helped to carry McQueen to the heights of fame. In 1996, he took over as head designer at Givenchy and continues to produce his own collections in London.

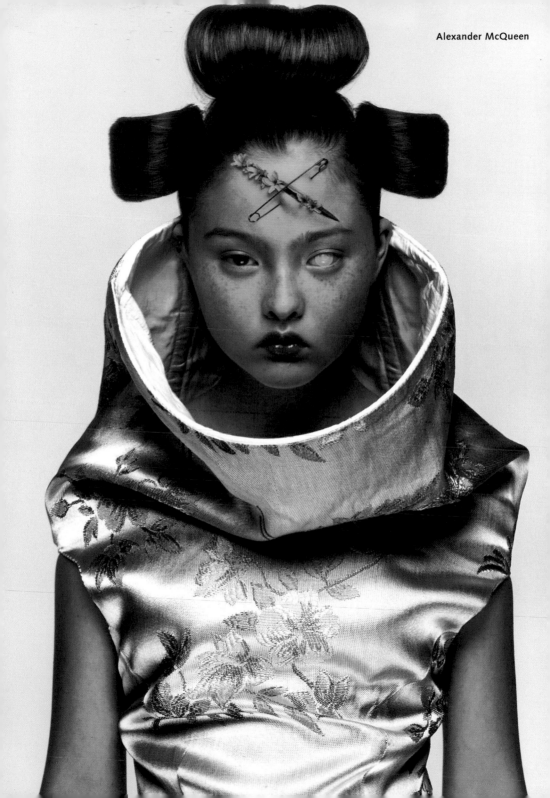

Dior

Dior and Givenchy

Causing upheavals in
Parisian haute couture,
in 1996, both Christian
Dior and Givenchy
acquired new artistic
directors for their haute
couture and ready-to-
wear collections. In a
daring gamble on the
future, the LVMH group,
which owns the two
houses and their
perfumes, chose two
young representatives of
the English fashion scene
to take over. Both John
Galliano and Alexander
McQueen are subversive
spirits, but both are
strongly inspired by the
history of costume.
The following year, the
two designers shared the
Best British Designer
award. Galliano was a
great success at Dior and
McQueen left Givenchy
to join Gucci in 2000
and was replaced by
another young British
designer Julien
MacDonald.

Gianfranco Ferre

Gianfranco Ferre

A Milanese designer to his fingertips,
Gianfranco Ferre was born in Legnano,
in 1944. In the Eighties, his career
took a new turn, culminating in
his appointment in 1989 as artistic
director of Dior's couture and ready-
to-wear collections. There he achieved
an international reputation with his
rigorously controlled style and almost
architectural treatment of fabric.
Targeting the mature self-assured
woman, Ferre's style has attracted,
both in Europe and the United
States, a clientele appreciative
of his reinterpretation of the basics
of the high-quality female wardrobe.

Alberta Ferretti

Alberta Ferretti was born in Gradara
Pesaro in Italy, in 1950. While still a
teenager, she worked in the family's
couture atelier and opened her own
boutique at the age of eighteen. In
1974, she produced a line of clothing
under her own name, which met
with growing success during the
Eighties, culminating in the launch
of the Ferretti Studio and Ferretti
Jeansphilosophy lines. Under the
name Aeffe, she also manufactures
clothes for Rifat Ozbek, Moschino
and Jean-Paul Gaultier. The designs
she shows in Milan are distinctive for
their elegance, simplicity and layering
of transparent lightweight fabrics.

Alberta Ferretti

Thierry Mugler

Thierry Mugler Couture and Jean-Paul Gaultier Couture

Two of the most brilliant representatives of Parisian ready-to-wear, Thierry Mugler and Jean-Paul Gaultier were admitted to the Chambre Syndicale de la Couture Parisienne in July 1997. While continuing to design their own lines, they contributed to haute couture shows from time to time, offering collections of the highest quality and injecting a breath of fresh air into the profession. Mugler's company, acquired by Clarins in 2003, is now devoted entirely to the perfume industry.

Jean-Paul Gaultier

Adeline André

Adeline André

In premises on the ground floor of an old apartment building in the Marais in Paris, Adeline André runs probably the smallest haute couture house in the world. Here the designer works with her two seamstresses, while her partner deals with the management and public relations sides of the business. Her style is no less original. At one time she pioneered a sort of minimalism derived from conceptual art, whereas now she concentrates on the rigorous relationship of proportions, careful finishing and precise fitting. All this is complemented by Adeline's inspired cutting that makes her one of the great innovators of the contemporary fashion scene.

Chanel

By gradually moving away from the style that Coco Chanel had dictated even into the Seventies, Karl Lagerfeld has succeeded in maintaining Chanel's position as one of the elite group of houses leading fashion into the twenty-first century. Chanel S.A. is a privately financed French company with subsidiaries in Japan and the United States. It embraces fashion, perfume and beauty products and is exceptional in having the Wertheimers as its sole owners. In conjunction with president Alain Wertheimer, the family makes all the decisions about the future direction of the label and controls its designs, production and worldwide distribution.

Chanel

Walter
Van Beirendonck
W & LT

Walter Van Beirendonck

Born in 1957, he erupted on to the international fashion scene in 1995 and has gone on to produce a series of resolutely futuristic designs under the label W & LT (Wild and Lethal Trash). Deliberately using fabrics developed by the very latest technologies, in violently contrasting colours, Walter produces clothes that are full of erotic and indeed sadomasochistic references, tinged with a mordant adolescent humour. His highly distinctive approach relates to a resurgence of anti-fashion, but this time there is nothing in the least ethnic about its origins; instead, it is science fiction that provides the inspiration for a display of such exuberant provocation.

Rifat Ozbek

Rifat Ozbek was born in Istanbul in 1953 but later moved to England, where he has established himself as one of London's most creative designers. A pupil of Central St Martin's College of Art and Design, he founded his own label in 1984. His work is a clever mixture of references to Africa, India and his native Turkey with witty takes on period clothing; it is expressed in a youthful style that is reminiscent of the hippest nightclubs and of the more outrageous street fashions. Ozbek's collections are cosmopolitan and they are different, constantly inventive and provocative. In recent years they have become increasingly streamlined and sophisticated, enjoying considerable success in both Milan and New York.

Rifat Ozbek

Donna Karan

Donna Karan

A dynamic personality and a star of the New York scene, Donna Karan brings a very personal and feminine approach to the plain, sober-coloured, casual style that dominates New York ready-to-wear. She was born in 1948 and worked as Anne Klein's chief designer, before setting up her own label in 1984. Her designs won immediate popularity among active urban women who appreciated the understated luxury of her clothes. Launching into mass production, the designer achieved even greater success with her second and more affordable line, DKNY. She has subsequently diversified into jeans, menswear, children's clothes and perfumes.

Gap

Established in San Francisco in 1969, the company caters for the silent majority who have neither the desire to be slaves to, nor the means to afford, high fashion. With 1,200 points of sale and many different ranges, all characterized by their simplicity and good taste, Gap has created a distinct style of its own, a casual look in which men, women and children are equally at home. Yet the no. 2 in the United States clothing industry does not lack glamour. When Sharon Stone received her Academy Award at the Oscars in 1996, she was wearing a black crew-neck from Gap.

Gap

Calvin Klein

Calvin Klein

Far more than a mere fashion
company and an exemplary success
story of our time, Calvin Klein
is a multi-product worldwide
phenomenon, whose exposure to
the media is second to none. In the
Seventies, as a young designer with
a physique as elegant as that of his
models, Calvin Klein launched his
first line of designer jeans, in a glare
of publicity. Who could forget that shot
of Brooke Shields in a provocative
pose, asking 'Do you know what
comes between me and my Calvin's?',
to which the reply was 'Nothing'? In a
similar vein are the carefully construed
advertisements for underwear, using
images tinged with eroticism. They
all help to promote the label of a
remarkable artistic director, a man
who casts a skilled eye across the
whole of his production process,
ensuring consistency throughout.
He is as attentive to the PR of his
mass-produced merchandise as he
is to the simplicity and sophistication
of its design.

In the Nineties, one of the first
to anticipate the globalization of
world markets, Calvin Klein began
to promote his fashions, perfumes,
accessories and home ranges right
across America and also in Asia
and in Europe. With his global
concept of pared-down simplicity
and sophisticated functionalism,
he has created an image that is both
glamorous and provocative, achieving
huge success among the urban youth
of the Nineties.

And Also

The vast majority of labels that have emerged in the Nineties have tried to revert to a product that corresponds more closely to the everyday needs of their female customers. In Paris, Eric Bergère promotes ready-to-wear whose androgynous elegance is full of references to Swinging London. The Dutch designer Josephus Melchior Thimister, on the other hand, recreates a spirit of couture elegance, with his fluid bias-cut dresses that are reminiscent of Madeleine Vionnet's designs. He and the Brazilian Ocimar Versolato were admitted in 1998 to the prestigious Chambre Syndicale de la Couture Parisienne, whose members include the houses of Christophe Rouxel, Dominique Sirop and Franck Sorbier. One of the few top designers to have launched his career in Spain is Narciso Rodriguez who, as well as operating under his own name, was asked in 1997 to produce a range of clothes for the luxury leather good manufacturer Loewe, which is part of the LVMH group. Following the examples of Dior and Givenchy, many of the older houses have called in young designers, with Cristina Ortiz moving to Lanvin, Nicolas Ghesquière to Balenciaga, Stella McCartney to Chloé, Peter Speliopoulos to Cerruti, Gilles Dufour to Balmain and Alber Elbaz to Yves Saint Laurent, for its Rive Gauche ready-to-wear collection. Of the labels launched recently in Paris, one of the most original is that of Isabel Marant, whose fresh and easy collections have met with a success that seems likely to last.

On the strength of his exuberantly imaginative collections, Todd Oldham is regarded as one of Manhattan's brightest contemporary talents. Since 1994 he has acted as a consultant to the Escada label.

Long dress in embroidered satin by Stella McCartney for Chloé
The young Englishwoman's style is classically romantic and refined. *Spring/Summer 1999*

Mule by Christian Louboutin
Operating on the fringes of fashion, the Christian Louboutin label upheld, since 1991, the quintessentially Parisian tradition of the designer shoe.

Giorgio Armani
His casual elegance
has become a
classic look.
Spring/Summer 1997

Eric Bergère
This simple, basic
style eliminates all
superfluous detail.
Photograph by Mario
Testino.

The ready-to-wear label of Dirk Bikkembergs, another designer of
the Antwerp school, was launched in 1989, initially for menswear only.
In 1994, the label was applied for the first time to similar garments for
women, which were presented in joint collections. Generally speaking,
the last years of the twentieth century saw most designer labels develop
menswear ranges to complement their lines of womenswear. These
often show considerably more imagination than mainstream ready-to-
wear for men, which seems to have exhausted all possible variations on
the theme of suit and tie. Nevertheless, they have come nowhere near
exploring the full potential of the experimental designs for the man of
the future that were produced back in the Sixties and Seventies.

The prevailing style continues to be unstructured and neoclassical, deriving from Giorgio Armani's radical reexamination of the fundamentals of the male wardrobe. The alternative is the deliberately neutral silhouette – faintly shabby, a touch awkward, crumpled and baggy – promoted by Yohji Yamamoto, Rei Kawakubo and their disciples. It appeals to a public that is ready to break once and for all with the James Bond triumphalism that has, for so long, been almost the only choice available to the man aiming to please, pull or persuade. Black has spread like wildfire, complemented by a white shirt, buttoned to the neck but with no tie; shoes meanwhile have become clumpier, more like Dr Martens.

Sportswear has continued its irresistible rise, carrying along with it footwear hitherto reserved for the sportsfield. Brand names abound, but Nike has achieved universal fame with its aggressive advertising campaigns and constant references to the use of cutting-edge technology. Men and women of all ages wear trainers in every situation and with any sort of outfit, not excluding evening gowns and dress suits. In their imagination, at least, these sports shoes bring them closer to the top sportsmen and women who are society's idols at the close of the millennium. Although one would like to see this as no more than an attraction to the ideal of athleticism, in practice, it is an inescapable fact that properly made leather shoes are expensive.

Xuly-Bët
Starting from the basis of clothes he has picked up in flea markets or in secondhand shops, the Mali-born designer fuses Western style with African tradition, in an entirely personal idiom.
Spring/Summer 1999

The various financial crises that have gripped wealthier countries and the low level of incomes in the third world were bound to push those managing on a modest budget towards this form of footwear, particularly when a prestigious image coincides with low production costs. Once again, street fashion rules, as represented by its humblest adherents. Faced with the choice between the patent-leather boot of the Belle Époque dandy and the air-cushioned trainer worn in the Bronx, the third millennium seems to have sided firmly with the latter.

The Future

Jérôme Dreyfuss

Now forming part of the huge collection of contemporary clothes being assembled within the precincts of the Louvre by the Musée de la Mode et du Textile is a selection of garments bearing the labels of unknown designers from all over the world. They were chosen by the fashion writers of the international press, filmed in July by American ABC News and exhibited during the summer of 1999 in the Rivoli wing of the old royal palace. What their creators have in common is a desire to breathe new life into fashion, by making innovations to cut; by developing

Raf Simons　　　**Atsuro Tayama**　　　**Fred Sathal**

alternative methods of construction; by exploiting the properties of new materials; and by giving a wholly personal twist to some of the classics of fashion history. Neither made-to-measure nor mass-produced, they increasingly render meaningless the boundary between couture and ready-to-wear. No more than hints of future promise, they will only bear fruit if the industrialists take care to give these designers their head. It is on the potential success of this collaborative project that the future of fashion – in Paris, Tokyo, London and Groningen – depends.

Véronique Leroy   Gaspard Yurkievich   Marc Le Bihan

3

1 Kate Moss and Johnny Depp, 1995. Anti-fashion for the stars, under the observant eye of François-Marie Banier.

2 Björk. With her unconventional personality and eclectic fashion sense, the Icelandic singer incarnates the spirit of the Nineties.

3 Princess Diana. For the mother of the future king of England, adulated by the masses, fashion was an instrument of power and prestige.

2

Conclusion

In 1999, the Italian luxury leather goods group Gucci acquired the house of Yves Saint Laurent, all except its haute couture department. On October 13, 2000, the world flocked to see the first YSL Rive Gauche collection created by the Texan Tom Ford. For the profession, this event was at once a symbolic death and a rebirth. Haute couture in all its grandeur and nobility was quitting the scene for lack of volunteers, as much among its practitioners as among its clientèle.

The luxury industry took note. The time favored commerce over art. The big names had to transform themselves into brands, and this was the price of their survival. The huge sums of money at stake no longer allowed them to fade away gracefully with their creators, as they had once done. The creators might become immortal in the collective memory, but their successors had to confront the hard realities of a planetary market. Another rule of the game: Yves was a man of the world, but Tom was a mondain, a man about town. Yves understood women. Tom communicated through them. Yves was sensual. Tom was sexy. And so on.

The words change, the system stays in place. Yet a gulf exists between the legend and the gloss that covers it. The history of fashion described in this book belongs to a period which lasted only one century. The next hundred years look like the century of anti-fashion. Perhaps it will be fashion in another guise – after all we create fashion, like prose, almost unawares. But the very fashion which is spontaneously inventing itself today outside the classic circuits is

Hussein Chalayan
The English designer is one of the hottest talents for the future. Photograph by Marcus Tomlinson.

already one step away from the world of chic and appearances. There will always be prestigious fashion labels, publicity experts to promote them and clients demanding perpetual novelty. But today the system has ceased to reproduce itself with the same regularity, or even by way of the same group mentality. Even the simple notion of a fashion 'season' has lost much of its sense; after all, today's consumers are on the move from country to country, all year round. Fashion is now a global concern. In the winter of 2004, people in shorts were seen walking in the snow, and ministers took their collars off for appearances on television.

We observe a couple walking down the Champs Elysées. It's a Sunday morning, they are about thirty years old, visiting Paris. The sun is out; she is wearing a long black satin bias-cut slip, stiletto-heeled mules, and a denim jacket. She hasn't just stepped out of a casino, nor has she come from a ball or a house of ill repute; she's merely walking hand in hand with her husband. He wears a tracksuit, dark glasses and a baseball cap. He has just gotten out of bed. Where's the fashion here? Yet the same couple can be seen in any big city, any time, anywhere in the world.

In the last hundred years, there have been more changes in the appearance of people than in the thousand years before. This occurred in successive shifts whose sediment settled with the utmost delicacy, and we have tried to describe each one in this book. But there is no certainty that the process will continue. Formerly, creators plunged straight into fashion as if from a diving board – carelessly, yet with the firm intention of getting as many people soaking wet as they could. Today innovation is still important, though less playful and more driven by cold strategy than it used to be. Indeed the new absolutely bristles with economic equipment, thereby forfeiting much of its suppleness and nearly all its spontaneity. Not surprisingly, we learn more from the business pages of the mainstream newspapers than from specialized publications about fashion matters, which are now much too serious in money terms to be left to mere designers.

Financially, the great fashion upheaval of the turn of the twenty-first century was the war between Bernard Arnault, president of LMVH, and Francois Pinault, the owner of Pinault-Printemps-Redoute. The bone of contention between these two luxury barons was control of Gucci N.V. Group, the Florence-based consortium whose turnover had quadrupled in five years under its managing director Domenico De Solé and its artistic director Tom Ford. This pair had become symbols of the mutation that can occur when the four cardinal points in any luxury business – creation, marketing, merchandising and communication – are merged into a single driving force. This was clear for all to see when Gucci took over Saint Laurent and everything about it was reshuffled. The only fixed point of reference thereafter was a general concept of shops all exactly alike, scattered throughout the world in favorable locations.

Who, in 2010, will control the luxury industry, already worth many hundreds of billions? Fashion's role in this struggle for dominion is largely one of packaging. The luxury wars are basically fought over images. In this perspective the smaller enterprise of Jean-Paul Gaultier, supported by its perfume branch (a subsidiary of Shiseido) and the stake in it owned by Hermès, has risen to the level of haute couture with two shows of made-to-measure clothing per year. At the same time Gaultier himself designs the Hermès ready-to-wear collections, at the risk of cannibalizing his own products. The time has come for the former *enfant terrible* of fashion to think about the future. Kenzo and Saint Laurent have retired; Thierry Mugler and several others of his generation are gradually relinquishing the limelight. Only the tireless Karl Lagerfeld at Chanel persists in his dazzling process of renewal, season after season – and always through labels other than his own, with which he has never reached quite the same heights. Meanwhile Azzedine Alaïa – Lagerfeld's diametrical opposite and the quintessential fashion freelance – carries steadily on with his work as

an artisan couturier and sculptor of women's silhouettes. He still has his own exclusive clientèle, though he now operates in partnership with the Italian firm of Prada.

Few new fashion houses (with the honorable exception of Peter and Rolf) have appeared since the turn of the century, though plenty of new labels have been formed around older structures. Hedi Slimane, a refugee from the former Saint Laurent team and now a coveted designer, is at the helm of the men's ready-to-wear department at Dior. Other successful grafts have been Nicolas Ghesquière at Balenciaga, Olivier Theyskens at Rochas and Vincent Darre at Ungaro. At the same time, several luxury groups – for the most part from the fine leather goods sector – have begun creating top quality ready-to-wear lines that are less crazy but certainly more effective than those of their predecessors. The best of these is Marc Jacobs at the luggage maker Louis Vuitton, which spectacularly celebrated its 150th anniversary in 2004. The union of Paris couturiers has fewer and fewer members, and some of the more recent candidates have been less than convincing; to the point, indeed, when we may expect a general revision of a concept that is rapidly becoming meaningless. Even though at Dior, in spite of – or perhaps because of – the mini-scandals unleashed by John Galliano every time he mounts a show, sales of accessories have been on the increase ever since his arrival in 1997. No doubt for a long time to come the future of fashion will be in the bag.

It remains to be said that by force of accumulations, mergers and acquisitions, of watching the competition too closely and pilfering its magic formula, fashion's geese may soon grow weary of laying their customary golden eggs. Such, at the very least, is the feeling on the street, where an obscure rebellion against the tyranny of appearances looks to be in the making. Out of all this systematic decomposition and decoupling there may one day arise a fresh array of postures and manners whose flux will elude, as fashion always has, all logic.

Marc Jacobs
Publicity photograph
with Sofia Coppola
Autumn 2000

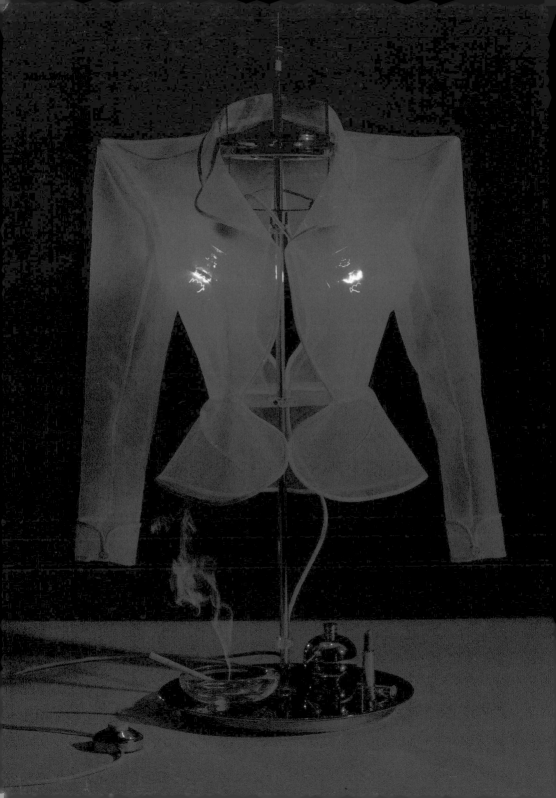

...

Agent Provocateur · Victor Alfaro · APC · Ann-Sofie Back · John Bartlett · Blundell · Boudicca · Véronique Branquinho · Ennio Capasa · Ally Capellino · Joe Casely-Hayford · Jimmy Choo · Corinne Cobson · Jasper Conran · Copperwheat · Doran Deacon · Alessandro Dell'Acqua · Timothy Everest · Nicole Farhi · Pearce Fionda · Shelley Fox · Bella Freud · Maurizio Galante · Owen Gaster · Elspeth Gibson · Andrew Groves · Olivier Guillemin · Eric Halley · Erickson Beamon · Abe Hamilton · Sarah Harmanee · Akira Isogawa · Betty Jackson · Richard James · Stephan Janson · Lainey Keogh · Daryl Kerrigan · Niels Klavers · Mark Kroeker · Christophe Lemaire · Jérôme L'Huillier · Ben de Lisi · Julien MacDonald · Marcel Marongiu · Benoît Méléard · Roberto Menichetti · Rodolphe Ménudier · Roland Mouret · Kostas Murkudis · Wim Niels · Sonja Nuttall · Jessica Ogden · Rick Owens · Lucien Pellat-Finet · Fabio Piras · Stéphane Plassier · Plein Sud · Jacqueline Rabun · Dai Rees · Clements Ribeiro · John Richmond · John Rocha · Dirk van Saene · Fred Sathal · Jeremy Scott · Seraph · Hedi Simane · Lawrence Steele · Anna Sui · Oscar Suleyman · Franck Sorbier · Olivier Theyskens · Isabel Toledo · Yuki Torii · Richard Tyler · Ronald Van der Kemp · A. F. Vandevorst · Tom Van Lingen · Amanda Wakeley · Junya Watanabe · Sharon Wauchob · Tristan Webber · Mark Whitaker · Matthew Williamson · Scott Wilson · Zucca ·

...

Jeremy Scott

Marcel Marongiu

Dirk van Saene

Alessandro Dell'Acqua

Zucca

Corinne Cobson

Moschino

Bibliography

General

ANSCOMBE Isabelle, *A Woman's Touch: Women in Design from 1860 to the Present Day*, New York, Viking Press, 1984

ASH Juliet and WILSON Elizabeth, *Chic Thrills: A Fashion Reader*, London, Pandora Press, 1992

BAILLEUX Nathalie and REMAURY Bruno, *Modes et vêtements*, Paris, Gallimard, 1995

BAINES Barbara, *Fashion Revivals*, London, B.T. Batsford Ltd., 1981

BALFOUR Victoria, *Rock Wives*, New York, Beech Tree Books, 1986

BALLARD Bettina, *In My Fashion*, New York, David McKay, 1967

BANNER Lois, *American Beauty*, New York, Alfred A. Knopf, 1983

BARWICK Sandra, *A Century of Style*, London, Allen & Unwin, 1984

BATTERBERRY Michael and Ariane, *Fashion. The Mirror of History*, New York, Greenwich House, 1977

BATTERSBY Martin, *Art Deco Fashion*, London, Academy Editions, 1974

BENAÏM Laurence, *L'Année de la mode 1987–88*, Paris, La Manufacture, 1988

— *L'Année de la mode 1988–89*, Paris, La Manufacture, 1989

BOUCHER François, *A History of Costume in the West*, London, Thames & Hudson, rev. edn, 1996

BRAIN Robert, *The Decorated Body*, New York, Harper & Row, 1979

CARTER Ernestine, *The Changing World of Fashion*, London, Weidenfeld & Nicolson, 1977

— *Magic Names of Fashion*, London, Weidenfeld & Nicolson, and Englewood Cliffs, New Jersey, Prentice-Hall, 1980

CHAPSAL Madeleine, *La Chair de la robe*, Paris, Fayard, 1989

CHENOUNE Farid, *A History of Men's Fashion*, Paris, Flammarion, 1993

COLCHESTER Chloe, *The New Textiles: Trends + Traditions*, London, Thames & Hudson, 1994

CORE Philip, *The Original Eye: Arbiters of Twentieth Century Taste*, London, Melbourne and New York, Quartet Books, 1984

DARIA Irene, *The Fashion Cycle*, New York, Simon & Schuster, 1990

DAVES Jessica, *Ready-Made Miracle*, New York, G.P. Putnam's Sons, 1967

DELBOURG-DELPHIS Marylène, *Le Chic et le Look. Histoire de la mode féminine et des mœurs de 1850 à nos jours*, Paris, Hachette, 1981

— *La Mode pour la vie*, Paris, Autrement, 1983

— *Le Sillage des élégances*, Paris, Jean-Claude Lattès, 1983

DESLANDRES Yvonne, *Le Costume image de l'homme*, Paris, Albin Michel, 1976

— and MÜLLER Florence, *Histoire de la mode au xxᵉ siècle*, Paris, Somogy, 1986

DIAMONDSTEIN Barbaralee, *Fashion: The Inside Story*, New York, Rizzoli International, 1985

DORFLES Gillo, *Kitsch: The World of Bad Taste*, New York, Universe Books, 1979

DORNER Jane, *The Changing Shape of Fashion*, London, Octopus Books Ltd., 1974

EVANS Caroline and THORNTON Minna, *Women and Fashion: A New Look*, London and New York, Quartet Books, 1989

EWING Elizabeth, *History of Twentieth Century Fashion*, London, B.T. Batsford, 1974

FAIRCHILD John, *The Fashionable Savages*, New York, Doubleday & Co., 1965

— *Chic Savages*, New York, Simon & Schuster, 1989

'La Filière textile-habillement en Europe' in *Perspectives stratégiques et financières*, Paris, Eurostaf, 1995

GAN Stephen, *Visionaire's Fashion. Designers at the Turn of the Millennium*, London, Laurence King Publishing, 1997

GARNIER Guillaume et al., *Paris-Couture, années trente*, Paris, Musée de la Mode et du Costume (exhibition catalogue), Éditions Paris-Musées, 1987

GIACOMONI Silvia, *L'Italia della Moda*, Milan, Mazzotta, 1984

GINSBURG Madeleine, *An Introduction to Fashion Illustration*, London, Victoria and Albert Museum Publications (exhibition catalogue), 1980

GLYNN Prudence, *In Fashion: Dress in the Twentieth Century*, London, Allen & Unwin, 1978

GOLD Arthur and FITZGERALD Robert, *Misia: The Life of Misia Sert*, New York, Alfred A. Knopf, 1980

GRUAU François-Marie, *Les Industries de l'habillement*, Paris, PUF, Que Sais-Je? Collection, 1996

GRUMBACH Didier, *Histoire de la mode*, Paris, Le Seuil, 1993

Guida internazionale ai musei e alle collezioni pubbliche di costumi e di tessuti, Venice, Centro internazionale delle arti e del costume, 1970

HAYE Amy de la (ed.), *The Cutting Edge. 50 Years of British Fashion. 1947–1997*, London, Victoria and Albert Museum Publications, 1996

HEAD Edith and HYAMS Joe, *How to Dress for Success*, New York, Random House, 1967

— and KESMORE Jane Ardmore, *The Dress Doctor*, Boston, Little, Brown & Co., 1959

HEBDIGE Dick, *Subculture: The Meaning of Style*, London and New York, Methuen Inc., 1979

HORN Marilyn J., *The Second Skin. An Interdisciplinary Study of Clothing*, New York, Houghton Mifflin Company, 1975

'L'Industrie mondiale du luxe', vol. II, in *Perspectives stratégiques et financières*, Paris, Eurostaf, 1995

JONES Mablen, *Getting It On: The Clothing of Rock 'n' Roll*, New York, Abbeville Press, 1987

KHORNAK Lucille, *Fashion 2001*, New York, Viking Press, 1982

KOREN Leonard, *New Fashion Japan*, Tokyo and New York, Kodansha International, 1984

LANZMANN Jacques and RIPERT Pierre, *Cent ans de prêt-à-porter*, Weill, Paris, P.A.U., 1992

LAVER James, *Taste and Fashion from the French Revolution to the Present Day*, London, Harrap & Co., 1945

— and HAYE Amy de la, *Costume and Fashion*, London, Thames & Hudson, rev. edn, 1995

LAW Lisa, *Flashing on the Sixties*, San Francisco, Chronicle Books, 1988

LEE Sarah Tomerlin (ed.), *American Fashion: The Lives and Lines of Adrian, Mainbocher, McCardell, Norell, Trigère*, London, André Deutsch, and New York, Quadrangle, 1975

LENCEK Lena and GIDEON Bosker, *Making Waves: Swimsuits and the Underdressing of America*, San Francisco, Chronicle Books, 1989

LIPOVETSKY Gilles, *L'Empire et l'éphémère. La mode et son destin dans les sociétés modernes*, Paris, Gallimard, 1987

LOBENTHAL Joel, *Radical Rags: Fashions of the Sixties*, New York, Abbeville Press, 1990

LURIE Alison, *The Language of Clothes*, London, Hamlyn Publications, 1982

LYNAM Ruth (ed.), *Paris Fashion*, London, Michael Joseph, 1972

— *Couture: An Illustrated History of the Great Paris Designers and Their Creations*, New York, Doubleday & Co., 1972

MARION G., *Mode et marché. Les stratégies du marketing du vêtement* (preface by Didier Grumbach), Paris, Éditions Liaisons, 1992

DE MARLY Diana, *The History of Haute Couture, 1850–1950*, London, B.T. Batsford, 1980

MARTIN Richard (ed.), *Contemporary Fashion*, Detroit, St James Press, 1995

McCONATHY Dale and VREELAND Diana, *Hollywood Costume*, New York, Harry N. Abrams, 1976

McDERMOTT Catherine, *Street Style: British Design in the 80s*, New York, Rizzoli International, 1987

McDOWELL Colin, *McDowell's Directory of Twentieth Century Fashion*, London, Frederick Muller, 1984

McROBBIE Angela (ed.), *Zoot Suits and Second-Hand Dresses*, Boston, Unwin Hyman, 1988

MELLY George, *Revolt Into Style*, London, Allen Lane, 1970

MENDES Valerie D., *Twentieth Century Fashion: An Introduction to Women's Fashionable Dress, 1900 to 1980*, London, Victoria and Albert Museum Publications (exhibition catalogue), 1981

MILBANK Caroline Rennolds, *Couture, The Great Fashion Designers*, London, Thames & Hudson, and New York, Stewart, Tabori & Chang, 1985

— *New York Fashion: The Evolution of American Style*, New York, Harry N. Abrams, 1989

La Mode et ses métiers du XVIIIe siècle à nos jours, Paris, Musée de la Mode et du Costume (exhibition catalogue), Éditions Paris-Musées, 1981

Moda italiana, 1946–1986, 40 anni di stile italiano, Rome, Palazzo Braschi (exhibition catalogue), 1987

Moments de mode, Paris, Musée des Arts de la Mode/Herscher (exhibition catalogue), 1986

Le Monde selon ses créateurs, Paris, Musée de la Mode et du Costume (exhibition catalogue), Éditions Paris-Musées, 1991

MORENO Elizabeth, *The Fashion Makers: An Inside Look at America's Leading Designers*, New York, Random House, 1978

MORISHITA Hiromo, *Inventive Clothes*, Kyoto, Chamber of Commerce, 1975

MULASSANO Adriana and ALFA Castaldi, *I Mass-Moda: Fatti e personaggi dell'italian look*, Florence, Spinelli, 1979

NUZZI Christina, *Parisian Fashion*, New York, Rizzoli International, 1980

O'HARA CALLAN Georgina, *Dictionary of Fashion and Fashion Designers*, London and New York, Thames & Hudson, 1998

PARKER Rozsika, *The Subversive Stitch: Embroidery and the Making of the Feminine*, New York, Routledge, 1989

PERROT Philippe, *Les Dessus et les dessous de la bourgeoisie: Une histoire du vêtement au XIXe siècle*, Paris, Fayard, 1981

— *Le Travail des apparences, ou les transformations du corps féminin, XVIIIe–XIXe siècles*, Paris, Le Seuil, 1984

POLHEMUS Ted, *Pop Styles*, London, Vermilion, 1984

— *Street Style: From Sidewalk to Catwalk*, London, Thames & Hudson, 1994

— *Style Surfing: What to Wear in the Third Millennium*, London, Thames & Hudson, 1996

REMAURY Bruno (ed.), *Repères mode & textile 96. Visages d'un secteur*, Paris, Institut Français de la Mode, 1996

— (ed.), *Dictionnaire de la mode au XXe siècle*, Paris, Éditions du Regard, 1994, rev. edn 1996

RILEY Robert, *The Fashion Makers*, New York, Crown, 1968

ROBINSON Julian, *Fashion in the Forties*, New York, Harcourt Brace Jovanovich, 1976
— *The Golden Age of Style. Art Deco Fashion Illustration*, London, Orbis Publishing Ltd., 1976
— *Fashion in the Thirties*, London, Oresko Books, 1978
ROCHE Daniel, *La Culture des apparences. Une histoire du vêtement, XVIIᵉ–XVIIIᵉ siècles*, Paris, Fayard, 1989, and Le Seuil, Points Histoire Collection, 1992
ROGER-MILÈS L., *Les Créateurs de la mode*, Paris, Eggimann, 1910
ROSELLE Bruno du, *La Mode*, Paris, Imprimerie Nationale, 1980
ROSCHO Bernard, *The Rag Race*, New York, Funk & Wagnalls, 1963
ROTHSTEIN Natalie (ed.), *Four Hundred Years of Fashion*, London, Victoria and Albert Museum Publications, 1984
SIMON Philippe, *La Haute couture. Monographie d'une industrie de luxe*, Paris, 1931
SIROP Dominique, *L'Élégance de Jacqueline Delubac*, Paris, Adam Biro, 1994
STEELE Valerie, *Paris Fashion: A Cultural History*, Oxford and New York, Oxford University Press, 1988
— *Women of Fashion. Twentieth Century Designers*, New York, Rizzoli International, 1991
STEGEMEYER Anne, *Who's Who in Fashion*, New York, Fairchild, 1980
TATE Sharon Lee, *Inside Fashion Design*, New York, Harper & Row, 1984
TÉTART-VITTU Françoise (ed.), *Le Dessin sous toutes ses coutures*, Paris, Musée de la Mode et du Costume (exhibition catalogue), Éditions Paris-Musées, 1995
THURLOW Valerie, *Model in Paris*, London, Robert Hale, 1975
TOUSSAINT-SAMAT Maguelonne, *Histoire technique et morale du vêtement*, Paris, Bordas, Cultures Collection, 1990
VEILLON Dominique, *La Mode sous l'occupation*, Paris, Payot, 1990
VINCENT-RICARD Françoise, *Clefs pour la mode*, Paris, Seghers, 1987
— *Les Objets de la mode*, Paris, Éditions du May, 1989

VREELAND Diana (ed.), *American Women of Style*, New York, Costume Institute, Metropolitan Museum of Art (exhibition catalogue), 1975
— *Allure*, New York, Doubleday & Co., 1980
— *D.V.*, New York, Alfred A. Knopf, 1984
WALKLEY Christina, *The Ghost in the Looking Glass: The Victorian Seamstress*, London, Peter Owen, 1981
WATKINS Josephine Ellis, *Who's Who in Fashion*, New York, Fairchild, 1975
WILSON Elizabeth, *Adorned in Dreams. Fashion and Modernity*, London, Virago Press, and Los Angeles, Berkeley, University of California Press, 1985
WISER William, *The Crazy Years: Paris in the Twenties*, New York, Atheneum, 1983
WOODHAM Jonathan M., *Twentieth Century Ornament*, New York, Rizzoli International, 1990
ZALETOVA Lidya et al., *Revolutionary Costume: Soviet Clothing and Textiles of the 1920s*, London, Trefoil Books, and New York, Rizzoli International, 1989

Monographs
BARILLÉ Elisabeth, *Lanvin*, London, Thames & Hudson, Fashion Memoir, 1997
BAUDOT François, *Chanel*, London, Thames & Hudson, and New York, Universe Publishing, Fashion Memoir, 1996
— *Alaïa*, London, Thames & Hudson, and New York, Universe Publishing, Fashion Memoir, 1996
— *Elsa Schiaparelli*, London, Thames & Hudson, and New York, Universe Publishing, Fashion Memoir, 1997
— *Paul Poiret*, London, Thames & Hudson, Fashion Memoir, 1997
— *Thierry Mugler*, London, Thames & Hudson, and New York, Universe Publishing, Fashion Memoir, 1998
— *Gruau*, Paris, Assouline, Mémoire de la Mode Collection, 1998
BLUM Eva, *Design by Erté*, New York, Dover Publications Inc., 1978

CASSINI Oleg, *In My Own Fashion, An Autobiography*, New York, Pocket, 1987
CHAPON François, *Mystères et splendeurs de Jacques Doucet, 1853–1929*, Paris, Jean-Claude Lattès, 1984
CHAPSAL Madeleine et al., *Rykiel par Rykiel*, Paris, Herscher, 1985
CHARLES-ROUX Edmonde, *Chanel: Her Life, Her World, and the Woman Behind the Legend She Herself Created*, New York, Alfred A. Knopf, 1975
— *Chanel and Her World*, London, Weidenfeld & Nicolson, 1981
CHENOUNE Farid, *Jean-Paul Gaultier*, London, Thames & Hudson, Fashion Memoir, 1996
DEMASSE Jacques, *Sonia Delaunay: Fashion and Fabrics*, London, Thames & Hudson, 1991
DEMORNEX Jacqueline, *Vionnet*, London, Thames & Hudson, 1991
DE OSMA Guillermo, *Mariano Fortuny: His Life and Work*, New York, London, Aurum Press Ltd., 1980, rev. edn, 1994
DESLANDRES Yvonne, *Paul Poiret*, London, Thames & Hudson, 1987
DESVAUX Delphine, *Fortuny*, London, Thames & Hudson, Fashion Memoir, 1998
DIOR Christian, *Dior by Dior*, London, Weidenfeld & Nicolson, 1957
DURAS Marguerite, *Yves Saint Laurent et la photographie de mode*, Paris, Albin Michel, 1988
ETHERINGTON-SMITH Meredith, *Patou*, London, Hutchinson, 1984
GARNIER Guillaume et al., *40 années de création, Pierre Balmain*, Paris, Musée de la Mode et du Costume (exhibition catalogue), Éditions Paris-Musées, 1985
— *Paul Poiret et Nicole Groult*, Paris, Musée de la Mode et du Costume (exhibition catalogue), Éditions Paris-Musées, 1986
— *Balenciaga*, Paris, Musée de la Mode et du Costume (exhibition catalogue), Éditions Paris-Musées, 1987
GIROUD Françoise, *Dior: Christian Dior*, London, Thames & Hudson, and New York, Rizzoli International, 1987

GUILLAUME Valérie, *Jacques Fath*, Paris, Éditions Paris-Musées, 1993
— *Courrèges*, London, Thames & Hudson, and New York, Universe Publishing, Fashion Memoir, 1998
HAEDRICH Marcel, *Coco Chanel: Her Life, Her Secrets*, London, Robert Hale, and Boston, Little, Brown & Co., 1972
Hommage à Elsa Schiaparelli, Paris, Musée de la Mode et du Costume (exhibition catalogue), Éditions Paris-Musées, 1974
HULANICKI Barbara, *From A to Biba*, London, Hutchinson, 1983
Issey Miyake, Body Works (texts by Diana Vreeland, Andy Warhol and Ettore Sottsass), Tokyo, Shozo Tsurumoto, 1983
Issey Miyake by Irving Penn, Tokyo, Miyake Design Studio, 1989, 1990 and 1993–95
JOUVE Marie-Andrée and DEMORNEX Jacqueline, *Balenciaga*, Paris, Éditions du Regard, 1988
KAMITSIS Lydia, *Paco Rabanne. Le Sens de la recherche*, Paris, Michel Lafon, 1996
— *Vionnet*, London, Thames & Hudson, and New York, Universe Publishing, Fashion Memoir, 1996
— *Paco Rabanne*, London, Thames & Hudson, Fashion Memoir, 1999
KOIKE Kazuko (ed.), *East Meets West*, Tokyo, Heibonsha, 1978
KRELL Gene, *Vivienne Westwood*, London, Thames & Hudson, and New York, Universe Publishing, Fashion Memoir, 1997
LACROIX Christian, *Pieces of a Pattern: Lacroix by Lacroix*, London and New York, Thames & Hudson, 1992
LEPAPE Claude and DEFERT Thierry, *Georges Lepape, ou l'élégance illustrée*, Paris, Herscher, 1983
LEYMARIE Jean, *Chanel*, New York, Rizzoli International, 1987
MADSEN Axel, *Living for Design: The Yves Saint Laurent Story*, New York, Delacorte Press, 1979
MARQUAND Lilou, *Chanel m'a dit*, Paris, Jean-Claude Lattès, 1990
MARTIN Richard, *Charles James*, London, Thames & Hudson, Fashion Memoir, 1997

Mary Quant's London, London, The London Museum (exhibition catalogue with an introduction by Ernestine Carter), 1973
MAURIÈS Patrick, *Jewelry by Chanel*, London, Thames & Hudson, 1993
— *Sonia Rykiel*, Paris, Assouline, Mémoire de la Mode Collection, 1997
McCARDELL Claire, *What Shall I Wear?*, New York, Simon & Schuster, 1956
MENDES Valerie (ed.), *Pierre Cardin: Past, Present and Future*, London and Berlin, Dirk Nishen, 1990
MORAIS Richard, *Pierre Cardin, The Man Who Became a Label*, London, Bantam Press, 1991
MORAND Paul, *L'Allure de Chanel*, Paris, Hermann, 1976
PALMER WHITE Jack, *Poiret*, London, Studio Vista, and New York, Potter, 1973
— *Elsa Schiaparelli*, London, Aurum Press Ltd., and New York, Rizzoli International, 1986
Paquin: Une rétrospective de soixante ans de haute couture, Lyons, Musée Historique des Tissus (exhibition catalogue), 1989
PELLÉ Marie-Paule and MAURIÈS Patrick, *Valentino: trent'anni di magia*, Milan, Accademia Valentino (exhibition catalogue), Bompiani, 1991
POCHNA Marie-France, *Christian Dior*, Paris, Flammarion, 1994
— *Dior*, London, Thames & Hudson, Fashion Memoir, 1996
POIRET Paul, *My First Fifty Years*, London, Victor Gollancz, 1931
— *King of Fashion: The Autobiography of Paul Poiret*, Philadelphia, J. B. Lippincott, 1931
QUANT Mary, *Quant by Quant*, London, Cassell & Co., 1966
— *Colour by Quant*, London, Octopus Books Ltd., 1984
RHODES Zandra and KNIGHT Anne, *The Art of Zandra Rhodes*, London, Jonathan Cape, and Boston, Houghton Mifflin Co., 1984
RILEY Robert, *Givenchy: 30 Years*, New York, Fashion Institute of Technology, 1982
ROUFF Maggy, *Ce que j'ai vu en chiffonnant la clientèle*, Paris, Librairie des Champs-Elysées, 1938

— *La Philosophie de l'élégance*, Paris, Éditions Littéraires de France, 1942
RYKIEL Sonia, *Et je la voudrais nue...*, Paris, Bernard Grasset, 1979
SAINDERICHIN Ginette, *Kenzo*, Paris, Éditions du May, 1989
Saint Laurent par Yves Saint Laurent, Paris, Musée des Arts de la Mode (exhibition catalogue), 1986
SAUNDERS Edith, *The Age of Worth, Couturier to the Empress Eugénie*, Bloomington, Indiana University Press, 1955
SCHIAPARELLI Elsa, *Shocking Life*, London, J.M. Dent, and New York, E.P. Dutton, 1954
SEEBOHM Caroline, *The Man Who Was Vogue. The Life and Times of Condé Nast*, New York, Viking Press, 1982
SIROP Dominique, *Paquin*, Paris, Adam Biro, 1989
SNOW Carmel and ASWELL Marie-Louise, *The World of Carmel Snow*, New York, McGraw-Hill, 1962
SUDJIC Deyan, *Rei Kawakubo and Comme des Garçons*, London, Fourth Estate, and New York, Rizzoli International, 1990
Thierry Mugler: Photographer, London, Thames & Hudson, 1988
Three Women: Madeleine Vionnet, Claire McCardell, and Rei Kawakubo, New York, Fashion Institute of Technology (exhibition catalogue), 1987
VAN DORSSEN Sacha and GIROUD Françoise, *Dior*, Paris, Éditions du Regard, 1987
VERMOREL Fred, *Fashion & Perversity: A Life of Vivienne Westwood and the Sixties Laid Bare*, London, Bloomsbury, 1996
VREELAND Diana, *Yves Saint Laurent*, London, Thames & Hudson, 1984
The World of Balenciaga, New York, Costume Institute, Metropolitan Museum of Art (exhibition catalogue), 1973
Yves Saint Laurent, New York, Costume Institute, Metropolitan Museum of Art (exhibition catalogue), 1983

Magazines and Fashion Photography

ALBERT-TERROU, *Histoire de la presse*, Paris, PUF, 1970

AVEDON Richard, *Evidence 1944–1994*, New York, Random House/Eastman Kodak, 1994

BEATON Cecil, *The Magic Image: The Genius of Photography*, London, Pavilion Books, 1989

CHASE Edna Woolman and Ilka, *Always in Vogue*, New York, Doubleday & Co., 1954

DAHL-WOLFE Louise, *A Photographer's Scrapbook*, New York, St Martin's & Marek, 1984

DEVLIN Polly, *Vogue Book of Fashion Photography*, London, Thames & Hudson, and New York, William Morrow and Co., 1979

DRAKE Nicholas, *The Sixties: A Decade in Vogue*, Englewood Cliffs, New Jersey, Prentice-Hall, 1988

HALL-DUNCAN Nancy, *The History of Fashion Photography*, New York, International Museum of Photography/Harry N. Abrams, 1978

HORST P., *Horst, Salute to the Thirties*, New York, Viking Press, 1971

HOWELL Georgina, *In Vogue*, New York, Schocken Books, 1975

KELLY Katie, *The Wonderful World of Women's Wear Daily*, New York, Saturday Review Press, 1972

Man Ray: les années bazaar, New York, Rizzoli International, 1988

MULVAGH Jane, *Costume Jewelry in Vogue*, London and New York, Thames & Hudson, 1988

— *Vogue History of 20th-Century Fashion*, Harmondsworth, Middx, Penguin Books Ltd, 1988

PACKER William, *Fashion Drawing in Vogue*, London, Thames & Hudson, 1983

TRAHAY Jane (ed.), *Harper's Bazaar: 100 Years of the American Female*, New York, Random House, 1967

VREELAND Diana and PENN Irving, *Inventive Paris Clothes, 1909–1939*, New York, Viking Press, 1977

William Klein. Mode In & Out, Paris, Le Seuil, 1994

Sociology and Fashion

BARTHES Roland, 'Histoire et sociologie du vêtement' in *Annales*, no. 3, July–September 1957

— *The Fashion System*, London, Jonathan Cape, 1985

BAUDRILLARD Jean, 'La Mode ou la féérie du code' in *Traverse*, no. 3, 1984

BELL Quentin, *On Human Finery*, London, Allison & Busby, 1992

BOURDIEU Pierre, *La Distinction. Critique sociale du jugement*, Paris, Éditions de Minuit, 1979

— 'Le Couturier et sa griffe: contribution à une théorie de la magie', Paris, *Actes de la recherche en science sociale*, no. 1, September 1974

CHAFE William, *The American Woman: Her Changing Social, Economic, Political Roles, 1920–1970*, Oxford and New York, Oxford University Press, 1972

DESCAMPS Marc-Alain, *Psychosociologie de la mode*, Paris, PUF, 1984

EVANS Sara, *Personal Politics: The Roots of Women's Liberation in the Civil Rights Movement and the New Left*, New York, Alfred A. Knopf, 1979

FLÜGEL J.C., *The Psychology of Clothes*, London, Hogarth Press, 1930

FRAZER Ronald (ed.), *A Student Generation in Revolt: An International Oral History*, New York, Pantheon Books, 1988

FRED David, *Fashion, Culture, and Identity*, Chicago, University of Chicago Press, 1992

HOLLANDER Anne, *Seeing Through Clothes*, New York, Viking Press, 1978

KÖNIG René, *Sociologie de la mode*, Paris, Payot, 1969

MELINKOFF Ellin, *What We Wore: An Offbeat Social History of Women's Clothing, 1950–1980*, New York, Quill, 1984

RIBEIRO Aileen, *Dress and Morality*, London, B.T. Batsford Ltd., 1986

ROACH Mary Ellen and BUBOLZ EICHER Joanne, *Dress, Adornment and the Social Order*, New York, John Wiley & Sons, Inc., 1965

WEINER Annette B. and SCHNEIDER Jane, *Cloth and Human Experience*, Washington, D.C. and London, Smithsonian Institution Press, 1989

Fashion and Art

Addressing the Century: 100 Years of Art and Fashion, London, Hayward Gallery (exhibition catalogue), 1999

Art et mode: attirance et divergence, special issue of *Art Press*, hors série no. 18, Paris, 1997

CRISPOLTI Enrico, *Il Futurismo e la moda*, Milan, Padiglione d'Arte Contemporanea (exhibition catalogue), Venezia Marsilio, 1988

GUILLAUME Valérie (ed.), *Les Avant-Gardes artistiques et la mode au xxᵉ siècle*, Paris, Musée de la Mode et du Costume (exhibition catalogue), Éditions Paris-Musées, 1997

HANSEN Traude and WIMMER Gino, *Wiener Werkstätte-Mode*, Munich, Christian Brandstätte, 1984

MARTIN Richard, *Fashion and Surrealism*, London, Thames & Hudson, 1989

— and HAROLD Koda, *The Historical Mode, Fashion and Art in the 1980's*, New York, Fashion Institute of Technology (exhibition catalogue), Rizzoli International, 1989

MORENO Elizabeth, *Sonia Delaunay: Art Into Fashion*, New York, George Braziller, 1986

SIMON Marie, *Mode et peinture. Le Second Empire et l'impressionnisme*, Paris, Hazan, 1995

THIEL Erika, *Künstler und Mode*, Berlin, Henschelverlag, 1979

VÖLKER Angela, *Moda. Wiener Werkstätte*, Florence, Cantini Editore, 1990

Picture Credits

4   Photo Jacques-Henri Lartigue
© Ministère de la Culture-France/
A.A.J.H.L.

8   © Illustration Ruben Toledo
for Louis Vuitton

10   © Photo David Seidner

12   © Photo Roxanne Lowit

13   © Photo Jean-Paul Goude

14–15   © Photo Liam Woon/
Gilbert and George for
Comme des Garçons

16   © Courtesy of *Harper's Bazaar*,
March 1938

17   © The Fabric Workshop
& Museum, Philadelphia

18   © Photo Frank Horvat

19   Gruau © Sylvie Nissen Archives

20   © Man Ray Trust/Adagp,
Paris/Telimage-1999

21   © *Il Tempo e la moda* (catalogue),
Skira

22   © Photo Ruben Afanador
for Isabel Toledo

24   Photo Baudoin Picard
© Lesage Archives

25   © Photo Serge Lutens

26   © Photo Pierre et Gilles, Paris

27   © Photo Karl Lagerfeld

28   Private collection © All Rights
Reserved

31   © Dymonds and Company/
Courtesy of the National
Portrait Gallery, London

32   © Photo RMN-Hervé Lewandowski

33   Photo Jacques-Henri Lartigue
© Ministère de la Culture-France/
A.A.J.H.L.

34   © Collection J.-L. Charmet

35   Photo Jacques-Henri Lartigue
© Ministère de la Culture-France/
A.A.J.H.L.

36   © Cliché Bibliothèque d'Art et
d'Archéologie Jacques Doucet-Paris

37   *Gazette du bon ton*,
March 1913 © All Rights Reserved

38   © Rue des Archives

39   © *L'Illustration*/Sygma

40   © Lipnitzki-Viollet

41   *Gazette du bon ton*,
March 1914 © All Rights Reserved

42   *Gazette du bon ton*,
March 1914 © All Rights Reserved

43   Photo Edward Steichen © All Rights
Reserved

44   *Gazette du bon ton*, January 1914
© Adagp, Paris-1999

45   © Man Ray Trust/Adagp,
Paris-1999. Collection UFAC

46   © All Rights Reserved

47   © Kathryn Abbe Photographs,
Glen Head, New York

48   © Fortuny Museum Collection,
Venice

49   © Fortuny Museum Collection,
Venice

51   © *L'Illustration*/Sygma

52   Metropolitan Museum of Art,
New York © All Rights Reserved

53   © All Rights Reserved

54   (above left) © All Rights Reserved
(above right) © Roger-Viollet
(below) © Harlingue-Viollet

55   (above left) © All Rights Reserved
(above right) © Photo Harris and
Ewing/Harry Winston Archives
(below) © Roger-Viollet

56   © Photo RMN-Hervé Lewandowski

57   Photo Baron Adolf de Meyer
© *Vogue*/The Condé Nast
Publications Ltd

58   © Rue des Archives

59   © Rue des Archives

61   © Hulton Getty/Fotogram-
Stone Images-Paris

63   SBM Archives © All Rights Reserved

64   © Rodchenko and Stepanova
Archives, Moscow. Courtesy
A. Lavrentiev

65   © Roger-Viollet

66   © Patrimoine Lanvin

67   © Photo Laziz Hamani/Assouline

68   © Patrimoine Lanvin

69   © Photo Hoyningen-Huene/
Hamiltons Photographers Limited

70   © Patou Archives

71   © Patou Archives

72   (above) SBM Archives © All Rights
Reserved
(below) © Hermès Archives

73   (above left) © Metropolitan
Museum of Art, New York
(above right) SBM Archives
© All Rights Reserved
(below) © Patou Archives

75   Private collection © All Rights
Reserved

76   © Hulton Getty/Fotogram-
Stone Images-Paris

77   SBM Archives © All Rights Reserved

78   © Chanel Archives

79   © Rue des Archives

80   (above) © Van Cleef & Arpels
Archives
(below) © Boivin Archives

81   (above left) © Jean Fouquet
Archives
(above right) © Boucheron Archives
(below left) © Cartier Archives
(below right) © Van Cleef & Arpels
Archives

82   Photo Tabard/ Musée
de la Mode et du Textile, Paris
© Collection UFAC

83   © Musée des Tissus, Lyon

84-85   © Photo Hoyningen-Huene/
Hamiltons Photographers Limited

86   Lelong private collection © All
Rights Reserved

87   © Man Ray Trust/Adagp/
Telimage-1999

88   © Lesage Archives

89   © Adagp, Paris-1999

90   © Schiaparelli Archives

91   © Photo Horst P. Horst/
Hamiltons Photographers Limited

92 © Metropolitan Museum of Art, New York

93 © Victoria and Albert Museum, London

94 © Guerlain Archives

95 © Coty Archives

96 © Photo Hoyningen-Huene/ Hamiltons Photographers Limited

97 Photo Joël Garnier © Charles Jourdan private collection

98 © Salvatore Ferragamo Museum, Florence

99 © Lipnitzki-Viollet

100 © Man Ray Trust/Adagp, Paris/ Telimage-1999

101 (above left) SBM Archives © All Rights Reserved
(above right) Man Ray Trust © Adagp, Paris-1999
(below) © Hulton Getty/ Fotogram-Stone Images-Paris

103 SBM Archives © All Rights Reserved

104 (above) © Hulton Getty/ Fotogram Stone Images-Paris
(below) © Photo Hoyningen-Huene/ Hamiltons Photographers Limited

105 (above left) © All Rights Reserved
(below left) © All Rights Reserved
(right) © AKG

106 Private collection
© Guyla Batthyany, Budapest

107 © Photo Bernard Richebé

108 © Keystone

109 © Keystone

111 © Collection Bibliothèque Nationale, Paris

112-113 © All Rights Reserved

115 © All Rights Reserved

116 © Photo Eugène Rubin

117 © Association Willy Maywald/ Adagp, Paris 1999

118 Photo published in *Look*, 1952
© All Rights Reserved

119 Photo Irving Solaro
© The Museum at the Fashion Institute of Technology, New York, gift of Dorris Duke

120 © Photo Lillian Bassman

121 Photo Galerie Chariau-Bartsch
© All Rights Reserved

122 © Photo Martin Muncaksi Estate/*Harper's Bazaar*

123 © Photo Norman Parkinson/ Hamiltons Photographers Limited

125 © Horst P. Horst /Hamiltons Photographers Limited

126 © All Rights Reserved

127 © Photo Louise Dahl-Wolfe/ Courtesy Staley-Wise Gallery, New York

129 © Harlingue-Viollet

130 © Hulton Getty/Fotogram-Stone Images-Paris

131 (above and below left) © Keystone
(below right) © Hulton Getty/ Fotogram-Stone Images-Paris

132 © Jacques Fath Archives

133 © All Rights Reserved

134-135 © *Album du Figaro* Archives, December 1951

137 © Robert Doisneau/Rapho

138 © All Rights Reserved

140 Gruau © Sylvie Nissen Archives

141 © Photo Burt Glinn/Magnum

142 © Hulton Getty/Fotogram-Stone Images-Paris

143 *Elle*, no. 326 © SCOOP

144 © Christian Dior Archives

145 © Photo Loomis Dean-*Life Magazine*/PPCM

146 © Rue des Archives

147 © Association Willy Maywald/ Adagp, Paris 1999

148 Photo Bellini © Christian Dior Archives

149 © Photo Frances McLaughlin

150 Lesage Archives © All Rights Reserved

151 © 1999 Archives of Milton H. Greene. LLC All Rights Reserved www.archivesmhg.com

152 © Roger Vivier Archives

153 © Photo André Ostier/ Roger Vivier Archives

154 © Lipnitzki-Viollet

155 Photo Jean Kublin
© Balenciaga Archives

156-157 Photo Jean Kublin
© Balenciaga Archives

158 Photo Jean Kublin
© Balenciaga Archives

159 © Collection Bibliothèque Nationale, Paris

160 Givenchy Archives © All Rights Reserved

161 Photo Willy Rizzo/*Paris Match* © SCOOP

162 © Photo Laziz Hamani/Assouline

163 © Photo Frances McLaughlin

164 © Photo Frances McLaughlin

165 © Photo Jean-Philippe Charbonnier/Rapho

166 © Musée des Arts Décoratifs, Paris

167 Lesage Archives © All Rights Reserved

168 (above) © Interpress/Kipa Press
(below) Photo Sam Levin
© Ministère de la Culture-France

169 (left) © Columbia/ Kobal/PPCM
(above right) Photo Louise Dahl-Wolfe © Courtesy of *Harper's Bazaar*
(below right) © Photo Edward Quinn, *A Côte d'Azur Album*, Scalo

171 © Rue des Archives

172 © Rue des Archives

175 Private collection © All Rights Reserved

176 Collection UFAC © All Rights Reserved

178 Photo Yoshi Takata
© Pierre Cardin Archives

179 Pierre Cardin Archives
© All Rights Reserved

180 (left) © Rue des Archives
(above right) Pierre Cardin Archives
© All Rights Reserved
(below right) © Photo Peter Knapp

183 (above left) © Hulton Getty/ Fotogram Stone Images-Paris
(below left) © Brioni Archives
(right) © Rue des Archives

184 © Photo Schwab/Dalmas/ Sipa Press

186 © Photo William Klein

187 Photo Mel Sokoluvsky

188 © *Women's Wear Daily* Archives

189 © Photo Jean-Marie Périer

189 © Rue des Archives

190 © Photo Charles Tracy

191 © Photo J.-P. Cade

192 © Photo Jean-Claude Sauer

193 © Photo Pierre Boulat/Cosmos

194 © YSL Archives

195 © Photo Jeanloup Sieff

196 © Photo Willy Rizzo/*Marie Claire*

197 © Photo Peter Knapp

198 © Keystone

199 Paco Rabanne Archives © All Rights Reserved

200 Emilio Pucci Archives © All Rights Reserved

201 © Photo William Claxton/ Fahey Klein Gallery

203 © Photo Ed Pfizenmaier

204 © Photo Peter Knapp

205 © Photo Peter Knapp

206 © Photo William Klein

207 © Photo Franco Rubartelli, taken from *Valentino: 30 anni di magia*, Leonardo

208 (above) *London Life* © All Rights Reserved
(below) © Hulton Getty/ Fotogram Stone Images-Paris

209 (above) Photo Dezo Hoffmann © Apple Corps Ltd
(below left) Photo Ronald Traeger
© *Vogue*/The Condé Nast Publications Ltd, 1965
(below right) © All Rights Reserved

210 © Cacharel Archives

313 Sketch by Yohji Yamamoto for the
Poupées Russes collection, 1989
© Yohji Yamamoto

314 (above left) Photo Jean-Pierre
Masclet © YSL Archives
(above right) © Photo
Roxanne Lowit
(below left) © Photo Roxanne
Lowit
(below right) © Chanel/Photo
Karl Lagerfeld

315 (left) © Photo Roxanne Lowit
(above right) © Photo Jacques
Bourguet/Sygma
(below right) © Photo Roxanne
Lowit

317 © Photo Peter Lindbergh

318 © Concept and photography:
Oliviero Toscani for United
Colors of Benetton

319 Photo Gilles Tondini
© Isabel Marant

320 Cartier Foundation for
Contemporary Art, 'Issey Miyake
Making Things' exhibition,
13 October 1998–28 February 1999
Photo Yasuaki Yoshinaga
© Issey Miyake Inc.

322 Photo Kazumi Kurigami
© Yohji Yamamoto

323 Photo Inez van Lambsweerde
and Vinoodh Matadin
© Yohji Yamamoto

324 Photo Rodriguez Duarte
© Versace Archives

325 Photo Richard Avedon
© Versace Archives

326 © Photo Keizo Kitajima
© Comme des Garçons

327 Photo Paolo Roversi
© Comme des Garçons

328 Photo Christophe Riher
© Martine Sitbon

329 Photo Nick Knight
© The Condé Nast
Publications Ltd

330 © Photo Michael Roberts/
Condé Nast PL/Tatler

331 © Photo Roxanne Lowit

332 © Photo Gucci Archives

333 Photo Mario Testino © Gucci

334 © Prada Femme Archives

335 © Prada Femme Archives

336 Photo Patrick Demarchelier
© Céline Archives

337 Photo Michel Momy
© Hermès Archives

338 Photo Isabelle Bonjean
© Vuitton Archives

339 (left) © Trussardi Archives
(right) © Loewe Archives

340 © Photo Nick Knight

341 Photo Tatsuya Kitayama
© Martin Margiela

342 (above) Photo Mario Testino
© Paul Smith
(below) Photo Tim Griffiths
© Philip Treacy

343 © Photo Christophe Kutner

344 © Photo Christophe Kutner

345 © Photo Michel Comte for
Dolce & Gabbana

346 © Marc Jacobs Archives

347 © Photo Michael Thompson

348 Photo Marleen Daniels
© Dries Van Noten Archives

349 © Ann Demeulemeester Archives

350 © Drawing Claire Smalley

351 © Photo Nick Knight

352 © Photo Michel Nafziger

353 © Photo Bruno Pellerin/Givenchy

354 Photo Michel Comte
© Gianfranco Ferré

355 © Alberta Ferretti

356 Photo Patrice Stable
© Thierry Mugler Archives

357 © Photo Peter Lindbergh

358 Photo M. Kishi © Adeline André

359 © Chanel/Photo Karl Lagerfeld

360 © W & LT Archives

361 © Photo Steven Meisel/
A+C Anthology

362 Photo Peter Lindbergh
© Donna Karan

363 © GAP Archives

364-365 Photo Mario Testino
© Calvin Klein

366 © Christian Louboutin Archives

367 Photo Pascal Therme © Chloé

368 © Armani Press

369 © Photo Mario Testino

371 Photo Gauthier Gallet
© Xuly-Bët

372-373 Musée de la Mode et du Textile
'Les "plus" de la mode' exhibition,
23 July 1998–6 September 1998
Photos Martine Richier © SCOOP

374 © Photo François-Marie Banier

375 (left) © Photo Davies & Davies/
Sygma
(right) Camerapress, London/
Imapress, Paris

376 Photo Marcus Tomlinson
© Hussein Chalayan

380 © Juergen Teller

382 Photo Graeme Montgomery
for Mark Whitaker

383 (from top to bottom)
1 © Totem Berlin
2 Photo Antoine de Parseval
© Marcel Marongiu
3 © Totem Berlin
4 © All Rights Reserved
5 Photo Frédérique Dumoulin
© Zucca
6- © All Rights Reserved

384 Drawing by Franco Moschino,
1991 © Moschino Archives

Acknowledgments

This book could never have been produced without the invaluable advice, patience and understanding of its many contributors, who, in their various ways, have helped to realize its publication. Sadly, the sheer number of people who have collaborated on the project prohibits them from all being listed here. Apologies to those whose names are not included – they are nevertheless sincerely thanked for their help and we are and shall remain extremely grateful to them.

The publishers would like to thank the following houses:
Adidas, Agnès B., Azzedine Alaïa, Adeline André, Giorgio Armani, Laura Ashley, Balenciaga, Balmain, Geoffrey Beene, Benetton, Anne-Marie Beretta, Eric Bergère, Manolo Blahnik, Boucheron, Brioni, Burberry, Cacharel, Pierre Cardin, Carita, Cartier, Jean-Charles de Castelbajac, Céline, Cerruti 1881, Hussein Chalayan, Chanel, Chloé, Corinne Cobson, Comme des Garçons, Converse France, Coty, Courrèges, Patrick Cox, Alessandro Dell'Acqua, Ann Demeulemeester, Dim, Christian Dior, Dolce & Gabbana, Dorothée Bis, Dr Martens, Jacques Fath, Louis Féraud, Salvatore Ferragamo, Gianfranco Ferre, Alberta Ferretti, Fiorucci, James Galanos, John Galliano, Gap, Jean-Paul Gaultier, Rudi Gernreich, Romeo Gigli, Givenchy, Grès, Gucci, Guerlain, Halston, Hermès, Marc Jacobs, Stephen Jones, Charles Jourdan, Donna Karan, Kenzo, Calvin Klein, Michael Kors, Krizia, Lacoste, Christian Lacroix, Karl Lagerfeld, Helmut Lang, Lanvin, Lesage, Levis, Loewe, Christian Louboutin, Isabel Marant, Martin Margiela, Marithé & François Girbaud, Marcel Marongiu, Mattel, Alexander McQueen, Missoni, Issey Miyake, Claude Montana, Moschino, Thierry Mugler, Nike, Rifat Ozbek, Jean Patou, Prisunic, Prada, Emilio Pucci, Paco Rabanne, Ralph Lauren, Oscar de la Renta, Sonia Rykiel, Dirk van Saene, Yves Saint Laurent, Jil Sander, Schiaparelli, Schott, Jeremy Scott, Martine Sitbon, Paul Smith, Sybilla, Angelo Tarlazzi, Isabel Toledo, Philip Treacy, Trussardi, Ungaro, Valentino, Van Cleef & Arpels, Tom Van Lingen, Dries Van Noten, Gianni Versace, Louis Vuitton, Junya Watanabe, Vivienne Westwood, Harry Winston, Mark Whitaker, W & LT, Xuly-Bët, Yohji Yamamoto, Zoran and Zucca.

And many thanks to all the photographers and illustrators:
Ruben Afanador, François-Marie Banier, Neal Barr, Lillian Bassman, Bellini, Isabelle Bonjean, Jacques Bourguet, Guido Brakema, René Burri, Paul Caranicas, Alex Chatelain, J.-P. Cade, R. Cauchetier, Jean-Philippe Charbonnier, William Claxton, Michel Comte, Louise Dahl-Wolfe, Marleen Daniels, Loomis Dean, Marie-Laure de Decker, J.-P. Decros, Patrick Demarchelier, Jack Deutsch, Rodriguez Duarte, Frédérique Dumoulin, Elliott Erwitt, Juan de la Fuente, Gauthier Gallet, Joël Garnier, Jean-François Gaté, Burt Glinn, Jean-Paul Goude, Annette Green, Tim Griffiths, René Gruau, Laziz Hamani, Horst P. Horst, Frank Horvat, Hoyningen-Huene, M. Kishi, Keizo Kitajima, William Klein, Peter Knapp, Nick Knight, Jean Kublin, Kazumi Kurigami, Christophe Kutner, Karl Lagerfeld, Inez van Lambsweerde and Vinoodh Matadin, Lisa Law, William Laxton, Sam Levin, Peter Lindbergh, Roxanne Lowit, Serge Lutens, Charlotte March, Jean-Pierre Masclet, Leonard McCombe, Frances McLaughlin, Steven Meisel, Duane Michals, Michel Momy, Graeme Montgomery, Sarah Moon, Ugo Mulas, Joan Munkacsi for Martin Munkacsi, Michel Nafziger, Helmut Newton, T. O'Neill, Carlo Orsi, André Ostier, Kourken Pakchanian, Norman Parkinson, Antoine de Parseval, Harri Peccinotti, Bruno Pellerin, Jean-Marie Périer, Ed Pfizenmaier,

Baudoin Picard, Pierre et Gilles, Edward Quinn, Bernard Richebé, Martine Richier, Christophe Riher, Willy Rizzo, Michael Roberts, Uli Rose, Paolo Roversi, Franco Rubartelli, Eugène Rubin, Jean-Claude Sauer, Francesco Scavullo, David Seidner, Kishin Shinoyama, Jeanloup Sieff, Claire Smalley, Mel Sokoluvsky, Irving Solaro, Karl Stoecker, Peter Tahl, Yoshi Takata, Pascal Therme, Michael Thompson, Marcus Tomlinson, Gilles Tondini, Oliviero Toscani, Charles Tracy, Ronald Traeger, Javier Vallhonrat, Tony Viramontes, Alain Vivier, Chris Von Wangenheim, Albert Watson, Bruce Weber and Liam Woon.

We are also grateful to all those who provided encouragement and support for the project, particularly: Beatriz Aristimuño, Maïmé Arnodin, Nadja Auermann, David Bailey, Brigitte Bardot, Jane Birkin, Björk, Jean Bouquin, Boy George, David Bowie, Marlon Brando, Naomi Campbell, Chris Carradine, Cher, Cindy Crawford, Angela Davis, Jacqueline Demornex, Catherine Deneuve, Johnny Depp, Devon, Deirdre Donohue, Jacques Dutronc, Edwige, Erin, Linda Evangelista, Marianne Faithfull, Loulou de la Falaise, Farida, Jane Fonda, Inès de la Fressange, Eric Ghysels, Gilbert and George, Hubert de Givenchy, Jean-Luc Godard, Bettina Graziani, Jerry Hall, Stéphane Houy-Tower, Kirsty Hume, Lauren Hutton, Bianca Jagger, Mick Jagger, Elton John, Beverly Johnson, Esther de Jong, Marie-Andrée Jouve, Anna Karina, Nina Lagdameo, Betty Lago, Madame Lucien Lelong, Donyale Luna, Kristen McMenamy, Elsa Martinelli, Kate Moss, Astrid Munoz, Jelka Music, Kirsten Owen, Tatjana Patitz, Elsa Peretti, Paloma Picasso, Pier Luigi Pizzi, Roman Polanski, Diana Ross, Martina Rossi, Isabella Rossellini, Shalom, Jean Shrimpton, John Travolta, Christy Turlington, Twiggy, Veruschka, Victoire, Gérard Benoit-Vivier, Diane Von Fürstenberg, Isabelle Weingarten and Charlotte and Emily Wheeler.

Finally, our thanks go to the many agencies, galeries and museums who have made this publication possible: Adagp, AKG Photo, Apple Corps Inc., The Archives of Milton H. Greene, Art Partner, Art+Commerce, the Association des Amis de Jacques-Henri Lartigue, the Association Française pour la Diffusion du Patrimoine Photographique, the Bibliothèque d'Art et d'Archéologie Jacques Doucet, the Bibliothèque Nationale de Paris, the Carla Sozzani gallery, the Chariau-Bartsch gallery, Cosmos, Edimédia, *Elle*, The Fabric Workshop & Museum in Philadelphia, the Fahey Klein Gallery, the *Figaro* archives, the Groninger Museum, Hamiltons Photographers Limited, *Harper's Bazaar*, Hulton Getty/Fotogram-Stone Images, Imapress, The Irene Lewisohn Costume Library, Jean-Loup Charmet, Kathryn Abbe Photographs, Keystone, Kipa Press/Interpress, The Metropolitan Museum of Art Library, Magnum, *Marie Claire*, the Michele Filomeno agency, the Musée des Arts Décoratifs de Paris, the Musée des Tissus de Lyon, the Fortuny Museum in Venice, the Musée Galliera in Paris, the Salvatore Ferragamo Museum in Florence, The Museum at the Fashion Institute of Technology, The National Portrait Gallery, Oakland Museum, Phaidon Press, PPCM, Rapho, RMN, Roger-Viollet, Rue des Archives, SBM, Scalo, Scoop, Sipa Press, Sotheby's, Sygma, the Sylvie Nissen agency, Télimage, Thames & Hudson, l'Ufac, The Victoria and Albert Museum, American *Vogue*, British *Vogue*, Italian *Vogue* and *Women's Wear Daily*; as well as to the following press agencies – Béatrice Keller, Karla Otto, Cristofoli Press, Elsa Girault, Kuki de Salvertes, Michèle Montagne and Quartier Général.

Index

*Asterisks indicate pages
where the reference is quoted
and illustrated, or illustrated
only.*

A

Adam, Pauline 114
Adidas 297*
Adolfo, F. Sardina 265
Adrian, Gilbert 104
Aeffe *see* Perretti, Alberta
Aghion, Gaby 177
Agnel 95
Agnelli, Morella 207
Agnès 51
Agnès B. 177, 268-269*
Aimée, Anouk 189
Alaïa, Azzedine 13*, 118,
282-285*, 318, 379
Albını, Walter 251 *, 254,
255*
Alby, Pierre d' 174, 176*,
235, 310
Alexandra, queen consort of
England 31*
Alexandre de Paris 312
Amies, Hardy 18*, 110
André, Adeline 358*
Anthony, John 258
Antonio 217*, 231*
Apollinaire, Guillaume 30
Aragon, Louis 38
Arbus, André 64
Arletty, Léonie Bathiat,
called 90
Armani, Giorgio 239, 251*,
252*, 254, 292-293*, 368*,
370
Arnault, Bernard 379*
Arnodin, Maïmé 212, 214*,
216

Ascoli, Marc 328
Ashley, Laura 232, 233*
Audibet, Marc 310
Auermann, Nadja 325*
Augustabernard 94
Avedon, Richard 325*

B

Bacall, Lauren 168*
Baez, Joan 189
Bailey, David 208, 219*
Bailly, Christiane 177, 213
Baker, Joséphine 62, 101*
Bakst, Léon 50, 55*
Balenciaga, Cristobal 24,
118, 134*, 154-159*, 160,
172, 196, 198, 204, 326, 366,
381*
Ballantine 242
Balmain, Pierre 86, 138*,
146, 150*, 152, 242, 366
Banier, François- Marie
374*
Banton, Travis 104
Bardot, Brigitte 164, 168*,
174, 188, 232
Barney's 318
Barychnikov, Mikhaïl 304
Bassman, Lillian 120*
Bates, John 208
Batthiany, Guyla 106*
Baudelaire, Charles 8
Baufumé, François 238
Beatles, The 190, 208,
209*
Beaumont, Étienne, Comte
de 56*
Beaurepaire, André 138
Beene, Geoffrey 262-263*
Belleteste 177
Benetton 318*
Bérard, Christian 89*, 90,

137*, 138*, 146, 178, 194
Béraud, Jean 32*
Beretta, Anne-Marie 308*,
310
Bergdorf and Goodman
122, 262
Bergé, Pierre 194, 210, 212
Bergère, Éric 366, 369*
Bernhardt, Sarah 38, 39,
54*
Bët, Xuly 371*
Bettina 133*, 135*, 160,
161*
Biagiotti, Laura 255
Bianchini-Férier 135*
Biba 18, 190, 208*
Biki 235
Bikkembergs, Dirk 369
Birkin, Jane 270*
Birtwell, Cecilia 208
Björk 375*
Blahnik, Manolo 296*-297
Blass, Bill 204, 258, 263-
265*
Bogart, Humphrey 168*
Bohan, Marc 238
Boivin 80*
Boldoni, Giovanni 56*
Bonabel, Éliane 138*
Boucheron 81*
Boulat, Pierre 193*
Bouquin, Jean 232*
Bousquet, Jean 210*, 214
Boussac, Marcel 146
Bowie, David 228, 249*
Boy George 288, 315*
Brancusi, Constantin 38, 39
Brando, Marlon 182, 183*,
224
Branquinho, Véronique 383*
Braque, Georges 38
Breton, André 38

Brioni 183*, 221 *
Brodovitch, Alexey 168
Brontë sisters, 232
Brooks, Louise 104*
Brown, James 228
Bruce, Stephen 226*
Brummell, George Bryan
8, 58, 59
Burberry, Thomas 265, 266*
Burrows, Stephen 190*,
228, 265

C

Cacharel 210*, 214, 220
Cadette 242
Caldaguès, Paul 136
Callaghan 254
Callot Soeurs 50
Campbell , Naomi 317*,
361*
Capucci, Roberto 207, 251
Cardin, Pierre 90, 177, 178-
181*, 220, 236, 272
Carel 242
Carita, Maria and Rosy
204*, 218*
Carnegie, Hattie 122, 150,
204
Cartier 80, 81*
Carven, Carmen de
Tommaso, called 164, 166
Casa Torrès, Marquise de
154
Casati, Marquise de 49
Cashin, Bonnie 124
Cassandre, Adolphe
Mouron, called 16*
Cassini, Oleg 204, 219*
Castelbajac, Jean-Charles de
177, 246*, 306-307*
Céline 336*, 346
Cerruti, Nino 254*, 366

Chakkal, Roland 244
Chalayan, Hussein 376*
Chanel, Gabrielle 29*, 50,
52, 65, 74-79*, 95, 96, 106,
123, 126, 162-163*, 172, 189,
192, 214, 236, 239, 240,
244, 298-301*, 314*, 318,
319, 358-359*, 379*
Charbonnier, Jean-Philippe
165*
Chaumet 30
Chéruit, Madeleine 50
Chloé 177, 242, 312, 328,
366, 367*
Chow, Tina 315*
Clarins 357*
Clark, Ossie 208, 244, 248*
Claxton, William 201*
Cligman, Léon 177
Coard, Marcel 39*
Cobson, Corinne 383*
Cocteau, Jean 30, 45, 58*,
62, 78, 90, 101, 138, 178,
194
Colette 45, 63
Colonna, Jean 310
Comme des Garçons 14
15*, 313, 326-327*, 370
Complice 254
Comte, Michel 345*
Condé Nast 101
Conran, Terence 216
Converse 266*
Coppola, Sofia 380*
Coty, François 95*
Courrèges, André 177, 189,
196-197*, 204, 208, 220,
224, 236, 238
Cox, Patrick 342-343*
Crawford, Cindy 317*
Crawford, Joan 122
Créateurs et Industriels,
242, 244, 246
Creed, Charles 50
Cunard, Nancy 100*

D
Dahl-Wolfe, Louise 127*,
169*
Dalí, Salvador 90, 118
Darré, Vincent 381*
Dassler, Adi see Adidas

Daumas, Jean-Rémy 310
Dautry, Raoul 136
Davis, Angela 227*, 228
Dean, James 182, 183*
De Chirico, Giorgio 38, 146
Delahaye, Jacques 177
Delettrez 95
Dell'Acqua, Alessandro
383*
Delman 152
Demarchelier, Patrick 336*
Demeulemeester, Ann 348*
Deneuve, Catherine 219*
Depp, Johnny 374*
Derain, André 45
De Solé, Domenico 332,
379
Dessès, Jean 135*, 164,
166, 167*
Diaghilev, Serge 30, 138
Diana, Princess of Wales
318, 324, 375*
Diba, Farah, Empress 207
Dietrich, Marlene 105*, 258
Dignimont, André 138
Dim 216*
Dior, Christian 86, 139, 142,
144-149*, 152, 154, 172, 173,
178, 181, 185, 192, 194, 203,
224, 238, 258, 352*-353, 366,
381
Doisneau, Robert 137*
Dolce & Gabbana 345*
Dorothée Bis 18, 214, 215*
Doucet, Jacques 34, 36*-39,
40, 44, 46, 86
Douking, Georges 138
Drecoll, Christoff von 51
Dreyfuss, Jérôme 372*
Dr Martens 230, 267*, 370
Du Pont de Nemours 310
Duchamp, Marcel 38, 88
Dufour, Gilles 366
Dufy, Raoul 40, 146
Dumas, Jean-Louis 336
Duncan, Isadora 49
Duse, Eleonora 49
Dutronc, Jacques 274*

E
Edward VIII 92, 102
Edwards, Blake 219

Edwige 314*
Ekberg, Anita 189
Elbaz, Alber 366
Elizabeth II, queen of
England 114, 152, 330
Ellis, Perry 312
Escada 369
Estérel, Jacques 164, 202
Evangelista, Linda 317*, 331

F
Fabergé 30
Faithfull, Marianne 188*,
189
Falaise, Loulou de la 314*
Falaise, Maxime de la 177
Farida 13*
Fath, Geneviève 132
Fath, Jacques 110, 111*, 132-
133*, 134*, 166
Fayolle, Denise 214*, 216
Fellini, Federico 206*
Fendi 242, 251
Féraud, Louis 191*, 202
Ferragamo, Salvatore 97,
98*
Ferré, Gianfranco 251*,
254, 354*-355
Ferreiro, Denise 99*
Ferretti, Alberta 355*
Feruch, Gilbert 272, 274
Fiorucci, Elio 228-230*,
234*
Foale & Tuffin 208
Fonda, Jane 271*
Fontana, Graziella 177
Ford, Tom 332-333*, 377*,
379
Fortuny, Mariano 46-49*
Fouquet 81*
Fragonard, Jean Honoré 152
Frank, Jean-Michel 64, 90,
318
Fratini, Nina 208
Fressange, Inès de la 314*
Furstenberg, Diane Von
271*

G
Gainsbourg, Serge 270*
Galanos, James 122, 261*,
265

Galitzine, Irène, Princess 94
Galliano, John 352*-353,
350*, 381
Gap 363*
Garavani, Valentino see
Valentino
Garbo, Greta 90, 105*, 258
Gaultier, Jean-Paul 244,
288, 290-291*, 310, 312, 341,
355, 357*, 379*
Gellé 95
Genny 254
Gernreich, Rudi 200-201*,
263
Ghesquière, Nicolas 366,
381*
Giacometti, Alberto 90
Gigli, Romeo 302-303*
Gilbert and George 14-15*
Girbaud, Marithé &
François 306*
Giroud, Françoise 141
Giudicelli, Tan 177
Givenchy, Hubert James
Taffin de 86, 90, 202, 218*,
244, 353*, 366
Godard, Jean-Luc 188,
189A, 219
Golo 226*
Goude, Jean-Paul 13*
Goya, Francisco de 158
Grau-Sala, Emilio 138
Gray, Eileen 39*
Gréco, Juliette 189
Grès, Alix 116-117*
Griffe, Jacques 164
Gris, Juan 39*
Gruau, René 19*, 140*
Grumbach, Didier 242,
244, 246
Gucci 23, 254, 332-333*, 336
Gudule 18
Guerlain 94*, 96
Guibourgé, Philippe 238,
239

H
Haines, Pat 224*
Halpert, Joseph 132
Halston, Roy Halston
Frowick, called 259*, 262
Hardy, Françoise 189

Hartnell, Norman 93*, 101, 110
Hayes, Isaac 228
Hayworth, Rita 169*
Head, Edith 104
Hechter, Daniel 177, 213
Hemingway, Ernest 62
Hemingway, Margaux 270*
Hepburn, Audrey 160, 189, 218*
Hepburn, Katharine 104*, 258
Hermès 23, 72*, 93, 169*, 336-337* 379*
Herrera, Caroline 312
Horst, Horst P. 91 *, 125*
Horva, Frank 18*
Hoyningen-Huene, George 69*, 84*-85*, 96*, 152
Hughes, Howard 104

I

Indreco 177
Invest Corp. 332
Irfé 94
Iribe, Paul 50, 53, 66, 68*

J

Jackson Five, The 227*
Jacobs, Marc 336, 338*, 340*, 380*, 381
Jacobs, Max 146
Jacobson, Elie and Jacqueline 214, 215*
Jagger, Bianca 314*
Jagger, Mick 274*
James, Charles 118-121*
Jeanmaire, Zizi 189
Jenny 94
John, Elton 228, 325*
Johnson, Betsey 204, 265
Johnson, Beverly 270*
Jones, Stephen 288*
Joseph 310
Jourdan, Charles 242

K

Kamali, Norma 265, 310*
Karan, Donna 362*-363
Karina, Anna 189*
Kawakubo, Rei see Comme des Garçons

Kelly, Grace 169*
Kennedy, Jacky 207, 219*
Kenzo 24, 239*, 240, 242*, 243*, 379*
Khanh, Emmanuelle 176*, 177, 213, 224, 226, 244
Klein, Anne 124, 204, 265, 363
Klein, Calvin 260, 293, 364*-365
Klein, Michel 244, 309
Klein, William 186*, 206*
Knapp, Peter 180*, 197*, 204*, 205*, 215*, 222*-223*, 235*, 237*, 243*, 248*
Knight, Nick 328-329*, 340*, 351*
Kochno, Boris 138
Kors, Michael 336*, 346-347*
Koshino, Junko 312
Krizia 242, 251*, 252, 253*, 254
Kublin, Jean 155*, 156*-157*,158*

L

Lacoste, René 102, 266*
Lacroix, Christian 280*, 304-305*
Lafaurie, Jeanne 110
Lagerfeld, Karl 24, 27*, 177, 239, 242, 244*, 245*, 251, 298-299*, 312, 314*, 358-359*, 379
Lago, Betty 278*
Lang, Helmut 344*-345
Lanvin, Jeanne 66-69*, 288, 366
Lanvin, Marie-Blanche 66*, 68
Lapidus, Ted 202
Larmon, Leila 226*
Laroche, Guy 152, 164-165*
Lartigue, Jacques Henri 4*, 33*, 35*
Lauren, Ralph 260, 294*-295
Lazareff, Hélène 173
Le Bihan, Marc 373*
Le Gardien 273*
Le Monnier 115*
Legrain, Pierre 39

Legroux 52, 115*
Lelong, Lucien 86-87*, 108, 146
Lempereur, Albert 143, 174-175*
Lenglen, Suzanne 70, 73*
Léonard 235
Lepage, Serge 202
Lepape, Georges 44*, 53
Leroux, Gaston 96
Leroy, Véronique 373*
Les 3 Suisses 216
Lesage 24*, 88*, 167*, 203
Leser, Tina 124, 125*
Let it Rock 18, 230
Levi-Strauss & Co. 224*, 259, 267*
Lewis 52
Lichtenstein, Roy 17*
Lifar, Serge 77*, 79*
Lindbergh, Peter 300*-301*, 317*, 357*, 362*
Lingen, Tom van 382*
Lipschitz, Ralf see Lauren, Ralph
Loewe 336, 339*, 366
Loewy, Raymond 216
Lombard, Carole 105*
Lopez, Antonio see Antonio
Lord & Taylor 132
Louboutin, Christian 366*
Louis, Jean 122, 169ᴬ
Louis XIV 8
Lowit, Roxanne 12*, 278*, 314*, 315*, 331
Lubin, Jean-François 95
Lucile 50
Luna, Donyale 219*
Lutens, Serge 25*
LVMH 346, 353, 366, 379*
Lyon, Sue 189

M

Madonna 324
Mafia 216
Mainbocher, Main Rousseau Bocher, called 92, 93*, 106
Malclès, Jean-Denis 138
Mallet-Stevens, Robert 50
Man Ray 20*, 87*, 88, 100*, 101

Mandelli, Mariuccia see Krizia
Mao Zedong 274*
Marant, Isabel 319*, 366
Mare, André 64
Margaine-Lacroix 51
Margé, Nicole de la 189
Margiela, Martin 24, 336, 341*
Marina de Grèce 92
Marongiu, Marcel 383*
Martial et Armand 94
Marzotto 250
Massaro, Raymond 162*
Masson, André 38
Mata Hari 54*
Matisse, Henri -45, 194
Maxwell, Vera 124
Maywald, Willy 117*, 147*
McCardell, Claire 124, 126-127*
McCartney, Stella 366, 367*
McDonald, Julien 353
McLaren, Malcolm 230, 330
McLaughlin, Frances 149*, 163*, 164*
McLean, Evalyn Walsh 55*
McMenamy, Kristen 325*
McQueen, Alexander 24, 350-351*, 353 *
Meisel, Steven 361*
Mello, Dawn 332
Mendès 210, 235, 238, 242, 244
Mérode, Cléo de 49, 55*
Meyer, Adolph, Baron de 57*
Mic-Mac 18
Michals, Duane 259*
Milhaud, Darius 58*
Miller, Lee 69*, 101
Miró, Joan 38
Missoni, Ottavio and Rosita 256*
Mitterrand, François 281
Miyake, Issey 49, 244, 245*, 320*
Mizrahi, Isaac 312
Molinard 95
Molyneux 50, 92, 110, 123
Mondrian, Piet 194*

Monroe, Marilyn 168*
Montana, Claude 244, 288-289*, 310, 312
Montesquiou, Robert, Comte de 56*
Morand, Paul 62
Morrison, Jim 227*
Morton, Digby 110
Moschino 355, 384*
Moss, Kate 374*
Mountbatten, Lady 101*
Mourgue, Pierre 115*
Mr Freedom 248*
Mugler, Thierry 118, 244, 279*, 286-287*, 288, 310, 312, 356*, 379
Muir, Jean 244
Muñoz, Anne-Marie 238
Mussolini, Benito 250

N
Naudet, Simone 114
Negrin, Henriette 46
Newton, Helmut 277*
Nike 316, 370
Norell, Norman 122, 150-151*

O
Oldham, Todd 366
Oliver, André 181
Ortiz, Cristina 366
Ozbek, Rifat 355, 360-361*

P
Pablo and Delia, 246
Paley, Natalie 86
Paquin 50, 51*, 166, 178
Paraphernalia 265*
Parkinson, Norman 123*, 231*
Patitz, Tatjana 317*
Patou, Jean 70-71*, 123, 242, 308
Paulette 114
Paulin, Guy 310
Peccinotti, Harri 211*
Peretti, Elsa 203*, 262
Périer, Jean-Marie 188*, 274*
Perugia, André 97*
Pianko, Zyga see Alby, Pierre d'

Picabia, Francis 38, 88
Picasso, Pablo 30, 39, 45, 62, 78
Picasso, Paloma 315*
Pierre et Gilles, 26*
Piguet, Robert 110, 146, 148, 166
Pinaud 95
Pinault-Printemps-Redoute 332*, 379*
Pipart, Gérard 177
Pizzi, Pier Luigi 221*
Poiret, Denise 45*
Poiret, Paul 30, 34, 39, 40-45*, 46, 50, 52, 54*, 74, 88, 96, 97, 140, 278, 350
Polanski, Roman 271*
Pollock, Alice 248
Pompidou, Claude 236
Pompidou, Georges 178, 236
Porter, Thea 208
Pougy, Liane de 49, 54*
Prada 23, 282*, 334-335*, 336, 381*
Premet 94
Prémonville, Myrène de 309
Price, Anthony 208, 249*
Prisunic 212*, 216
Promostyl 216
Proust, Marcel 30, 49, 62
Prouvost, Jean 132
Prussac, Lola 166
Pucci, Emilio 200*
Putman, Andrée 246

Q
Quant, Mary 18, 189, 208, 209*, 224
Quorum 248

R
Rabanne, Paco 198-199*
Rambova, Natasha 47*
Rateau, Armand-Albert 66, 68*
Ravel, Maurice 63
Rébé 152
Reboux, Carolin 52, 96*, 97
Redfern, Charles Poynter 50, 239

Réjane, Gabrielle Réju, called 38*
Rémy, Suzanne 152
Renta, Oscar de la 204, 258, 260*, 312
Reverdy, Pierre 38
Revillon 93
Rhodes, Zandra 208, 248*
Ricci, Nina 93, 110, 136, 152, 177, 312
Ricci, Robert 93, 136
Rigaud 95
Roberts, Tommy see Mr Freedom
Rochas, Marcel 110, 381*
Rodier, Eugène 235
Rodriguez, Narciso 336, 339*, 366
Roehm, Carolyn 312
Roger et Gallet 95
Rolling Stones, The 208, 228
Rosier, Michèle 177, 211*, 213
Ross, Diana 228, 229*
Rostand, Edmond 59*, 66
Rouff, Maggy 110
Rousseau, Henri, called Le Douanier 39, 240
Rouxel, Christophe 366
Roversi, Paolo 327*
Russell, Jane 104
Ryklel, Sonia 214, 240*, 318

S
Sade, Marquis de 330
Saene, Dirk van 383*
Saint Laurent, Yves 10*, 18, 118, 152, 177, 185*, 189, 192-195*, 203, 210, 212, 213*, 224, 225, 238*, 242, 244, 366, 377*, 379
Saint-Cyr, Claude 114, 115*
San Giorgio 254
Sanchez, Fernando 244
Sander, Jil 340*-341
Sant'Angelo, Giorgio di 203*, 204
Santos-Dumont, Alberto 30
Sassoon, Vidal 208
Sathal, Fred 372*
Sauguet, Henri 139, 146

Scherrer, Jean-Louis 203
Schiano, Marina 195*
Schiaparelli, Elsa 65, 88-89*, 107*, 123, 134*
Schlumberger, Jean 142
Scholte 102
Schön, Mila 251, 256
Scott, Barrie 228
Scott, Jeremy 383*
Scott, Ken 254
Seberg, Jean 189, 218*
Seidner, David 10*, 290*
Sem, Georges Goursat, called 34*
Sheppard, Eugenia 251
Shiseido 379*
Shimada, Junko 312
Shrimpton, Jean 189, 218*, 222-223*
Sieff, Jeanloup 195*
Simonetta 206*, 207
Simons, Raf 372*
Simpson, Wallis see Windsor, Duchess of
Sirop, Dominique 366
Sithon, Madine 328-329*
Slimane, Hedi 381
Smith, Paul 342*
Snow, Carmel 147
Sonny and Cher 227*
Sorbier, Franck 366
Sorel, Cécile 38
Speliopoulos, Peter 366
Steiger, Walter 312
Stiebel, Victor 110
Stieglitz, Alfred 88
Sting 324
Stone, Sharon 363
Strange, Steve 288
Stravinski, Igor 30, 55*, 78
Süe, Louis 40, 50, 64
Swanson, Gloria 122
Sybilla 302*

T
Takada, Kenzo see Kenzo
Tapie, Bernard 116
Tarlazzi, Angelo 244, 308-309*
Tate, Sharon 271*
Tayama, Atsuro 372*
Testa-Taroni 221*

Testino, Mario 333*, 364*, 369*
Thatcher, Margaret 330
Thimister, Josephus Melchior 366
Thimmonier, Barthélemy 51, 377
Thomass, Chantal 309
Thompson, Michael 347*
Tiffany, Charles Lewis 262
Timwear 242
Toledo, Isabel 22*
Toledo, Ruben 8*, 23
Tomlinson, Marcus 376*
Tommaso, Carmen de see Carven
Torrente 202
Toscani, Oliviero 273*, 318*
Touchagues, Louis 138
Toussaint, Jeanne 80
Townley Frocks 126
Travolta, John 276*
Treacy, Philip 342*
Trigère, Pauline 204, 265
Trussardi 339*
Turlington, Christy 317*
Twiggy 187*, 189, 208*

U
Ungaro, Emanuel 203, 205*, 210, 381*

V
Valentina 94
Valentino 205, 207*, 242, 244, 251
Vallhonrat, Javier 303*, 305*, 328
Valois, Rose 115*
Van Beirendonck, Walter 360*
Van Cleef & Arpels 80*, 81*, 142
Van Dongen, Kees 45
Van Noten, Dries 348*-349
Vaskène, Georges 177
Vautrin, Line 164, 166*
Vélasquez, Diego de 158
Venet, Philippe 202, 244
Verdura, Fulco di 78*, 142
Versace, Donatella 324
Versace, Gianni 254, 324-325*
Versolato, Ocimar 366
Veruschka 189, 207*, 238*
Victoire 192*

Vincent, Françoise 214
Viramontes 288*
Viollet 95
Vionnet, Madeleine, 51, 65, 82-85*, 92, 106, 123, 126, 366
Visconti, Simonetta see Simonetta
Vivier, Roger 152-153*
Vlaminck, Maurice de 45
Vogel, Lucien 53
Vramant, Madeleine 110
Vreeland, Diana 12*, 18
Vuitton, Louis 8*, 23, 336, 338*, 346, 381*

W
Wakhevitch, Georges 138
Warhol, Andy 259
Watson, Albert 298*
Watteau, Antoine 36
Weber, Bruce 294*
Weill, Jean-Claude 143, 170
Weinberg, Salomon, called Samy 235
Wertheimer, Alain 358
West, Mae 90
Westminster, Duke of 77

Weston 275
Westwood, Vivienne 230, 248, 330-331*
Whitaker, Mark 382*
Wild and Lethal Trash, see Van Beirendonck, Walter
Windsor, Duchess of 90, 92
Wood, Natalie 89
Worth, Frederick 8, 24, 34, 36, 40, 50, 192
Worth, Gaston 378

Y
Yamamoto, Kansai 310
Yamamoto, Yohji 313*, 318, 322-323*, 326, 370
Youssoupoff, Félix 94
Yurkievich, Gaspard 373*

Z
Zoran, Ladicorbic) 298*
Zucca 383*
Zuckerman, Ben 265
Zurbarán, Francisco de 158